Understanding Communist China

Tai–chün Kuo
Ramon H. Myers

Understanding Communist China

Understanding Communist China

*Communist China Studies in the United States
and the Republic of China,* **1949–1978**

TAI-CHÜN KUO
and
RAMON H. MYERS

**Hoover Institution Press
Stanford University
Stanford, California**

The Hoover Institution on War, Revolution and Peace, founded at Stanford University in 1919 by the late President Herbert Hoover, is an interdisciplinary research center for advanced study on domestic and international affairs in the twentieth century. The views expressed in its publications are entirely those of the authors and do not necessarily reflect the views of the staff, officers, or Board of Overseers of the Hoover Institution.

Hoover Press Publication 334

Library of Congress Cataloging in Publication Data
Kuo, Tai-chün, 1952–
    Understanding Communist China.

    Bibliography: p.
    Includes index.
    1. China—Study and teaching—United States.
2. China—Study and teaching—Taiwan.   I. Myers,
Ramon Hawley, 1929–   II. Title.
DS734.97.U6K86   1986   951'.0072073   86-3126
ISBN 0-8179-8341-4 (alk. paper)
ISBN 0-8179-8342-2 (pbk. : alk. paper)

Design by Elizabeth F. Gehman

CONTENTS

■ Preface   *ix*

1 ■ The Problem and Our Approach   *1*

2 ■ Understanding by Means of Typologies:
Research in the United States   *16*

3 ■ Understanding by Means of Typologies:
Research in the Republic of China   *40*

4 ■ Verification of Typologies   *52*

5 ■ Understanding Communist China
by Means of Prediction   *64*

6 ■ Understanding by Means of Interpretation
of the Event   *84*

7 ■ Understanding the Chinese Communist System   *109*

8 ■ Conclusion   *125*

■ Notes   *135*

■ Index   *167*

We dedicate this book
to the scholars, staff, and directors
of the Institute of International Relations
in Taipei, Taiwan, the Republic of China
and of the Hoover Institution
at Stanford University, California, U.S.A.

PREFACE

Attempts to understand Communist China have resulted in confusion and frustration. In fact, interpretations of events and developments in this society have been as varied as the conflicting accounts given by witnesses of the murder in the movie "Rashomon."

In 1972 John King Fairbank, former doyen of Chinese Studies at Harvard University, described the Maoist revolution as "on the whole the best thing that has happened to the Chinese people in many centuries. At least, most Chinese seem now to believe so, and it will be hard to prove it otherwise."[1]

Writing in 1971 for *Successo,* Galeazzo Santini described the then-current enthusiasm for the Maoist revolution in China. "China is now the fashion around the world, and in no uncertain terms. Everywhere politicians of the most conservative and bourgeois kind are attempting to rebuild for themselves a compromised career by singing the praises of Mao Tse-tung."[2]

After interviewing refugees in Hong Kong in the late 1960s and early 1970s, Miriam and Ivan London presented this view of Communist China:

Beyond the bland facade of China's great open cities and the green abundance of its show-place communes lies a vast country *in obscuro*—a China through the looking-glass. In this, some say imaginary, country, people do not converse in *People's Daily* platitudes, but use a distractingly earthy language, enriched with sly puns and ancient proverbs; young men sing melancholy songs and brood over lovers and lost illusions; sons and daughters esteem their families above the Party; there are thieves, pick pockets, and prostitutes; village cadres keep "one eye open and one eye shut" to sideline business activities; women quarrel hysterically over their works in communal kitchens; speculators slip in and out of towns buying and selling ration coupons; underground factories operate; farmers lavish care on their private plots while neglecting the collective lands; and massive numbers of the Chinese peasantry, immemorially patient and industrious, labor daily under hardship and deprivation for three meals of rice gruel and sweet potatoes a day.[3]

On October 1, 1979 one of Communist China's top leaders, Yeh Chienying, was quoted in *Jen-min jih-pao* (*People's Daily*) as saying that "the 'Cultural Revolution' forced the country to endure an entire decade of oppression, tyranny, and bloodshed."[4]

Here we have a distinguished American China scholar, a foreign journalist, several American social scientists, and a leader of Communist China's regime offering conflicting views on the meaning of the Cultural Revolution for China's leaders and people. If interpretations in the 1970s were so mixed and varied, what about the earlier years of the regime? Were not these years also open to question? This book surveys the attempts of experts in both the United States and the Republic of China on Taiwan to try to understand Communist China—a society that was cut off from the outside world for nearly thirty years and that published very little information about its people during that time. It is intended for the intelligent lay person and non-China scholar who is interested in learning about the ways in which experts have tried to understand Communist China. It is also a survey and appraisal of the many competing interpretations about Communist China that appeared between 1950 and 1978.

The idea for this book germinated in letters between Dr. Chang Kingyuh, then director of the Institute of International Relations in Taipei, Taiwan, and Dr. Ramon H. Myers, curator-scholar of the Hoover Institution's East Asian Collection. They agreed on the importance of evaluating the efforts of scholars in the United States and the Republic of China to understand the major events and developments in Communist China. They believed that such a study could improve the future research capabilities of both groups of scholars.

The authors are most grateful for the help received from these two organizations. In addition, they wish to express their thanks to the following individuals who offered valuable criticisms and suggestions to improve drafts of this manuscript.

Harry Harding, Jr., senior fellow at the Brookings Institution, read the original draft and offered many encouraging remarks. Stanley Rosen of the University of Southern California commented on our methodology, as did Thomas A. Metzger, Lowell Dittmer, and Thomas Rawski. Andrew Nathan, Richard Baum, Chalmers Johnson, and Robert Scalapino also examined our original draft and provided important suggestions for improvement.

We thank Joyce Kallgren for making it possible to present several chapters of our book to the China Studies Colloquium hosted by the Center for Chinese Studies at the University of California, Berkeley, in November 1983.

We are also grateful to the following other readers, who took time from their work to comment on an early draft of this study: Franz Michael, Yuan-Li Wu, Jürgen Domes, J. G. Bell, and A. Doak Barnett. Finally, we thank Dr. Charlene Seifert for her editorial comments, which greatly improved the clarity and the arguments of the text. None of the above-mentioned scholars are responsible for errors or interpretations.

1

The Problem and Our Approach

How can the members of one society understand the behavior and interpret the events of another society that is very different in culture, language, and history from their own? This question has loomed ever larger as the world has divided into opposing camps and become possessed of enormous mutual destructive capabilities. It was, however, raised as early as the late nineteenth century, when scholars in Germany and other European countries began trying to explain why and in what ways Western capitalist societies were so different from other societies.

By the turn of the twentieth century a controversy had already been raging for several decades on the ways in which different foreign regions and civilizations should be studied. Certainly the most ambitious attempt to develop the concepts and typologies for this task was Max Weber's *Economy and Society,* a work of enormous erudition and complexity.[1] Similar efforts in other countries tried to meet this. By the 1920s and 1930s French scholars Marc Bloch and Lucien Febvre had launched a new journal, *Annales,* which addressed the origins of Western capitalism and outlined how comparative historical studies could explain why societies differed. The success achieved by *Annales* enabled Lucien Febvre to establish the Sixth Section of the Ecole Pratique des Hautes Etudes in 1948, which, in 1975, became the Ecoles des Hautes Etudes en Sciences Sociales.[2] This organization now cosponsors the social science and historical studies of Europe's distant past and of non-Western societies.

During the same period similar research, on an unusual scale, was also being conducted by states that were relative latecomers to modernization. At the turn of the century a brilliant Japanese official in the Taiwan colonial service, Gotō Shimpei, was already building a modern library and encouraging officials to use it for comparing the various administrative policies and experiences of European colonial regimes. Gotō believed that the Japanese might be able to avoid the mistakes made by these colonial regimes and learn how they successfully managed millions of non-Westerners. The Japanese continued their research on foreign societies by creating (in April 1907) a special research department in the new South Manchurian Railway Company located in Dairen, Manchuria.[3] For the next four decades one of its chief tasks was to study Chinese society in all its complexity, so that Japanese policy-makers would be able to promote Japanese interests in that country.

Immediately after World War II the United States found itself in the unique position of rehabilitating the war-shattered economies of Europe and Japan and of forestalling violent political revolution in various parts of the developing world that had potential strategic importance for the West. The United States knew very little about these foreign regions. The great political upheavals and the civil war in Russia had long posed a new challenge to the West. But when a new regime came to power in China in 1949 and allied itself with the Soviet Union rather than the West, this challenge became more serious.

That new challenge forced the United States to understand the intentions of the new Chinese leaders and developments in their society. Here was a country with a half-billion people, making up nearly one-quarter of the earth's population, occupying a large, strategic portion of the Asian mainland, and bordered by several thousands of miles of Soviet territory and by the Pacific Basin. One of the great civilizations of human history, China possessed a difficult language and a complex culture that differed radically from those in the West. When China's new leaders began to restrict information about life and events in this great country, the task of understanding China became even more difficult.

AMERICAN EFFORTS TO UNDERSTAND COMMUNIST CHINA

In the 1950s national and private efforts merged to find new ways to train experts and establish the means by which policy-makers and scholars could better understand the behavior and developments taking place in the Soviet Union and the People's Republic of China (PRC). Asian studies had formerly concentrated on Japan. American interest in Communist China lagged until George Taylor, John K. Fairbank, and other scholars persuaded private foundations to promote Communist China studies. The year 1958 marked a watershed for Chinese Communist area studies in the United States. In that year a ten-member Contemporary China Committee chaired by Professor Taylor began to coordinate activities in both the American Council of Learned Societies and the Social Science Research Council (SSRC).[4] This committee advised on the allocation of foundation funds to establish new centers of research and training in Communist China studies.

Between 1959 and 1970 China area studies exploded, and the Ford Foundation alone gave more than $23 million to assist China centers and programs at American institutions, sponsor research projects, and train students in language and field research. The U.S. government also advanced about $15 million—mainly for student fellowships. More than a score of U.S. universities also made major commitments to Communist China studies. In sum, in this decade nearly $41 million was spent for the promotion of China area studies in American institutions of higher education—more than half of it for contemporary China studies.[5]

The SSRC's Committee for Contemporary China Studies played a crucial role in conceptualizing and organizing Communist China studies in the United States. On the committee's suggestions, the SSRC funded and managed a Chinese language program for a select group of potential China experts, prepared reports urging support for major libraries to build China collections, initiated bibliographical projects, funded selected scholars to produce articles and monographs, and made possible the training of pre- and post-doctoral candidates in Taiwan and Hong Kong.

China centers in major universities sprang up in the northeast, midwest, Pacific northwest, and the far west; many began awarding China area studies degrees and doctoral degrees to candidates in the humanities and social sciences. Many students specialized in Communist China studies and eventually found work in government, academe, or the private sector.

Even after the 1960s the SSRC continued to serve as the moving force behind several hundred Chinese-language and research fellowships for advanced students, a small proportion of whom specialized in Communist China studies. Between 1969 and 1979 over one hundred academics with doctoral degrees received financial support for research on Communist China. The SSRC had made available roughly $4.6 million for research, conferences, and bibliographic support of Communist China studies, with additional sums allocated for language-fellowship support.[6]

By 1979 this remarkable expenditure had spawned a dozen or so distinguished China centers with libraries and interdisciplinary programs offering in-depth training in Communist China studies. Many eminent scholars from these institutions had organized more than a dozen major conferences on Communist China, the results of which had been published by the major academic presses. Many workshops had also developed research on events and trends in contemporary China. Similarly, during this period public and private monies also helped to create Hong Kong's United Research Institute. The institute's excellent library and the nearby Union Service Center provided facilities for hundreds of American scholars and China experts from other countries to search the documentation and interview refugee informants from Communist China. Similar funding went to Taipei for the establishment of the important Stanford University-Taipei Language Center, where nearly a generation of American students have received Chinese-language training.

Thanks to this public and private funding, probably more than a thousand students received several years of intensive Chinese-language study, and many hundreds more received substantial financial support for their research on Communist China. Some of these students eventually found careers in law, journalism, and public service in the Central Intelligence Agency, the Department of Defense, or the Department of State; and hundreds more taught and conducted research in institutions of higher learning.

Did this huge expenditure of resources greatly increase our understanding of the behavior and events of Communist China? The main purpose of this study is to provide a reasoned analysis of this question. But other factors also motivated the writing of this book. We believe that an evaluation of American research on Communist China could elucidate more clearly the difficulties that must be overcome when either public or private efforts are directed toward understanding another society. We must constantly remind ourselves of these difficulties, so that we can maintain high standards of foreign-area research in the future. Further, we see this study as a means of summing up what experts have really learned about Communist China, evaluating the mistakes of interpretation they have made, and examining how similar mistakes could be avoided in the future.

Experts in other countries have also tried to understand the meaning of events in Communist China, and their motives for doing so have been as important as those of the experts in the United States. Some of the same difficulties that have confronted the Americans have also beset these scholars. But special circumstances have often made their research style and findings very different from those of American researchers. We therefore contend that to evaluate American research on Communist China, a comparative study of similar research done in another country is a legitimate and useful undertaking. Why? First, a comparative approach can identify those particular problems and difficulties that make understanding a foreign society so elusive and challenging. Second, a comparative approach illustrates that there are many ways of understanding a foreign society and that different research methodologies will provide different levels of understanding of a foreign society.

For our study we have compared the research findings of a large sample of scholarship produced in the Republic of China (ROC) with the findings of a sample of scholarship produced in the United States during the years 1949 through 1978.[7] We have selected this time period because it represents a convenient period of political continuity, particularly because during this period China was closed to much of the outside world.[8] The following reasons prompted us to select scholarship from the Republic of China. First, the ROC government has always monitored developments on the Chinese mainland because of its long-standing rivalry with the PRC's communist regime. Ever since the Chinese Communist Party was formed in 1921, the ROC government has competed with the Chinese Communists. Many ROC researchers—particularly those who have had personal dealings with the Chinese Communist Party (CCP)—have understood the true meaning of Chinese communist terms and clichés. They have also been very knowledgeable about the complex political activities within the CCP and have been familiar with the personal lives of many high-ranking party cadres. Finally, because Communist China experts in the ROC are able to understand Chinese political culture, history, and language, they have been able to read enormous quantities of CCP documents and government publications and to grasp the real meaning of these materials.

On first view, then, we would expect ROC scholarly research to be of very high caliber, and we therefore contend that a representative sample of this research could serve as a high standard by which to judge a large sample of American research on Communist China.

ROC EFFORTS TO UNDERSTAND
COMMUNIST CHINA

After their move to Taiwan, it was natural for the ROC authorities to try to understand Chinese Communist Party activities and to observe developments on the mainland. ROC experts on communist affairs quickly noted that Beijing's leaders were increasingly relying on Soviet aid and moral inspiration. Although the ROC leaders realized that the CCP lacked sufficient naval and air-force power of its own, they feared a Soviet-backed communist military invasion of the island. The ROC leaders also recognized that communist subversion had been notably successful in undermining Nationalist support in the cities and behind Nationalist lines during the civil war. Accordingly, Taipei's leaders feared an upsurge of communist infiltration and sabotage on the island.

For these reasons, in early 1950 the central committee of the Nationalist party established special agencies to carefully study all developments on the communist-ruled Chinese mainland that might relate to subversion or armed attack and to recommend appropriate policies of response. These agencies also began to examine the new regime's policies and to pinpoint weaknesses in the emerging communist system that the Nationalist government might use to its advantage if its forces were ever able to re-enter the mainland.

Whereas the Ministry of National Defense assumed the responsibility for intelligence-gathering activities on the mainland, communist-affairs experts comprised only a small group of officials and civilians. Some members of this group were actually former members of the Communist Party.[9] These experts mainly relied on information from Hong Kong and Nationalist intelligence sources. They also tapped public sources: newspapers and magazines published throughout the mainland, radio broadcasts and other Communist Party publications, refugee and defector interviews, and documents on official relations between the USSR and the PRC.

From these sources—and particularly from the first-hand intelligence information gathered by the ROC government—these China-watchers assessed current conditions and the prospects for change on the mainland. In the 1950s these reports rarely circulated publicly. In the Chinese bureaucracy, as in any bureaucracy, subordinates evolved a pattern of not reporting any news that might distress or embarrass their superiors. An example of this practice occurred in 1960. Government officials publicly stated that Communist China was merely replicating the organizations and policies long established in the Soviet Union and that the foreign-policy interests of the two communist giants were identical. China experts, however, correctly predicted a likely split between the two powers, but they did not report this finding to their superiors.[10] This example merely highlights the difficulty of reporting accurate intelligence assessments when these assessments conflict with the foreign-policy claims or intentions of the leadership.

By the early 1960s a number of events began taking place that slowly influenced how China-watching was to be conducted within the ROC. The split between Moscow and Beijing divided communist parties all over the world, and the expansion of a Moscow-led global communist movement appeared to be losing momentum. Beijing's Great Leap Forward campaign had just failed, and its regime had turned increasingly inward. As a result, the flow of published information from Communist China began to decline just as Western interest in understanding this new regime was intensifying. Countries like the United States were making a substantial effort to train Communist China experts. At the same time many of the youth and intellectuals within the ROC were beginning to take an interest in Communist China. Taipei officials tried to respond to these new demands for more information about life and conditions on the mainland. Finally, ROC China-watchers were becoming eager to expand their contacts with foreign scholars, and there were, therefore, new pressures to produce accurate accounts of mainland trends and to engage in debates with foreign experts on differing interpretations of conditions in Communist China.

The ROC established the Institute of International Relations (IIR) in 1961 and, shortly thereafter, the Institute for the Study of Chinese Communist Problems (ISCCP). Located in Taipei, both institutes made use of the same small core of government in-house experts of the 1950s, and these senior researchers quickly became the nucleus of expanding research programs. Drawing upon universities, government agencies, and departments of the military, these institutes expanded staff and built libraries to include materials acquired by government intelligence operations on the mainland. They also began to publish their research findings in journals and monographs written in Chinese and other languages.

Since our sample of research writing is taken primarily from the IIR and the ISCCP, a few comments about these organizations are in order. The IIR is closely affiliated with National Chengchi University, from which it draws many young staff for further training. Chengchi trains selected students to write master's theses. Once chosen by the IIR, a promising graduate student will be encouraged to obtain a higher degree abroad and develop a command of a foreign language in order to communicate with other scholars. The IIR has about seventy researchers; thirty-three focus on communist Chinese affairs (twenty full time and thirteen adjunct). The institute's senior experts have included, among others, Li T'ien-min, Chang Cheng-pang, Yin Ch'ing-yao, and Chu Wen-lin.

The ISCCP has about eighty researchers, seventeen of which are senior China-watchers—for instance, Tsai Hsiao-ch'ien, Hsuan Mo, Chen Yu-ch'ang, Hsiao Yeh-hui, and Lin Chen. The ISCCP has five research groups which analyze Communist Party affairs and the PRC's political system, military, economy, and cultural affairs. The ISCCP differs from the IIR in one notable respect: its research concentrates on current events. The ISCCP has made a concerted effort to collect relevant PRC documents, such as tabloids published by Red Guards during the Cultural Revolution, texts of central and local broadcasts of Chinese mainland radio since 1949, and other primary source materials.

Other institutes and archives with communist Chinese studies could also be mentioned, but the IIR and ISCCP constitute the two largest and best representatives of ROC research on mainland affairs.

In the 1950s only about 50 experts worked full time on mainland studies, but by the 1970s their number had risen to about 150. These researchers demonstrated a solid understanding of Chinese history and culture. They were well versed in Marxist-Leninist theory and the history of the Chinese Communist Party, and many had received training in the social sciences in the West. At present, the most educated experts are at the IIR; most of the staff possess either a master's degree or a more advanced degree.

As a result of the upgrading of academic skills over the past two decades, a new generation of experts has begun to replace those elder scholars who predominated in the 1950s, continued to work in subsequent decades, and only began to retire in the last five years. This new generation of Communist China experts has different perspectives and diverse skills. Some members of this new group who have already distinguished themselves are Yung Wei (methodology), Chao Hung-tse and Wu An-chia (history of the CCP), Chou Yu-shan, Liu Sheng-chi, and Chiang Chen-ch'ang (culture and society under communist rule), Chiang Hsin-li and Hsiung Tse-chien (communist ideology and theory), and Yeh Po-T'ang (PRC foreign policy).

Finally, we should mention that institutes like the IIR and the ISCCP contain the best storehouse of records on Communist China. A few examples underscore this point. In an article in a 1966 issue of the *China Quarterly,* Henry G. Schwarz drew attention to a small newsletter entitled *Ts'an-k'ao hsiao-shi* (*Reference News*) that circulated among the upper elite of the CCP to keep them well informed about events in other parts of the world. Schwartz quoted an unnamed leading authority on Communist China, who said he "never heard of anyone outside of the mainland having copies" of *Reference News.*[11] This newsletter's existence was also news to other professionals in the United States, who wrote Schwarz that major Chinese libraries had never acquired copies.

In the ROC, however, experts had been reading *Reference News* throughout the 1950s, and in the 1960s copies abounded in every major research center. ROC scholars had long realized this newsletter's real function: the CCP leadership kept its members informed about the outside world in a highly selective way. Something long known in the ROC was not realized in the United States until the mid-1960s.

As early as the 1950s ROC experts also were reading intraparty documents that had circulated within the CCP Central Committee, at important CCP meetings, and in lower organs of the party and government—all obtained by means of government intelligence operations. One of these documents told of Beijing's preparations to intervene in the Korean War.[12] Another group of materials, acquired during the night of March 4, 1964 by a Nationalist commando raid, contained official policies pertaining to fourteen rural communes of Lien-chiang county in Fukien.[13] These documents made it possible to identify new rural organizations and understand how they had operated in the countryside since 1958. Among this same collection of records were the Landing Craft Documents, which described how People's Liberation Army units had helped the CCP cope with the severe food shortages and declining party morale produced by The Great Leap Forward campaign.[14]

ROC experts also had the opportunity to read the texts of the CCP's constitution, adopted at the Ninth Party Congress, and the draft of the constitution of the PRC even before officials had made it public.[15]

The ISCCP also published documents released by the CCP Central Committee on the Lin Piao incident. In April 1972 *Chung-kung yen-chiu* reprinted in photo offset the *Chung-fa* (Central Committee Document) that described Lin Piao's aborted coup and his death.[16] Several months later this same journal reprinted additional documents describing how Lin and his associates tried to oust Mao Tse-tung from power.[17]

In one of these documents, entitled "Outline of 'Project 571'" (which in Chinese was the code name for armed uprising), Lin Li-kuo (Lin Piao's son) and his associates tried to justify their reasons for launching an armed uprising. The document describes both the favorable conditions and the difficulties facing the insurrectionists and discusses the various strategies that could be used. Most foreign experts doubted the veracity of this document, and some even claimed that Taipei had forged it to discredit their rival on the mainland. But Chou En-lai referred to these same materials in his political report at the Tenth CCP Party Congress, which verified their authenticity.[18]

The researchers in the ROC have tried to make these classified CCP documents available to their Western counterparts. For example, by the end of December 1979, the IIR had translated and published a total of 249 classified CCP documents in its two English-language journals (*Facts and Features* and *Issues & Studies*).[19] We have gone to some length to describe the unique, authentic CCP documents obtained by Nationalist intelligence and housed in the ROC and the wide use made of these documents by ROC experts. Our reason for doing this will become clearer when we discuss the difficulties that have confronted experts on Chinese communist affairs in the United States and the Republic of China.

THE DIFFICULTIES OF UNDERSTANDING A FOREIGN SOCIETY

We have briefly outlined how American and Chinese experts were trained to study Communist China. What kinds of difficulties did these experts have to overcome to understand the events and behavior in this society? We note three major difficulties: (1) prejudice or bias, (2) limited information, and (3) problems associated with mastering a foreign language and understanding a foreign culture. Let us examine these singly as they apply to each group of experts.

Prejudice or bias refers to the tendency of researchers to, for various reasons, deliberately or unconsciously ignore certain evidence in their research; stress certain concepts, terms, or typologies to the exclusion of others; and present their findings in flamboyant or rhetorical terms. Although this definition may not cover all forms of bias or prejudice that are capable of distorting serious research findings about a foreign society, it will allow us to cite examples from our two groups of Chinese communist-affairs experts.

We will first consider the American experts. For a long time many American experts refused to use the research findings and primary CCP documentation of ROC scholarship. Several things explain this prejudice. First, many suspected that Taipei had forged CCP internal documents as part of its propaganda war with Beijing. Second, many strongly distrusted ROC scholarship because of its shrill anticommunist rhetoric and its moral condemnation of the Beijing regime. The following example conveys the typical rhetoric of many ROC China-watchers. After evaluating the Four Clean Movement that preceded the Cultural Revolution, one researcher could not resist stating: "Mao Tse-tung has become a leader driven by desperation because he has lost popular support. The Chinese Communists have lost the backing of the people. The Communist regime is now in severe danger."[20]

In our sample of American research published in the 1960s, very few scholars cited ROC scholarship; it was not until the mid-1970s that the situation began to change. American experts remained skeptical of ROC research because of its overt anticommunist tone, but there were also other reasons for this skepticism. Many dismissed ROC research methods because they were narrative-descriptive instead of hypothesis-testing. Others viewed the power-struggle thesis of the Taipei researchers as too simplistic.

Another bias or prejudice of American experts consisted of the preferred usage of certain key concepts to characterize the dynamics of the Chinese communist regime. In the 1950s most American experts insisted on calling Communist China a totalitarian state, which was a reflection of the anticommunist temper of that decade and the perceptions of many that the Moscow-Beijing alliance was a holy crusade bent on expanding its influence worldwide. In contrast, in the late 1960s and 1970s some American researchers projected certain virtues on the Beijing leadership, praising the policies of these leaders because they believed these policies would also be suitable for their own country. Instead of analyzing the Chinese regime on its own merits, these researchers concentrated on lauding China's development performance as one worthy of emulation by other countries.

Finally, there was a marked reluctance on the part of many American researchers to critically evaluate and morally judge the catastrophes produced by the CCP—like the famine of 1959–61, when between twenty to thirty million Chinese died (see below). Perhaps because of little reliable data, many experts preferred to focus on the positive, functional aspects of the Chinese communist regime. We will not probe further into the reasons behind these prejudices or biases. The factors that attract or repel a researcher when studying a foreign society and the ways in which these sentiments shape perceptions—and eventually research findings—is a task we will leave to others.

Turning to ROC experts, we should first note the language they used to present their findings. They often used emotive terms to describe the communist regime's illegitimacy and the amoral qualities of both leaders and CCP members. Researchers openly expressed their value judgments about the mainland regime's behavior. Further, many scholars exhibited a strong tendency to stress the negative impact of CCP policies on culture, society, and living standards. At other times they also presented their findings in a tendentious way, postulating that the regime would soon collapse because it suffered from acute disorders. For example, one scholar writing about CCP policies toward minorities concluded that "the new policy demonstrated a growing contradiction and struggle between the Chinese Communist Party and the minorities . . . If this new conflict is fueled by the peoples' hatred of the Communist regime, the overthrow of that regime is only a matter of time."[21]

Did this propagandistic style really distort and incorrectly explain the behavior and trends inside Communist China? By neglecting to use ROC research and documents, were American researchers misled in their attempts to understand Communist China? To what extent did the powerful anti- or procommunist bias frequently exhibited in the research writings of both groups of scholars produce misunderstanding about Communist China? Our study tries to answer these questions.

Limited information constituted a second serious handicap for both groups of researchers. Not only did the communist regime release little authenticated information about developments, but it virtually published nothing officially about the lives and habits of the CCP leadership. CCP meetings were closed affairs, and even the many investigations conducted by the party about conditions in the country were never published in any detail. Foreign visitors were never allowed to move freely, to live in the countryside for long periods, or to interview officials unless they were regarded as friendly to the regime and had obtained permission from someone at the top. Of the country's 2,300 counties, perhaps only 200 had ever been visited by foreigners, and then only on a very superficial basis.[22]

American researchers had to make do with even less information than their Chinese counterparts, who at least had access to Nationalist government intelligence materials. Even though most of this Nationalist information was made available to the West, many Westerners ignored it or did not take it seriously. Aside from refugees interviewed in Hong Kong and letters from relatives of Nationalist Chinese, foreign researchers had very limited contact with the people. Before 1978 few high-ranking communist officials had defected. Prisoners were rarely released from labor camps or jails and allowed to leave the country to report their experiences. Because of the paucity of reliable information on life and events inside China, American researchers have been forced to rely on fragmentary evidence to reconstruct events and interpret the impact of CCP policies on both the Chinese people and the leadership.

In understanding Chinese language and culture, experts in the ROC had an obvious advantage. These experts were not studying a foreign society but a world they already understood well. They also knew a great deal about the behavior and thoughts of the new ruling elite; some had even been members of the CCP and had had personal ties with the top leaders. They understood how those with power and authority behaved under different circumstances and how those in subordinate positions reacted to policies that threatened their privilege and power. These experts were also at home in the Chinese language; they digested huge quantities of information, carefully pieced together intricate details to show how social and political action was unfolding, and used their intuition to judge the motives of the leading actors who dominated the political stage at any one time.

In contrast, considerable time and resources had to be expended to teach American experts the Chinese language in Taiwan and Hong Kong; even then, few achieved more than a minimal reading comprehension of newspapers and CCP documents. Language skills, of course, varied greatly, and some researchers were able to competently conduct refugee interviews and ferret out important information. But many American experts seemed to depend on language services—first established in Hong Kong and later developed in the United States—to translate selections from mainland Chinese magazines, technical journals, newspapers, and broadcast reports. Furthermore, it was difficult to understand and relate Chinese culture to behavior. Therefore, American researchers experienced enormous handicaps in trying to extract pieces of reliable information and make sense of it. As a result, many opted to rely on sophisticated methods of research to overcome their deficiency of language and lack of cultural understanding.

RESEARCH APPROACHES
FOR UNDERSTANDING
A FOREIGN SOCIETY

Research methods for understanding any foreign society vary greatly depending on what one wants to know. Military experts want to know about manpower, weaponry, and strategy. Economists want to know about the amount and distribution of wealth and how the economic system produces it. Policy-makers are interested in leadership motives, intentions, and strategies. Political scientists want to know how power is held and distributed and whether institutions exist to legitimize authority. Despite these different foci, approaches that will produce understanding are limited. We discuss some of these briefly below, because they will serve as the framework to organize our comparative study.

To achieve a rudimentary understanding of a foreign society, it is necessary to identify its essential traits or dynamics. This requires grasping the essential features of how another society is ruled, how wealth is produced and distributed, how stable the social order is, and how culture and ideas influence the performance of these tasks. An understanding of these general dimensions of human activity gives us only an initial, approximate knowledge of events, trends, and behavior in another society. One method used to provide this general level of understanding is to construct descriptive typologies.

A descriptive typology abstracts from reality certain essential characteristics or traits and relates them in some logical order to describe the human behavior or action taking place.[23] Such a typology naturally oversimplifies, but it serves to direct our attention to common patterns of human action. If a descriptive typology has been well constructed, and further investigation verifies the validity of its key attributes and their logical relationship to each other, this typology can then be used to explain why and how certain developments take place. To be sure, not everything can be analyzed in this way. Nevertheless, a descriptive typology can help both to identify major trends in a society and to interpret the past.

Another approach of great utility is the narrative approach, which depends on the collection of pertinent, correct facts, a mastery of language to allow one to authenticate and understand these facts, and a profound understanding of a given culture and the ways in which it influences behavior. To analyze and interpret the past by means of the narrative approach, it is necessary to arrange facts in some sequence. This sequence should accurately reflect the flow of human behavior and the events that actually happened. If some reliable facts do not conform to this sequence of events, another narrative must be constructed that does incorporate the relative facts. If new facts become available, they too must be used to construct an updated narrative of the past.

The analytical power of narrative can be enhanced by keying it to a typology. The narrative approach, however, can also be used independently to explain an event and impute meaning to it. If a narrative has incisively explained a past event, it can be used as a model to predict the future. In recent years the narrative approach has not been popular. But this approach still has great merit for the purpose of analyzing political events, changes in foreign policies, and political rivalries among elites in a foreign society.

A third approach relies on social-science theory to explain events and behavior in a foreign society. Human behavior that is regular and uniform can be measured and classified into definable patterns by the use of socioeconomic indicators. Hypotheses can be formulated to explain observable relationships between these patterns, and statistical procedures can be used to verify the existence of these relationships. When these hypotheses have been successfully tested, it becomes possible to advance theories about events or behavior. If these theories are supported by the available historical evidence, we can attempt to predict future behavior or events.

The three approaches reviewed above can be used independently or in conjunction to understand behavior in a foreign society—either for purposes of pure intellectual curiosity or for other interests. Our task now is to examine these approaches and judge how well American and Chinese researchers have succeeded in achieving an understanding of Communist China.

THE APPROACH OF THIS STUDY

First, how can we summarize and evaluate the major findings of the large, disparate body of literature produced by these two groups of researchers? We are dealing, after all, with hundreds of journal articles, scores of monographs, and many conference volumes written by each group of scholars. We have chosen to use the descriptive typology method to gain a proximate understanding of the essential traits of the Chinese communist regime, including political dynamics, economic behavior and development, social stability and integration, and the role played by ideas and culture. We have constructed five typologies, each of which are based on a cluster of research findings that come to common conclusions about the characteristics of Chinese society.

Our typologies, then, are derived from insights and interpretations advanced by various groups of researchers. For each group of research findings we have constructed a typology that describes the essential characteristics of the communist regime between 1949 and 1978. We offer a word of caution, however, about this approach. We never imply that a particular researcher's interpretation of Communist China entirely corresponds to the interpretation our typology might imply. Rather, we view our typologies as distillations of a wide range of research findings. We might relate a single scholar's findings to more than one typology. Nor do we mean to impugn the integrity of any scholar by associating his or her work with a particular typology. We fully recognize the danger of isolating a part of a researcher's findings from the context of his or her work to support the typology we advance. In spite of these risks, however, we believe that our constructions of descriptive typologies have the following merits.

Our five typologies identify different interpretations of the key events and predominant behavioral patterns in Communist China between 1949 and 1978. A careful reading of Chapter 2 will show that various typologies have competed through time, some predominating in one period but not in others.

How do we verify these typologies so that we can judge how well researchers in the United States and the ROC have actually understood Communist China? To judge which typologies were most valid, we consulted the new evidence that has become available since 1978. Part of this new evidence has come from candid statements by communist leaders about their own regime. Some has also come from Western observers who have been privileged to reside for long periods in China and to collect far more information about local conditions than had ever been gathered before. By relating this evidence to each typology, we were able to test which typologies were valid.

We only examined research that sought to predict certain major trends, such as political change. If researchers are able to accurately predict likely developments, they must obviously have some understanding of how the ruling leaders have already behaved, what impact their policies have had on society, and what patterns of behavior have flowed from these actions. By comparing a variety of predictions made by American and ROC experts, we try to evaluate how frequently these predictions have been vindicated and what kinds of predictions have seemed valid.

When researchers use the narrative method with certain concepts of political and social behavior, they are attempting to understand the origins and meaning of particular events. The 1949–56 socialist transformation, the 1958–60 Three Red Banners Campaign, and the 1966–76 Great Proletarian Cultural Revolution were unique events. Both party and state attempted to impose a special kind of dominance over society by creating different kinds of organizations to influence human behavior. Researchers often implicitly used elements of our five typologies to narrate these events and explain what had occurred inside Communist China. In Chapter 6 we summarize, compare, and evaluate American and Chinese narrative-method research.

Finally, we review other approaches that have tried to explain change in Communist China. For example, we examine research based on refugee interviews that developed socioeconomic quantitative indicators to measure patterns of behavior and trends and that tested hypotheses.

The concluding chapter summarizes our general findings by outlining the achievements and shortcomings of the scholarship produced by both groups of researchers. By relating these findings to the difficulties both groups have tried to overcome, we have returned full circle to the fundamental problem of this study: Between 1949 to 1978, how well did American scholars understand Communist China?

2

Understanding by Means of Typologies: Research in the United States

By describing a society as modern or traditional, developing or advanced, or capitalist or communist, we differentiate among societies according to generally agreed-upon, but implied, characteristics. These characteristics might denote the predominant features of governance, describe how resources are allocated and goods and services are produced, depict how social units are organized and how their members behave, or indicate the cultural values and ideals that exist in a given society.

Furthermore, we can select certain patterns of these characteristics and arrange them in a causally connected way to describe the general behavior of the leaders of a society, their policies, and the reactions of the people to these policies. This level of conceptualization, which involves the construction of a descriptive typology, allows us to describe key changes in a foreign society and interpret them in some judgmental way. A descriptive typology contains one or more statements about the actions and behavior of the leadership in a foreign society. These statements will describe leadership behavioral patterns in this society in a logical manner. These patterns will be considered rational, in that they are oriented toward certain goals and represent a choice of appropriate means to achieve these goals.

Our descriptive typologies also imply judgmental evaluations of the key characteristics of a society. Different standards can be used, but they should be made explicit. We offer four standards.

First, there is economic development. This can be evaluated in terms of whether or not a high, sustained growth of output per capita occurred over time, whether or not income became more equally distributed, whether output per capita rose because of productivity or because of the allocation of more resources to production and distribution, and whether or not economic development was associated with environmental destruction.

Second, there is political development. This can be evaluated in terms of whether power became concentrated in a few hands or became more dispersed over time, whether effective checks to power were weakened or strengthened, whether more or fewer people engaged in political participation, and whether the political system was stable or unstable, functional or dysfunctional.

Third, there is social development. This can be evaluated in terms of whether different groups in society had to bear higher costs or experienced positive changes in life expectancy, social status, and freedom of choice; whether new or old social organizations influenced these costs and benefits; and whether social values and norms were or were not changed.

Fourth, there is cultural and artistic development. This can be evaluated in terms of whether more or less artistic creativity and diversity evolved; whether there was more or less artistic and cultural expression; and whether there was more or less conformity to a single doctrine of thought.

Descriptive typologies help to organize a large number of research findings, to summarize them, and to interpret them by certain criteria. To sum up: Descriptive typologies allow a limited conceptualization of important events and trends in a society; they help to explain relationships that elucidate the past and predict future changes in the society; and they provide insights that convey meaning to certain events and trends in the society.

For American research writings, we have constructed four descriptive typologies: communist-totalitarian, which characterized research of the 1950s; the modernizing communist regime, which became the major typology of the 1960s and 1970s; the revolutionary-socialist regime, which challenged the last-named typology in the late 1960s and 1970s; and finally, the Chinese communist regime, which represented the work of a small group of scholars and coexisted with the last two typologies.

COMMUNIST-TOTALITARIAN CHINA

In 1956 Carl Friedrich and Zbigniew Brzezinski advanced a descriptive typology that they believed identified the key features common to communist and fascist dictatorships in the twentieth century.[1] These included

- An official, standard ideology
- A single mass party, typically led by one man
- A terroristic system of police control
- Party control of mass communications
- Party control of the army and of weapons
- Party control of the economy

When all these features coalesced, society achieved a "totalitarian breakthrough" and was set on a trajectory that was virtually irreversible.

   Most scholars used this typology to describe the behavior and developments in the Soviet Union prior to World War II, and experts researching
Communist China believed the emerging features of this society merely du-
plicated those of the Friedrich-Brzezinski typology. They thought that Communist China was simply trying to replicate the Soviet Union. Writing in
1954, Walter Rostow and his collaborators pointed out that in China the "top
leadership seeks to repeat on the Chinese scene the pattern of domestic transformation carried out by Stalin in the early 1930s, with a specially urgent
emphasis on the creation of a Chinese industrial base for the maintenance of
its modernized armed forces."[2] These same authors saw Communist China
as expansionist and as seeking to "increase the independent authority of
Peking in Asia within the limits permitted by the need to maintain the Sino-
Soviet alliance, and by the resource requirements of the industrialization
program."[3]

   Scholars of the 1950s perceived that China's leaders were trying to extend the Communist Party's control over the whole of Chinese society in an
unprecedented manner. Intellectuals were subjected to ideological remolding
and compelled to conform to party dictates. In 1953 an article in *Problems
of Communism* pointed out that the "party presumes to dictate not only what
a man may write, and how he may write it, but how and where he must
spend his time in pursuit of inspiration."[4] The middle class was singled out
for harrassment, and their authority and privileges were soon eliminated.[5]
Writing in 1955, Richard L. Walker characterized China in the first five years
of communist rule as "a totalitarian dictatorship."[6] Walker described how the
Communist Party ruled China: it imposed a doctrine through controlled communications; manipulated a variety of "mass support organizations"; and relied on the military, the judiciary, and the Ministry of Public Security to apply
the necessary force and coercion to maintain authority and elicit obedience
to party policies.[7]

   In 1956 Arthur Steiner wrote that "the 'labor movement' in Communist
China has lost any resemblance to the free world concept of a workers' organization seeking economic betterment for its members. It is clearly and
simply a tool of the Chinese Communists for the manipulation of labor to
their own ends."[8] In 1956 Norris P. Smith accurately predicted the "virtual
completion of collectivization during 1957."[9]

   Mao Tse-tung, the party's preeminent leader, was also perceived as
building a totalitarian society that would allow only small pockets of noncon-
formity. Benjamin Schwartz noted Mao's totalitarian vision of the new society in Mao's speeches of the early 1950s.

   What, then, is the overall vision presented in Mao's speeches? It is the
   vision of a totalitarian society by consent, so to speak, a society in which

the state may hold its authority in reserve in certain well-defined areas of culture (such as natural sciences). The "fundamental" harmony of the society will be preserved all the more effectively by allowing an area of slack—that is, by recognizing that certain clashes of interest and a certain degree of ideological error are normal, and that there may be certain areas of the arts and sciences where Marxism-Leninism does not immediately yield any answers.[10]

But Schwartz also reminded his readers that "the authority of the state, however, remains supreme, and the basic concept is still fundamentally totalitarian."[11] Sinologists who knew something about traditional imperial rule concluded from the political developments of the early 1950s that "the new order, in seeking *absolute* uniformity and conformity, excludes any such outlet. With modern techniques and instruments of coercion at its command, the Communist regime is seeking to impose a system that surpasses in its totality anything that China has experienced in the past" (emphasis in the original).[12]

Other experts merely saw Mao's tactics of rule as Stalinist. Writing in 1958, Roderick MacFarquhar emphasized the Stalinist-totalitarian features of Communist China.

The inescapable conclusion from all this is that at no point in the development of Chinese Communist totalitarianism—past or present (and the writer is tempted to add, future)—have economic factors been (or will they be) decisive. What has been decisive so far has been the Chinese leaders' partiality, primarily for political reasons, to the Stalinist form of totalitarianism.[13]

Aside from Mao's reliance on Stalinist methods, most experts during this decade viewed Communist China as a monolithic state. Robert C. North appraised the party's Eighth Congress in 1956 in just these terms.

What emerges from the Eighth Congress, therefore, is the picture of a totalitarian government dedicated in purpose, confident in its success, Machiavellian in its foreign relations, and ruthless in domestic regimentation and the exploitation of human lives for ends of state. How Chinese Communist leaders will deploy their rapidly developing strength is difficult to predict.[14]

And when Mao ordered the organization of communes in 1958, the party's capacity to restructure China's rural society only confirmed that "Party control in China is greater today than it has ever been, exceeding even that in the Soviet Union."[15]

Interpreting Communist China as a totalitarian society persisted even into the early 1960s. In 1961 A. Doak Barnett commented, "the regime that the Chinese Communists have established is the first effective totalitarian regime, at least in the modern sense, in Chinese history."[16] Barnett argued, however, that special circumstances had influenced China to choose the totalitarian path. He pointed out that China had been organized according to Soviet organizational principles but "with significant Chinese variation," which flowed from different party tactics to reorder social relations and remold ideology. The historian John K. Fairbank also concluded that the China of the 1950s was a product both of her past and of selective factors borrowed from the West that added up to "a totalitarianism which is something quite new in China's experience."[17]

If the experts viewed the Chinese system as an "ideal" totalitarian system, how did they evaluate the impact of this new system on society? Here, again, there seemed to have been a widely shared view that the new burdens imposed on Chinese society by this regime were exceedingly high and that certain classes paid a heavy price for the regime's early success in extending its authority and insisting on doctrinal conformity.

Some experts saw the party's tactic of giving land to the farmers and then collectivising that land as a cruel hoax played on the rural people. "For the sake of an outmoded doctrine maintained by the tiny minority in power, the Chinese peasant is to be brought under a system which has proven a failure in application, as the post-Stalin Soviet leadership has itself revealed."[18] Others tried to estimate the loss of human life, pointing out that between February 1951 and mid-1952 at least two million so-called counter-revolutionaries had been slain and that between mid-1952 and mid-1954 another fifteen million had lost their lives. In addition to this slaughter, a huge number of people were incarcerated by the regime (an estimated twenty-three million).[19] Millions more were rounded up and sent to the new corrective labor camps for supervision and thought reform. "We can say that in six years of Chinese Communist rule about 15 million persons out of a total population of around 600 million—one out of every 40 citizens—have entered the regime's prisons or corrective labor camps."[20] Yuan-li Wu described how the regime used slave labor for water conservancy projects and other economic activities.[21]

As early as 1952 A. Doak Barnett provided a graphic report of how labor had been mobilized to build the Chungking-Chengtu railroad line. His informant, a civil engineer who had fled to Hong Kong, revealed that the laborers for this project had been recruited from nearby villages as corvée labor. Although workers were paid in both rice and currency, "the pay did not provide any surplus to send home to their families. And secondly, the pace of work was considered unreasonable."[22] This engineer said that the construction of railroads around the country in this way would entail poor-quality transport, which would rapidly deteriorate and require constant repair in the near future. Barnett's interviews with refugees led him to conclude in 1952 that the new regime was probably exacting far too high a price from its citizens for its programs.

> As stated earlier, these accomplishments, and the revolutionary energy behind them, have made a deep impression on a considerable number of people. To the extent that one can judge Chinese "public opinion" from Hong Kong (a difficult task, at best), however, the majority of Chinese feel that the price paid for such accomplishments—ruthless disregard of the individual, thought control, regimentation of society, etc.—is too high. Mr. Wu, for example, believes that most people in Szechwan are bitterly dissatisfied with the Communists, despite the Chungking-Chengtu railway and other development projects now being carried out. He himself decided over two months ago that, although he occupied a fairly advantageous position as a technician under a regime that glorifies technicians, he did not want to continue living in the oppressive atmosphere the Communists have created. He decided to leave his country for the first—and conceivably the last—time, and he is now a "White Chinese" refugee in Hong Kong.[23]

Barnett repeated this same assessment in 1962, when he summarized his impressions of how well the new regime had succeeded in meeting the needs of the people. "The price in terms of economic austerity, overwork, rigid political control, and unprecedented regimentation has been extremely high. The entire twelve-year period since the Communist take-over has been one of almost continuous struggle, tension, and uncertainty in China, and these are not 'easily' endured for a prolonged period of time."[24] Although a number of writers sympathetic to the new regime did not agree that the Chinese people had experienced such high costs during the 1950s, most leading U.S. China-watchers judged the new regime negatively, chiefly because they viewed Communist China as a totalitarian system.

THE MODERNIZING
COMMUNIST REGIME

The training of more China experts after 1958 occurred just as social-science departments began insisting on training graduate students to formulate testable hypotheses or to construct analytical models and verify them by quantitative procedures. This new generation of China experts was acutely sensitive to the importance of methodology. They also witnessed the remarkable events in China during 1966–67, which convinced many that describing China as a totalitarian system with features similar to the Soviet Union had been too simplistic and, at times, erroneous.

The descriptive type we call a modernizing communist regime contains the following propositions about Communist China during its first thirty years.

- This regime sought to modernize China by means of competing visions, ideas, and policies that were either transformative or accommodative.
- Because the regime primarily pursued transformative policies, economic policies fluctuated greatly when the leaders created new organizations and mobilized human and physical resources. These policies, however, did not seem to be associated with any long-run, serious dysfunctions in Chinese society.
- The pattern of instability and mixed success at modernization owed much to the absence of traditional Chinese values and institutions, for which the leadership had not yet found appropriate substitutes.

Let us be clear about our terms. "Modernization" denotes the process by which society is transformed by scientific and technological advances.[25] This leadership vision of the new society and the policies needed to create it quickly is termed "transformative." Thomas A. Metzger's pioneering study *Escape from Predicament* first introduced this concept.[26] In other words, if leaders have in mind an ideal society very different from the existing one, and if they believe that people can adapt quickly to different norms and values to conform to this ideal future society, they will pursue policies to create this society. We refer to these policies as transformative. These leaders also believe that people will be able to change their beliefs by means of incessant struggle if the correct policies are introduced and new organizations are created to make human behavior conform to that of the new society.

"Accommodative" leaders and their supporters share the same vision of the future society as their transformative-minded colleagues. But accommodative leaders contend that society ought to be gradually reformed by slowly building the appropriate new institutions, consolidating gains, and gradually reshaping these institutions as new conditions—made possible by the adoption of new science and technology—allow. They argue that much time has to elapse before society's values can be fundamentally changed. This process cannot occur, however, until the economy's productive capabilities have been greatly enhanced by rapid modernization.

During the 1950s transformative and accommodative leadership behavior often coexisted in Communist China, but transformative behavior gradually began to predominate—first in the late 1950s and again in the late 1960s and early 1970s. Accommodative behavior revived only after 1978. These swings in leadership behavior produced great changes in organizations and, more characteristically, in the participation of a large proportion of the society in the new experiments. The key goal for both transformative and accommodative groups, however, was to create the new values and norms necessary to build a modern communist society. We have found that the majority of articles and books in our sample focused on the competing ideas and policies of Mao and his colleagues and their alleged impact on society. What follows covers only a small portion of these writings.

By 1960 some China-watchers began suggesting that the Chinese Communists were behaving differently from Communists in Moscow. Benjamin Schwartz noted that the party's attempts to impose Stalinist policies on China had proved difficult because the "subjective outlook of Mao Tse-tung and his entourage are equally important." Schwartz then said that "one of the peculiar features of Chinese communism is the whole area of phenomena known as 'thought reform' and 'remoulding.'"[27] This new line of thinking suggested that certain leaders—namely, Mao and his followers—placed enormous importance on policies to make the people think as Mao did. Yet Mao's emphasis on "mind over matter" and the Stalinist method of initiating a "revolution from above" could still converge, as in the Greap Leap Forward campaign of 1958–59.[28]

By 1965 a new generation of China experts began to develop the insights offered by Benjamin Schwartz. John Wilson Lewis saw Mao's "revolutionary struggle" as an effort to force the CCP to take the view that "the redistribution of power and accompanying ideological and organizational changes must precede and lay the foundation for industrialisation."[29] Schwartz reemphasized his view of five years earlier by saying that "Mao Tse-tung and those closest to him have played a leading role in determining basic policy shifts during the last fifteen years."[30] Mao's hopes of achieving the good society were dependent upon a spiritual transformation of the people and the radical collectivization of society. Others like Mao pressed for a "modernization which can be incorporated into the Maoist vision" by the substitution of human energy for weapons and physical capital.

The violence of the Great Proletarian Cultural Revolution surprised most U.S. China experts. Especially surprising was the way communist leaders attacked one another. Many saw Mao and his supporters as attempting to alter the norms and values of society so that "every person must actively participate in the political system and processes." Mao, however, needed political power if he was to impose his grand design on society.[31] It became fashionable to interpret the activities of the early 1960s as intraparty differences in policy and perspectives that were becoming increasingly intense over time. Some experts saw the intense intraparty debates between 1963 and 1965 as a clash between two different strategies for modernizing China. One sought to rekindle a revolutionary ideology; the other sought to solve "new, post-revolutionary socio-economic problems" by means of institutionalized, routinized state and party policies.[32] Mao's later use of Red Guards to attack party leaders, his attempts to develop a cult of personality, and his vigorous efforts to legitimize his control both within and outside of the party showed the "significance of political ideology and the difficulty of challenging an established doctrine and evolving a new one in a totalitarian system."[33]

Mao's transformative vision of the new society required the creation of new attitudes and behavior that would somehow eventually accommodate a new technology and science without being dependent upon them. Lloyd Eastman contrasted Mao with Marx by noting that Mao's future society would still require authority but would require that intellectuals work; differences between mental and physical labor would actually be erased.[34] Richard M. Pfeffer called Mao *"a radical in power*—perhaps the first in history who has substantially retained his radical purity after being in power for over a generation" (emphasis in original).[35]

Even in the late 1960s Mao's transformative ideas and policies still prevailed in the party. Gordon A. Bennett described 1969 as a conflict-ridden year, but "the political initiative has been recovered by Mao-oriented socialists. They may share power in given organs and given localities with leaders of somewhat different persuasions; nevertheless, the revolution will go on."[36] John Bryan Starr argued that Mao's ideology had to be taken seriously as a powerful motor force for political action and social behavior; Mao's transformative ideas merely served as a corpus of thought to justify "permanent revolution" for as long a time as it would take to create the new society.[37] Harry Harding, Jr. insisted that the political violence of recent years had not been simply a power struggle but had been "instead, an idealistic and visionary program, designed to reverse trends toward inequities in China's economic system, and toward rigidities in her political institutions."[38]

The demise of Mao in late 1976 produced many interpretations of his programs and new speculations on how they might influence China's future. James R. Townsend saw Mao's legacy in three forms: the policy of the "mass line" to elicit grass-roots support for party policies; the institutions of the "mass line" that called for decentralized organs of the state and popular political study and criticism; and finally, a movement toward egalitarian social relationships that was to be accomplished by narrowing social status and rewarding all occupational groups equally. He concluded that "the mythic Mao will be both populist and prophet, a man of the people, who saw the anti-popular tendencies of our time and struggled against them."[39] Some political scientists even pointed out that the debates and struggles among party leaders in the 1970s were perceived by Mao as a new Marxist interpretation of Chinese reality, which propounded that society's "superstructure" had become increasingly important and which blocked economic modernization. According to this theory, if political and cultural changes were initiated first, modern economic growth would follow naturally.[40]

Certain China-watchers, however, pointed out that even in the 1950s party leaders of different ideological persuasions had compromised, and leaders of accommodation-style behavior had sometimes had their way. Roderick MacFarquhar commented that at the Eighth Party Congress in 1956, the Liu Shao-ch'i and Teng Hsiao-p'ing reports never mentioned Mao's thoughts. Liu even stated that "the principal contradiction in China was no longer between the proletariat and the bourgeoisie, but between an advanced socialist system and backward productive forces."[41] Liu's interpretation of Chinese reality at that time already differed from Mao's; he emphasized that the party should develop the economy through science and technology.[42] Andrew Nathan went so far as to argue that during much of this early period "leftist and rightist policies . . . more often co-existed than not," which is simply to say that party leaders shared a complex mix of transformative-accommodational ideas.[43]

Although China-watchers might not always have agreed on the result of these conflicting ideas and policies, many agreed that when the party pushed transformative policies, Communist China (unlike other communist societies) experienced extremely large economic fluctuations. The economist Alexander Eckstein theorized that when the leadership perceived that certain resource scarcities had worsened, they responded with policies to overcome these scarcities. Because leaders often differed in their perceptions, however, their policies ranged from those calling for "scaling down the pace of development" to those "for more intensive mobilization of the population in order to speed up development."[44] Yuan-li Wu also referred to these same ideological disputes within the top leadership.[45] Kuan-I Chen used regression analysis to demonstrate that fluctuations in net domestic product between 1952 and 1965 were highly correlated with large variations in food-grain and industrial production. Despite the party's reliance on central planning, China's economy experienced unusually large swings in economic activity.[46]

Most experts did not associate these violent swings in economic policy and activity with any severe setbacks for the people's welfare or with a decline in goods, services, and physical capital. Because China began its development in 1949 at an economic disadvantage, building an advanced industrial base required a prodigious effort. Viewed from this perspective, leading economists considered the first two decades to be periods of moderate growth. Alexander Eckstein asserted that "the rate of farm production growth in China may be considered as eminently respectable although, placed against the formidable pressure of population and the rather rapid rate of population growth, it does not seem adequately to have met the requirements of the country's industrialization."[47] Because the economy had annual rates of growth between two and three percent for per capita-output, Eckstein conjectured that "China's economy advanced at a moderate speed."

Robert M. Field estimated that between 1949 and 1974 industrial production grew at an average annual rate of 13 percent, but between 1960 and 1974 the rate of growth slowed to 6 percent per annum (as compared to 22 percent for the years 1949–60).[48] Field also reported that regional development of industry had continued over the entire period at breakneck speed.[49] Leo A. Orleans gave the regime high marks for its environmental policies, noting the government's efforts to provide good water, enforce antipollution measures, and protect China's environment.[50]

Not all China-watchers analyzing economic trends agreed with these favorable assessments, but those we have cited certainly did not think that economic development suffered under a leadership committed to transformative policies. Some economists, however, tried to separate the short-term fluctuations from the long-term effects of transformative policy changes on the economy. Robert Dernberger pointed out that "serious disruption in transportation and production" occurred after 1966, and industrial production "did not regain the peak level of 1966 until 1969."[51] But according to Dernberger, in aggregate terms industrial output still grew at 8.8 percent per year and agricultural output at 3.1 percent per year between 1963 and 1971. He conjectured that in the near future China could join the advanced countries in "a pentagon of world powers."[52]

Communist China's transformative leadership also began to try to develop new organizations, create new social behavior, and shape new rural-urban relationships. In this regard, legal reforms were crucial. Victor Li saw two types of legal systems evolving. One, which evolved in the 1950s, followed a mixture of pre-1949 and Soviet legal precepts, by which the state tried to enforce law and settle disputes. Another, which evolved in the 1960s, sought to instill new norms and social values in order to reform behavior.[53] But in the area of economic activity, reforms of organizations took precedence over legal reforms. For example, Carl Riskin pointed out that the "years following the (Great) Leap have seen a re-gearing of small industry to serve agriculture, and a rationalization of technique to enable 'expanded reproduction' to replace 'primitive accumulation' as the basis for further growth."[54]

Another new organization, the small study group (*Hsiao-tsu*), seems to have originated partly from Bolshevik party rituals and partly from the trial-and-error procedures worked out by the Chinese Communists to bring the party and the masses closer together. According to Martin King Whyte, the *Hsiao-tsu* "do imply a high degree of authoritarian regimentation, of pervasive scrutiny of and control over individual behavior by higher authorities. Yet they are also expected to facilitate a de-emphasis on commands, coercion, and material incentives and to lead to mass enthusiasm and involvement."[55] This, and other, organizations created by the party also altered social relationships.[56]

Ezra Vogel argued that the party's mobilization campaigns in the first fifteen years had enabled the regime to penetrate and influence the private lives of its citizens, even to the extent of creating a new social ethic, which he called "comradeship" and defined as "a universal morality in which all citizens are in important respects equal under the state, and gradations on the basis of status or of closeness cannot legitimately interfere with this equality."[57] Vogel sensed that there had been a decline in friendship and a rise in comradeship in Communist China. "What is unique about Communist China is not the presence of a universalistic ethic governing personal relations, but the absence of a private ethic to supplement the public ethic and support the commitment of the individual to his friend."[58]

To realize the party's goal of wide political participation, the Maoist cadres redefined worker-management relations and altered the career patterns of new bureaucrats. The communist regime had already exhibited a remarkable capacity to mobilize resources, as seen in the great corvée labor projects of the 1950s. These types of activities continued in later decades. But one particular transformative policy sent urban youth to work and live in the countryside, often in other provinces. Initiated on a very small scale in the 1950s, this program to alter urban-rural relationships grew on an unprecedented scale during the 1960s and early 1970s and amazed foreign observers. The party leadership hoped that sending youth to the countryside (known as *Hsia fang*) would ease congestion in cities, minimize elitism, and raise the cultural level of farmers. Some observers predicted that if the experiment was successful, other countries might adopt it.

Hsia fang is a Chinese application of Marxist theory for modernisation purposes. The Chinese Communist regime has instituted the system in an effort to forestall the growth of parasitism and to promote modernisation values among its elite, to utilise in production manpower which would otherwise be wasted in unnecessary administrative posts and to inculcate in its elite a style of work which both grasps the practical problems of production and raises the productive spirit of the workers and peasants. Insofar as *Hsia fang* succeeds in its purpose it may be a developmental formula of great significance, not only for China but for other underdeveloped countries as well.[59]

Some China experts believed the movement helped to slow up urban population growth. Paul Ivory and William Lavely estimated that the rural rustication program contributed to a lowering of female fertility in Shanghai because of greater female participation in the work force to compensate for the departure of around 1,290,000 young people from the city between 1968 and 1976.[60]

As for the absence of appropriate values to accommodate these new transformative policies, Lucian Pye has argued that the Chinese have never been able "to reconcile the manifest accomplishments of their traditional civilization with the requirement that their society would have to be radically made over."[61] Pye perceives that since 1949 there has been a continual interplay among ideology, personality, and decision-making in shaping agriculture, education, socialization, and military affairs. For the early decades of communist rule Pye draws a picture of a very unstable communist system, which "had done . . . little to institutionalize and routinize authority." There was therefore a need for a powerful leader like charismatic Mao Tse-tung.[62]

According to Pye, Mao's repeated stress on class conflict replaced the old appeals for harmony that had predominated in traditional China. Mao tried to mobilize the entire population by drawing upon people's long-suppressed emotions of anger. For brief moments these popular sentiments supported Maoist transformative policies and accounted for the regime's short-lived successes. Unlike other people, the Chinese have never been troubled by any crises of identity; they have always faulted their leaders for not creating that "complete and absolute form of government, strong enough to bring China back to its rightful place in the eyes of the rest of the world."[63] Leaders who failed quickly fell from grace.

Pye contends that until different values toward authority replace traditional Confucian values, the Chinese leadership will not be able to create a highly specialized and differentiated modern society. Such a society requires a complex division of authority, and these conditions run counter to traditional Chinese values that find comfort in an omnipotent authority. "This is the basic problem Mao confronts when he talks of the 'red and expert' issue. He continues to insist that the specialist must be the complete servant of the political authority and that no form of specialized knowledge can be allowed to compromise the authority of his revolution, which is embodied in his own person."[64] Because the Chinese do not find it easy to divide authority, believe that any division of authority will produce conflict, and feel a compelling urge to re-establish a monopoly of authority to minimize this conflict, Pye argues that China will not be able to modernize until new cultural values replace older ones.

THE REVOLUTIONARY
SOCIALIST REGIME

By 1968 U.S. involvement in the Vietnam conflict had begun to outrage many students and professors. One by-product of campus protest of this war was the publication (in May 1968) of a newsletter that later became a scholarly periodical devoted to contemporary Asian studies—the *Bulletin of Concerned Asian Scholars*. Students and faculty specializing in Asian studies established forums to debate not only American involvement in Vietnam but also American policy toward the Far East and China-related research and teaching. They used the *Bulletin* and other scholarly journals to challenge the Joint Committee for Contemporary China's organized China studies and the then-current interpretation of developments within Communist China.[65] The new perspective that emerged in their writings conveys the key characteristics of a descriptive typology that we call the revolutionary socialist regime:

- The Chinese revolutionary socialist regime, strongly influenced by Maoist thought and policies, initiated revolutionary strategies that greatly improved the welfare of the Chinese people and created a more egalitarian society.
- These developments were not associated with any severe difficulties for this new leadership and society.

These analysts of Communist China argued that the party leadership, influenced by Mao Tse-tung's writings and arguments, formulated policies aimed at developing better human beings. Furthermore, they said that party policies were aimed at raising the material welfare standards for all the people at the same time.

Perhaps the most striking difference between the capitalist and Maoist views concerns goals. Maoists believe that while a principal aim of nations should be to raise the level of material welfare of the population, this should be done only within the context of the development of human beings, encouraging them to realize fully their manifold creative powers. And it should be done only on an egalitarian basis—that is, on the basis that development is not worth much unless everyone rises together: no one is to be left behind, either economically or culturally. Indeed, Maoists believe that rapid economic development is not likely to occur *unless* everyone rises together. Development as a trickle-down process is therefore rejected by Maoists, and so they reject any strong emphasis on profit motives and efficiency criteria that lead to lopsided growth (emphasis in the original).[66]

When the Communist Party first began to unify China under its control, it redistributed wealth and income by taking the land and other properties of the rural elite and giving them to poor families and by confiscating the assets and property of the urban capitalists and elite and using them for state programs. With these assets the party and the state were able to finance economic recovery, initiate a planned economy, and undertake the construction of large-scale industrial projects and new factories. Land reform played a key role. According to Victor Lippit, land reform redirected income from recipients who had formerly spent most of it on consumer luxuries and corrupt activities to the new state, whose sound economic plan for building key industries was eventually to produce consumer goods for the benefit of all the Chinese people.

> The change in property relations wrought by the land reform in the agricultural sector of the economy and by increasing socialization in the industrial sector redirected income flows which had sustained luxury consumption in the financing of both higher levels of investment and higher consumption for those most in need. In this way the long-range development needs of the economy and the immediate and pressing needs for the alleviation of poverty were reconciled in the Chinese revolution.[67]

Lippit also criticized some American economists for stating that the high rate of investment in capital accumulation had restricted consumer expenditures and retarded the improvement in welfare for the Chinese people during the 1950s. Lippit contended that the redistribution of rural income had enabled the state to raise the ratio of investment to income and had even helped rural households raise their consumption expenditures. He favored these policies, and he did not believe they imposed a great burden on the people.

Even the Great Leap Forward policies of Mao and the party between 1958 and 1960 bestowed some benefits on the country. Carl Riskin suggested that "for the present . . . there is no evidence that workers were not motivated to upgrade skills during the Great Leap (introduction of industrial technology to peasants during the 'backward iron and steel movement' is one of the few generally conceded virtues of the movement)."[68] Contrary to the views of other China-watchers, who commented that these same policies had been brutally imposed on the people, Stephen Andors asserted that "the policies of the Leap found crucial sources of support within Chinese industry, both from amongst the leading cadres at the enterprise level as well as some economic planners."[69] Andors attributed this positive reception to managers allegedly unhappy with the Soviet-style factory management practice of giving a single manager power over foremen and their workers.

Others praised the Great Leap Forward policies for bringing a huge influx of women into the rural and industrial labor force, thereby changing the socioeconomic relations between women and men. Phyllis Andors lauded this campaign for drastically changing women's roles and forcing the party to provide more resources to support women's commitment to work and their participation in the labor force.[70]

In evaluating the next great political campaign, the Cultural Revolution, Carl Riskin admitted that industrial production had declined in 1967. He conjectured, however, that "the performance suggested by 'official' statistics, on the other hand, is not one of rapid growth, but of sufficient increase to maintain low but adequate consumption standards, and a moderate but positive response of food-grain output to increasing amounts of inputs."[71] Stephen Andors was impressed by the intent of certain factories to eliminate piece wages and bonuses and the party's efforts to initiate new committees to manage factories and to develop a different web of work rules. He argued that "the Cultural Revolution put emphasis on cooperation and collective *esprit* as motivating factors for both workers and managers. Large-scale, detailed discussions were held to revise rules and regulations to maintain discipline and order without a control apparatus to supervise every detail. Rules and regulations formulated with worker participation were strictly and eagerly obeyed because they were realistic."[72]

Andors regarded these industrial-management changes as very significant. He introduced a volume of translated documents on this issue with the following statement:

> This volume is an attempt to let the revolutionary vision that has been so much a part of the politics of Chinese industrial development speak for itself through books and documents published and widely read in China. The nature of politics in the post-Mao Tse-tung era is still impossible to discern, but it is certain that this vision will continue to play a crucial role in shaping the patterns of conflict even as it did before Mao's death.[73]

Andors argued that, regardless of the turmoil associated with China's many great campaigns, in each of them "there was a mass learning process going on, technical as well as political . . . In all of the campaigns in industry, the distribution and purpose of technical knowledge was a prime issue of political concern and conflict."[74]

Other concerned Asian scholars applauded the party-state policies that developed regions in which there were high and stable food-grain yields by making resources available to the collective-farming system and establishing procedures whereby workers in this system were paid according to egalitarian principles.[75] Still others reported that Communist China did not suffer from the stagflation that beset many Western countries in the 1970s. The party, they said, adhered to a balanced budget during this period and only financed the amount of economic growth the country could afford. More importantly, these measures allegedly benefited the countryside. "Perhaps in no area of the economy have China's achievements been so strikingly successful as in their handling of agricultural collectivization and, with special emphasis since the Cultural Revolution, in raising the standard of living in the countryside to bring economic and social conditions in the rural areas closer to those of the towns."[76] The terms of trade had steadily improved. Therefore, commune members purchased more products from the cities, increased savings, and expanded investment in their small-scale industry.

These scholars argued that these revolutionary policies had promoted progress on nearly all fronts in the country since 1949. John Gurley described the success of these policies in providing more welfare gains for the populace.

> The truth is that China over the past two decades has made very remarkable economic advances (though not steadily) on almost all fronts. The basic, overriding economic fact about China is that for twenty years it has fed, clothed, and housed everyone, has kept them healthy, and has educated most. Millions have not starved; sidewalks and streets have not been covered with multitudes of sleeping, begging, hungry, and illiterate human beings; millions are not disease-ridden. To find such deplorable conditions, one does not look to China these days but, rather, to India, Pakistan, and almost anywhere else in the underdeveloped world. These facts are so basic, so fundamentally important, that they completely dominate China's economic picture, even if one grants all of the erratic and irrational policies alleged by its numerous critics.[77]

THE CHINESE COMMUNIST REGIME

Our final typology contains four principal elements:

- Since 1949 the Communist Party has exerted pervasive control, completely dominating society in spite of periodic political campaigns to purge local and top-level leaders.

- The essence of this single-party regime has been to retain control, and all other concerns are tied to this fundamental issue.
- Chinese Communist Party politics have always been characterized by factionalism and the struggle for power.
- Single-party control, the power struggle to retain control, and the complex group factionalism this struggle has produced have been associated with severe, long-term difficulties for the Chinese regime and its people.

This new typology (associated with the 1960s and 1970s) differed from the totalitarian typology of the 1950s. It recognized that a new pattern of behavior characterized the party after 1960—a struggle for power and party factionalism. Various party leaders and their supporters began to differ sharply over how Chinese society should move toward communism in the future, and some resorted to irregular means to regain their power within the party.

Whereas the party seemed monolithic in the 1950s, it changed during the next two decades. Even so, many experts contended that the party never really lost its control over society and that it was still able to maintain its dominance, even in the smallest community. In fact, tight party control continued in spite of the coalitions competing for leadership. After 1960 the frequent power struggles influenced not only the political norms of party behavior but also the people the party ruled, making the party's management and development of society and the economy more difficult.

But control over society was still a major objective of the Communist Party. Paul Harper described how the party used mass organizations to control various sectors of society in the 1950s; trade unions served as the party's transmission belt to control the urban industrial work force. Nevertheless, tensions arose between union representatives and higher party leaders in the late 1950s, when more workers demanded professional considerations. By 1965, however, unions were again made "wholly subservient to the Party and the transmission belt was to move in one direction only—downwards."[78] But the Cultural Revolution enabled some urban unions to regain a certain amount of power; this revived the old tensions. Harper remarked that "the union cadres will perceive their interests to lie with furthering the livelihood of the workers and the advance of production, in which professional and bureaucratic attitudes comprise the day-to-day approach rather than the political and ideological, despite sporadic emulation drives and mass movements."[79] He speculated that union cadres might even seek "operational independence from the Party" because of the new relationship between the party and the unions established during the Cultural Revolution. But in conclusion, Harper's analysis confirmed the longstanding capability of the party to manipulate the unions to its own ends.

Similarly, the party used the system of people's courts to make control of party organs wholly political. Allan Spitz points out that "in sum, the People's Courts in China function to suppress the enemies of the state and to help solve the contradictions among the people."[80] He also says that "as an integral part of the political-legal front, [these courts] operate in response to the policies and goals of the Party in Communist China."[81] Using mainly Russian sources, George Ginsburg and Arthur Stahnke examined the new People's Procuratorate and concluded that the coincidences between the Soviet and communist Chinese versions of the procuratorate by far outnumbered their differences.[82] After 1952 the People's Procuratorate became an instrument of state and party power.

By virtue of the enormous control established over society by the mid-1950s, the party proved capable of intruding into personal relationships, marriage, and childbearing and dictating moral behavior. Privacy was not allowed. According to Paul Hollander, "the main pillar of the Chinese Communist ideological position is the Party's view of human nature, which it insists upon as the indispensable precondition of a correct approach to questions of morality and interpersonal relations. This view has remained unchanged since the early 1950s and—barring a fundamental transformation of the political system—is not likely to undergo modification."[83]

The party tried to control intellectuals by selecting leading writers and spokespersons for harsh punishment; these examples were a warning to others who might try to resist party dictates. Adam Oliver stressed that "intellectuals have been used as pawns for broad thought remolding drives by the Chinese Communists ever since Ting Ling went through the wringer of the original Cheng Feng movement in 1942."[84] The party periodically initiated these campaigns as a "stupendous effort to reshape the patterns of thought of an entire people."[85] Religion was not tolerated either, because the party feared that various associations of believers would impede societal control. "With the advent of the Communist regime, there has been a steady decline in theist religion."[86]

In addition to controlling labor, youth, intellectuals, morality, and religion, the party used its power to enforce policies on the small-scale administrative unit of the county. In county administrations the party appears to have successfully mobilized policies to create an infrastructure and new projects. Take the example of Fukien Province. Even though "a substantial degree of de facto decentralization exists in the Chinese system because of the inability of the Centre directly to administer programmes at the basic level," the party created in Fukien Province a remarkably fine-tuned, sensitive, administrative instrument capable of adjusting policy to the vicissitudes of reality without sacrificing the policy itself.[87]

The party could not have effectively controlled society without the assistance of the Public Security Bureau. Branches of this bureau were "set up on every level from the central government down to the villages and streets."[88] Even during the Cultural Revolution, when the People's Liberation Army (PLA) had to restore order, there is no evidence that revolutionary committees ever tried to manage the Public Security Bureau units. These units continue to provide police control and backup support for the party even today.[89]

Since the party controlled behavior so tightly, it was only natural that individuals of high party rank would try to make the party work for them. Every leader realized that he had to be effective or the party apparatus would become the instrument of another leader—perhaps an adversary. Because leadership posts in the party were so crucial, the ambitious competed for necessary votes either in the Political Bureau or in the Central Committee. Failing this, they might resort to irregular means, such as calling on organs outside the party to crush their opposition and regain party control. The struggle for power within the party became most conspicuous during the 1960s.

Chu-Yuan Cheng, writing in late 1966, described the events of that year as "a fierce power rivalry among the potential heirs of Mao Tse-tung."[90] The rise and fall of a powerful provincial communist official could also be attributed to Mao's effort to control the various political levels of power. Peter Moody described the career of the Kwangtung official T'ao Chu as an attempt to exploit political opportunities within the context of a continuous struggle for power.[91] Franz Michael viewed Mao's efforts since 1958 as a continual contest with his party colleagues, which finally compelled Mao to take unprecedentedly violent measures to purge his foremost rival—Liu Shao-ch'i—and his supporters. "Looking back over the course of events in Communist China since 1958, the present [1966–67] spectacle of madness and chaos appears as the natural climax to Mao's losing battle to impose his brand of radical, utopian communism at home and to assert his claim to world Communist leadership abroad."[92] According to Michael, after having built up his power to lead the CCP in the 1950s, Mao finally "became a maverick in his own party and in the world Communist movement." To regain control over the party, Mao had to struggle to wield his influence once again.

The struggle for power sometimes took the form of a top leader ousting an heir apparent suspected of aligning with the leader's enemies and plotting to take power prematurely. CIA analyst Philip Bridgham recounted how Mao removed his designated successor, Lin Piao, when Mao was trying to rebuild the party and press forward his Cultural Revolution programs, because he suspected Lin of becoming the leader of a disloyal opposition.[93] "Lin, Ch'en Po-ta, and the top military command should have joined forces in an attempt to prevent their impending downfall."[94] They did not, and this error in judgment cost Lin his life and his would-be allies their careers.

Before Mao died, China-watchers like Parris H. Chang postulated that a new power struggle between Teng Hsiao-p'ing and Hua Kuo-feng was already underway. Hua was "walking a precarious political tightrope."[95] He aligned himself with the party radicals to destroy Teng, but the radicals had no assurance that Hua would not follow Teng if they tried to seize power after Mao died. We know, of course, that Hua quickly turned on the radicals after Mao died; he arrested them and then tried to use Teng to retain his power in the party.[96] But the gentlemen's agreement between Teng and Hua (if there had been one) quickly dissolved; Teng rehabilitated his disgraced supporters, who subsequently re-entered the party and government and aligned with him. Teng eventually eased Hua out and, after consolidating his power base, appointed Hu Yao-pang and other strong supporters to the Political Bureau, the Central Committee, and various prestigious councils.

These violent power struggles coincided with the political activity of factions formed by the party elite within and without the party. Factional struggles also reflected bruising power struggles between individuals, and much has been written on the dynamics of political factionalism in Communist China. Although we cannot summarize the literature on this issue, we will demonstrate the great importance given to this political behavior in China by American China-watchers.

William Whitson contended that the assignments of field army officers to military posts reflected bonds of confidence and in-group security between military commanders and their subordinates.[97] To ensure their power, influence, and prestige, party military leaders selected personnel for their field armies. But although factions existed within the PLA, these factions never became serious enough to threaten the composition of factions within the party itself.

Different party factions have been identified, however. Michel Oksenberg and Steven Goldstein identified four main groups of party leaders: (1) militant fundamentalists, who wanted to mobilize the populace to meet the Western threat; (2) radical conservatives, who wanted to borrow selectively from the West; (3) eclectic modernizers, who were even more eager to borrow from the West; and (4) Westernized Chinese, who advocated the "pursuit of national greatness as a Westernized country."[98] Oksenberg and Goldstein opined that "by early 1973, then, conditions appeared to be evolving firmly in a direction favorable to the eclectic modernizers—perhaps even shifting the political center of gravity toward them and away from the radical conservatives."[99] They predicted that factional struggles among these groups would continue throughout the decade.

The politics of the mid-1970s, for example, hinged on whether the ultraleftist faction in the party could wield enough military power to force their policies on other party factions. In analyzing the relations between the ultraleftists and the military, Alan P. L. Liu concluded that the ultraleftists had interfered "with virtually every issue handled by the High Command, from the military budget to the style of navy uniforms."[100] By doing so, he said, the ultraleftists mortgaged the real support needed to maintain their power. Harry Harding, Jr., writing about the post-Mao era, predicted a prolonged struggle between the moderate and radical factions in the party because of the many controversial issues that divided Hua and Teng and their supporters.[101]

The party greatly concentrated power in a few hands, designed new instruments of control to preserve a hierarchy of power, and retained power in the hands of top party leaders and their supporters. More importantly, this power mass was used to destroy many traditional institutions and create new ones in their place. Because the start-up and trade-off costs of drastic socioeconomic reforms are always very high, they place a heavy burden on both the society and the economy. Therefore, a communist system of this type soon becomes prone to numerous maladies, which can worsen over time rather than disappear. Some of these maladies are cited in the China-watching studies mentioned below.

Ten years after the regime's founding, Choh-ming Li concluded that the rate of economic growth had exceeded that of the population, "but the development programme, calling for heavier and heavier sacrifices, was determinedly imposed upon the people from above. Discontent was growing and widespread. The regime may indeed face an internal situation far more serious than at any other time since 1949."[102] Yuan-li Wu confirmed these same disasters for the years 1958–60,[103] and Edwin F. Jones stated that the food shortage had become so bad by 1960–61 that "the regime will probably have to resort to 'hard' policies, imposing social discipline by force, but they will be directed at securing conformity to established institutions rather than spurring social changes."[104]

These severe economic disasters were also described in a unique set of documents obtained by Nationalist intelligence called *Kung-tso t'ung-hsun* (Bulletin of Activities) and interpreted by John Wilson Lewis and J. Chester Cheng.[105] These documents stressed the decline in military and party morale, which was starting to cause a crisis of leadership. They also mentioned that the many large-scale water conservancy projects built by corvée labor did not provide reservoirs for regions suffering drought and produced large areas of highly alkaline soil. The alleged stability of the late 1950s owed more to "the greater political controls which are exerted over the people, including, of course, coercion."[106] The huge decline in labor productivity associated with the economic activity of these same years led one observer to note that these policies "produced an excess of cost over gain; the Chinese Communists had, in effect, lowered themselves by their own bootstraps."[107]

For the years 1952 to 1977 Anthony M. Tang found that agriculture just managed to meet the essential food needs of the expanding population, but "agriculture productivity, as measured by the index of total factor productivity, declined at an average rate of 0.65 percent. This is in sharp contrast to the productivity gains recorded by Japan, South Korea, and Taiwan."[108]

Organizations like the PLA were also damaged. Ralph L. Powell described how soldiers joined the revolutionary committees to run factories in the late 1960s. These activities apparently interfered with their combat training.[109] Assigning PLA units to construct plants also impaired their combat readiness.

Some China-watchers cited estimates from Taipei sources claiming that nearly 80 million people had spent time in forced-labor camps between 1949 and 1967; as many as 12 million had lived in these camps at any single time; and around 5.3 million had died in these camps.[110] The regime utilized the camps to re-educate prisoners, many of whom had been incarcerated for their political opinions. The party organized these camps to prevent the formation of any inmate subculture, which made it difficult for a criminal tradition or any opposition group to arise.

The normative rules that had long governed party political behavior gradually broke down, and in 1966–67 they were completely abandoned.[111] Frederick C. Teiwes argues that, originally, there was a formal code of political behavior. Members could dissent, but once collective leadership had agreed on a basic policy, all members had to obey higher directives. Lenient rectification and confession of errors by members had precedence over ruthless purging by imprisonment or death. According to Tiewes, these rules first began to change in 1957–58, when many provincial leaders were purged for alleged disloyalty. They changed even more dramatically in 1959, when Mao dismissed P'eng Teh-huai for his criticism of the Great Leap.[112] Minority rights practically disappeared and then ended in the Cultural Revolution years of 1966–67, when many top cadres ended up in prison and lost their lives. The formal code of conduct was in ruin, and party membership began to lose its desirability.

Intellectuals, in particular, bore the brunt of party wrath. The party frequently targeted an outstanding scholar for scathing public humiliation and criticism to intimidate other intellectuals into toeing the party line. Merle

Goldman recounted the bitter struggle waged by the party against the scholar Hu Feng in the early 1950s, pointing out that intellectuals who had served the Party well were often eventually victimized by it. "The long conflict between Hu Feng and the CCP illustrates the familiar tragedy of a man who supported the Communist revolutionary aims, little realising that his life of protest would no longer be possible once the party came to power."[113] Unlike the last two typologies, this fourth typology, like the totalitarian typology, describes the enormous suffering of the Chinese people because of the policies of the Communist Party.

3

Understanding by Means of Typologies: Research in the Republic of China

In the 1950s the first echelon of China-watchers in the Republic of China had worked with government intelligence documents and had published their research findings mainly for government use. Most of them had participated in the communist movement or had had personal connections with the CCP. They understood the CCP's internal operations and could derive unusual insights from Communist Party documents and publications. Therefore, when these experts analyzed the intelligence information from the mainland, they interpreted it in ways very different from those with only a social science background and perspective.

Beginning in the early 1960s a second generation of Communist China experts emerged, some of whom had been trained by their seniors but who had also received social-science training abroad. In the 1970s a third generation of researchers came onto the scene. Although better trained in social-science methodology and quantitative techniques, they lacked the rich personal experience and empathy with the CCP possessed by their seniors. Like their senior colleagues, however, they also had good training in the history of the CCP, communist ideology, and Marxian dialectics. They also understood Chinese political behavior, culture, and language. Therefore, it is not surprising the ROC experts would develop a very distinctive interpretation about the behavior of the mainland regime. We have summarized these views in the following typology.

THE CHINESE COMMUNIST TOTALITARIAN SYSTEM

There has so far been no attempt to examine the research on Communist China produced by ROC China-watchers on Taiwan. Our approach constitutes merely a preliminary effort to advance a typology that we believe appropriately summarizes their key findings. This typology has six basic, interrelated propositions:

- The CCP has completely dominated the state and, by means of its organs—especially the military and the Public Security Bureau—has tried to control all action and behavior in Chinese society. This control, however, has led to the bureaucratization of society and the creation of a privileged stratum very dependent on party power.

- The CCP, however, was enormously influenced by the leadership of a single man—Mao Tse-tung—who eventually exerted dictatorial power over the party and the state alike. Certain structural features of the party permitted enormous power to be concentrated in the hands of Mao and his followers.

- Because the party leadership and the rank and file had always comprised a mixture of Marxist-oriented intellectuals, rural poor, and social deviants, many party members were both influenced by the powerful, charismatic leadership of Mao and also craved power, privilege, and security; they frequently supported party leaders who opposed Mao.

- Therefore, powerful tensions always existed between the dominant leader Mao and other party leaders. This power struggle within the party has always characterized the CCP and will continue to do so as long as the Communist Party tries to maintain its total dominance over state and society.

- Because the party has been, and still is, faction-ridden and obsessed with maintaining its dominance over state and society, a peaceful, gradual transition to a different kind of political system cannot occur without great violence.

- Finally, because the party and state have greatly reduced private property rights and altered the structure of traditional incentives, and because the economy has been seriously affected by low productivity and enormous waste, Chinese cultural values have greatly deteriorated; social anomie has been widespread.

ROC China-watchers have constantly warned their readers (and, perhaps unconsciously, each other) that understanding CCP aims and behavior requires a thorough reading of communist texts and a profound understanding of how the CCP acquired power, controlled its members, and ultimately dominated those under its rule. One has to grasp the true meaning of party tactics and of the clichés that party leaders constantly cite—such as "the endless class struggle," "the omnipotence of war," and so forth—and also have a thorough knowledge of how the CCP applies dialectical thinking to party policies. Warren Kuo reminded his readers that:

> In order to analyze Chinese mainland issues, we often must resort to the same dialectical logic which the Communists have used . . . That logic had proved to be effective for studying the CCP's intra-Party struggle and Party personnel changes by using such concepts as the "law of contradiction," and the principle of "dividing one into two"; we also can examine the continuous violence on the mainland by using their theory of "endless class struggle"; we can appraise Party behavior by referring to "struggle-criticism-transformation (tou-p'i-kai)" and "one strike and the three anti-movement"; we can interpret how power has shifted within the Party and the state by the theory of "continued revolution"; we can also analyze the CCP's foreign policy and the Party's concept of co-existence with other states by the "united front tactics" and other double-dealing techniques.[1]

Other experts agreed with Kuo.

At a seminar on the methodology for studying Communist China held in Taipei in June 1982, Yin Ch'ing-yao, Ts'ao Po-i, and Chao Hsien-yün concurred that even though training for different areas of study—such as textual analysis, communist behavior, and matters of communist ideology—might vary, it was necessary for all China-watchers to develop a profound knowledge of Marxist-Leninist theory, the use of dialectical logic, and the history of communist parties in general.[2] Chao Hsien-yün, in particular, strongly emphasized that "dialectical logic is especially useful for analyzing the materials published by the Communists."[3] Cheng Hsüeh-chia and Li T'ien-min also pointed out that prerequisites for undertaking Communist China studies were (1) a thorough comprehension of how the communist systems in different countries actually worked and (2) an ability to differentiate the special characteristics by which the Chinese Communist Party controlled the state and the society.[4]

Bearing these injunctions in mind, we note that the ROC experts placed primary emphasis on the capability of the CCP to dominate state and society in a totalitarian fashion. After seizing power, the party quickly eliminated the national political legislative body, ended freedom of the press, forbade freedom of movement in society, regulated choice of housing, controlled entry into work occupations, and dominated the judicial process by means of its many instruments of state and mass popular control. As for individual choice within the party, Chen Yü-ch'ang pointed out that "in the Chinese Communist power apparatus, the Party decides virtually everything."[5]

Because the party has been obsessed with achieving total control over state and society, CCP leaders have always stressed the importance of political action; they have frequently urged that "politics takes command," implying that the driving force for all human activity must be politics. Throughout much of the period of CCP control, party leaders have regarded the population they ruled as simply putty to be remolded; the method for doing so was to use political education to create a new, uniform, mass ideology. Political campaigns were also mounted to release productive power and create the appropriate incentive structure for people to work harder and consume less. According to Wu An-chia, the great political campaigns—like the land reform (1950–52), the Three-anti Five-anti Movement (1952), the Three Reform Movement (1953), the Three Red Banners Campaign (1958–60), and the Three Revolutionary Movements (1963)—were initiated partly to develop the economy by releasing greater productive forces.[6] These movements, however, greatly damaged the economy. "The Party red line had become a panacea, and political movements had been endless. As a result, these movements produced serious economic backwardness, and the inefficient economic policies associated with each [movement] made it impossible to have stability."[7]

This regime also had to depend on military power and a country-wide secret police system to extend its total dominance over society. Warren Kuo has noted that "under the CCP's centralized leadership, the military and the police have turned out to be inseparable instruments for governing the people and identifying any possible enemies opposed to the Party."[8]

Such pervasive party control, however, led to a massive bureaucratization of society, which replaced the former private exchanges through free associations and markets. Without any strong checks on bureaucratic control and privilege, small fiefdoms of bureaucratic power quickly emerged, composed of a few individuals within a privileged class that took its rights for granted. "The principal malpractices by the Party leaders are those of bureaucratism, the excessive concentration of power into the hands of a few, patriarchical leaders, life-long tenure for cadres holding positions of leadership, and all kinds of special privileges."[9] Wu An-chia also noted that the establishment of a party dictatorship created widespread bureaucratism and a society without any formal law.[10]

This Communist Party ruled the Chinese people very differently from any previous regime, and its dominant style of leadership, governance, and ideology represented an aberration in Chinese political history. According to the ROC experts, Peking's rulers relied excessively on foreign political theories, particularly the Marxist-Leninist interpretations that had evolved in the Soviet Union and had been borrowed by China as the "exported products of the Soviet Communist revolution."[11] But this Sovietized Marxist theory was further modified by communist leaders like Mao Tse-tung. Consequently, those Chinese Communists who prided themselves as followers of Mao practiced an "excessive, leftist-oriented and fiercely adventuristic type of Marxism-Leninism."[12]

Because of this two-stage transmutation of Western Marxist theory—first, by the Soviet Communists and, later, by Mao and his supporters—ROC communist-affairs experts contended that the Maoist leadership and its policies bore little relationship to traditional Chinese statecraft principles and political philosophy. Many ROC experts were therefore stunned and dismayed to read accounts by Western China-watchers stressing the continuities between Maoist political-cultural goals and Chinese political-cultural traditions. As Teng Kung-hsuan acidly stated, "We are most astonished about the theory that Maoism should be regarded to be an extension of China's cultural tradition rather than an imported ideology."[13] Teng went so far as to argue that the Peking regime bore a close similarity to the Stalinist regime; that its key organizations and policies were greatly influenced by the Soviet experience of the 1920s and 1930s. He pointed out that the "inception, organization, and growth of the CCP were planned and hatched all along by Soviet Russia; in particular, Stalinism exerted a profound influence upon Mao."[14]

To differentiate the post-1949 communist regime from previous Chinese political systems, ROC experts stressed that the new regime under the Communist Party never represented a change in dynasty or simply another ordinary government. Instead, the Communist Party tried to impose a completely different social system on the people. Additionally, the communist theories developed in China on the continuous class struggle, the need for violent revolution, and the justification for a proletarian dictatorship were entirely incompatible with traditional Chinese political rules of governance. These former principles had dictated that the ruling elite should practice benevolence, seek to establish social harmony, and stress a neo-Confucian morality. Finally, political campaigns like the Cultural Revolution simply showed the contempt Mao and his followers shared for Chinese political traditions.[15]

Nevertheless, Mao and his followers were Chinese. Mao and other leaders borrowed from the experience of the Russian revolution and the writings of Lenin and Stalin in transforming communist ideas to conform to China's reality. The resultant combination drew upon a singularly negative strain in Chinese political culture—namely, those Machiavellian practices that perpetrated despotism and unbridled cruelty. As Warren Kuo has written,

> Mao Tse-tung was deeply imbued with the dark side of traditional Chinese society, and he engaged in those same dictatorial practices once used by the ancient tyrants of Chinese history. In building up his control over mainland China, Mao really had created a personality cult as well as having intro-

duced a personal style of dictatorship that was based upon his using an absolute power that exceeded any held by the previous tyrants in Chinese history.[16]

ROC experts attached considerable importance to Mao Tse-tung's one-man autocratic rule. Chu Hsin-min described Mao's personality as full of contradictions and considered him an egomaniac.[17] For Warren Kuo, Mao was "obsessed by super-egotism."[18] Hsing Kuo-ch'ang considered Mao to be of "radical and unstable mentality."[19]

But if Mao was obsessed with power and, unlike the previous Chinese tyrants, used it in unlimited ways, he also eulogized the great upheavals of the past—especially the revolutions fomented by the peasantry to topple monarchs and replace them with new leaders of greater power. Yung Wei pointed out that "it was the peasant revolts in Chinese history in which Mao found his deepest empathy and identification."[20]

According to the ROC experts, then, this peculiar combination of ideas—developed, on the one hand, from Mao's reading of foreign communist sources and, on the other, by his penchant not to employ tactics used by former Chinese leaders to outsmart their rivals—account for much of Mao's intense desire to transform the world. But Communist Party organizations also gave Mao the latitude to achieve a degree of supremacy over his colleagues and rivals never achieved by previous Chinese rulers. Warren Kuo has described how the special structural features of the Communist Party allowed individuals like Mao to accumulate enormous power without being held accountable to anyone.

First, the party was always ruled by an inner core of leaders whose power was never curtailed by any institutions within the party. "Because the plenum of the Central Committee of the CCP is not annually held and meetings of the Politburo are rarely convened, the decision-making power naturally falls into the hands of those within the Standing Committee of the Politburo . . . The Party Chairman, in turn, can exercise absolute power in the Standing Committee."[21] Second, the party chairman also dominated the party's Central Committee. Once this committee decided on a particular policy, all party members were compelled to comply.

The very fact that the CCP persists in subordinating the individual to the organization, the minority to the majority, and lower organs to higher organs, creates the favorable conditions for the Central Committee to behave in an absolutist manner. To make matters worse, it is the Chairman of the Central Committee who has the last say in everything . . . The actual processes of policy-making within the top elite, in reality, negate collective leadership.[22]

Finally, these structural features of the party made it possible for a dictator to emerge and impose his personal style of leadership. A man of Mao's capabilities and strong personality found it easy to gradually build a personality cult.

> The dictatorial traits inherent in the Chinese Communist leadership hierarchy will never change. Viewing the current Chinese Communist apparatus in this perspective explains how Mao could establish a tightly controlled organization, instill iron discipline, and subordinate individuals to the Party . . .[Such conditions demanded] the sacrifice of individuals to the Party dictatorship. Because Mao personally took over the reigns of the Party, Party dictatorship became tantamount to being his personal dictatorship.[23]

For these reasons, ROC China-watchers believed that Mao and his leadership clearly counted; that no historical analysis of the post-1949 period could ignore his monumental influence on party affairs and on society itself. But Mao could not have acquired such enormous power if the organizational structure and behavioral norms within the party had not combined to allow a concentration of power in the hands of the very top leadership.

The party also possessed a social mixture that ROC experts believed was related to the special process of party development, the strong personality of Mao, and the Leninist features of party organization. The party consisted of a blend of different social groups committed to violence and the philosophy that the ends justify the means. The party had never appealed to members of the industrial working class. In the formative years of the party, membership was limited primarily to disgruntled students and alienated intellectuals—many with a distinct Marxist ideological orientation—who hated authority and were seeking power to transform society according to their utopian ideals. After the party left the cities and switched to guerrilla warfare in the remote areas of the country, various social deviants and community outcasts joined its ranks and became committed to using violence to achieve party goals. Cheng Hsüeh-chia remarked that ever since the party's August 7, 1927 conference, when the CCP leaders adopted a policy of rural violence, the party "consisted mainly of peasants and rascals" and was not a party of urban industrial workers or proletarians.[24] In July 1971 K'ung Teh-liang wrote: "For the past 20-odd years, peasants have occupied roughly 70 percent of the total CCP membership; if intellectuals are included, the figure is more than 80 percent. With these non-proletarian, petty bourgeoisie elements in its ranks, the CCP has always been plagued by 'intra-Party contradictions.'"[25]

This new social mixture greatly contributed to a pattern of deviant behavior that represented the worst features of Chinese social behavior. "By inheriting the traits of the peasants, rascals, and the petty bourgeoisie, the CCP membership became inclined to possess such characteristics as seeking revenge, engaging in sabotage, and resorting to force. Party members tended to indulge in Leftist, adventuristic policies. The Three Red Banners Campaign and the Cultural Revolution were events which in part represented this particular social and behavioral trait of the CCP."[26] Devoid of the social-moral constraints of traditional Chinese society to check individual greed, deceit, and violence, these new party members brought with them their own standard of moral relativism and a willingness to submit to the new code of morality demanded by the party leadership.

A powerful leader bent on becoming an autocrat, a party that contained no institutional checks on the accumulation of power by a few leaders, and a membership representing the most undesirable behavioral traits in society combined to produce cleavages and tensions within the CCP among different leaders and their supporters. Factions or groups formed, dissolved, and re-formed. They competed with each other for power, the winner took all and the loser was purged. The CCP therefore became a party constantly subjected to group rivalry and factional struggle for power and influence. As Li T'ien-min put it, "The purge is one of those measures used by the Communist Party for consolidating its organizations, or, to be more specific, a procedure which the ruling stratum of the Communist Party uses to substitute for elections."[27]

ROC experts attached great significance to this particular party pathology, which they contended would exist as long as a party structured like the CCP tried to rule China. "The history of the Chinese Communists is one of intra-Party struggle . . . Intra-Party struggle is not only a built-in feature of the CCP; it is also a mechanism by which the power-holders compete with each other to consolidate their control. Looked at in this way, all intra-Party struggles are basically power struggles, but they have been carried out under the guise of ideological-line struggles."[28]

Certainly, party leaders like Mao have insisted on a political style of action conducive to continual competition for party power. This competition should be viewed in two ways. First, the party leadership has always encouraged its members to criticize each other's, as well as their own, thinking and conduct. This criticism could be friendly or rancorous, but this persistent habit was bound to encourage party members to strike at their opponents first rather than wait to be criticized, thus losing credibility and respect in the eyes of others.

Second, tactics and ideas mattered. The different argumentative positions or points of view about party goals and policies expressed by the membership were typically classified as the "left" or the "right" course of political opinion or action. Therefore, leadership disputes over the resolutions of key problems were continually phrased in the metaphorical language of a "line struggle" between "rightist" or "leftist" leaders and their factions. Party debates consequently always took the form of struggles among party leaders and their factions over which particular political "line" the party should take. These debates could become strident, and even brutal; opponents changed sides, hurled accusations at each other, and often used devious methods to humiliate their rivals. Warren Kuo has argued that such debates merely reflected an underlying struggle for the reins of party power and enabled a leader and his faction to impose his ideas and his will upon his opponents.

> All evidence indicates that while every one of the [party] struggles began as differences over "line," they always ended as a struggle for leadership in which either one group of new power-holders or another emerged victorious to defeat the other challengers. It seems only reasonable to say that any differences of "line" between rival factions are merely of secondary importance and that the struggle for power is of primary importance.[29]

To win the debate over which political line the party should adopt, a group of party leaders had to capture enough votes to impose their view on the Central Committee and then convince the membership. The struggles over political line among the top leaders of the Political Bureau's Standing Committee could take many forms, ranging from friendly discussion and a show of hands to a vicious use of force to purge opponents, including sending them to languish and die in prison. In 1966, for example, Mao organized the Red Guards and called in the PLA to impose his course of political action on his rivals in the Political Bureau. As a result of that struggle, many military officers acquired positions of power in both the party and the state; some even acquired more power than Mao found acceptable. When Mao perceived that the party was being taken over by the military, he then acted to reverse this trend.[30]

By denying that theoretical disagreements over which political line to follow ever really mattered, some ROC experts went so far as to argue that the so-called line struggles should be interpreted merely as naked power struggles between particular leaders. For example, when Lin Piao perished in 1971, Mao Tse-tung announced that the conflicts between Lin and himself had been "the severest line struggle since the founding of the CCP." Yet, Yao Meng-hsuan wrote that "there has never been a Lin Piao 'line' in the CCP's history"; he, like many other experts, interpreted this event as merely the end of a bitter struggle for power.[31] K'ung Teh-liang concurred. "Every power struggle has been concealed by reference to a two-line struggle . . . The so-called leftist, rightist, and counter-revolutionist lines have merely been used by Mao to label his enemies or to eliminate dissent within the Party."[32] If theoretical debates simply concealed those struggles for party power by which one leader tried to impose his course of action upon rivals, were any specific tactics developed by competing leaders and their factions to win such struggles?

ROC China-watchers have often referred to the "united-front" tactics of Mao and the CCP as a means by which a weak contender could wear down and isolate a stronger rival and eventually gain supremacy. Warren Kuo and others have cited countless examples of Mao's use of this strategy before 1949 to assert his power whenever he was outvoted in the Central Committee. A tactic that worked well for Mao against rivals within the party could certainly be utilized against enemies outside the party. The party successfully used the united-front tactic during the Sino-Japanese War and again when they defeated the Nationalist party. It is not surprising that ROC China-watchers have been adamant in their claims that the CCP has continually used the united-front tactic as a strategy for conducting Peking's foreign policy.

After a meticulous study of PRC publications pertaining to the united-front tactic, ROC experts like Warren Kuo described it in this way:

> First, enemies must be clearly identified by differentiating between the primary enemy and the secondary or weaker enemies. In order to deal with the primary enemy, one had to make compromises on a temporary basis and cooperate with the secondary enemy, even if on a weak alliance basis, in order to marshall all power to deal with the primary enemy. In effect this tactic really meant teaming up with tomorrow's enemy to eliminate today's more powerful opponent—with an eye to crushing the secondary enemy sometime in the future. Second, this strategy also meant adopting a sequential set of activities to crush one's enemies on a one-by-one step basis. In effect, one dealt with a series of enemies by aligning with several weaker ones, then crushing the primary enemies through such an alliance, and finally turning against one's allies and crushing them. Third, this strategy involved both relying upon alliance and struggle at the same time. When the CCP offers friendship to either a party or state to form an alliance against a common but superior foe, they are really utilizing this alliance on a short-term basis and will scrap it when expedient. To ally with a minor foe and to struggle simultaneously against a superior foe really means just doing that.[33]

Kuo warned that in interpreting foreign-policy statements in dealing with the CCP on any political-military-economic issues, one should never take their public statements at face value. "In line with their principle of dialectics, the Communists can devise and modify that tactic depending upon how time, space, and conditions change. If certain objective conditions are required, they will unequivocally negate what they asserted yesterday. Therefore, the public statements uttered by the Communists are hardly credible."[34]

Warning that PRC statements of foreign policy should be interpreted as tactics of the united front, Yin Ch'ing-yao stressed that this tactic had been used by the CCP to deal with its enemies when it rose to power in China and was being used again in the 1970s to compensate for China's position of weakness in the world. According to Yin, "the United Front tactic is a disguised form of Mao's class struggle."[35] When the PRC normalized relations with the United States in 1978, ROC experts warned that Peking's overtures to cooperate with the United States against the Soviet Union must be understood as a tactic of the united-front strategy. "We should avoid their traps in negotiations that merely conceal a ploy of a United Front-type struggle."[36] By linking the regime's foreign policy to a tactic long used by party leaders to unseat their rivals both inside and outside the party, ROC experts were compellingly suggesting that there was a connection between leadership tactics and the periodic crisis of intra-party power struggle.

This power struggle results from several pathologies. First, the Communist Party has continually been subjected to internal factional struggle and constantly changing political policies. One assumes that members of the Communist Party experience endless insecurity as they try to ally with this or that faction in hopes of retaining their power and guaranteed privileges. Party members are also constantly being scrutinized and tested by their peers; if found wanting, they are disciplined, punished, or purged. Members have to be especially careful to conceal any information about their family-social background, their personal relationships, and their individual views that might be used by party rivals to humiliate and disgrace them, thereby ruining their party careers.

Second, the party has so far been unsuccessful in legitimizing its rule over the country. ROC experts have long maintained that the party has ruled mainly by virtue of its power and control over society. By continually changing policies, by creating and dismantling institutions, and by switching leaders from one position to another, the Communist Party has failed to develop any routine procedures that would inspire popular confidence in either the party or its leaders. These two pathologies have created uncertainty, fear, and cynicism throughout Chinese society.

ROC experts also contend that it is virtually impossible for this kind of totalitarian regime to evolve into a different kind of political system without great disorder and violence. Because party leaders constantly compete for the mantle of leadership, strong leaders come and go without any arrangements for succession according to prescribed procedures. Further, because the party holds total power in this society, it is unlikely that it will ever peacefully relinquish power to other groups in the society; political change can only be effected by a violent seizure of power by some group inside or outside the Communist Party.

After the turbulence of 1966–67 and the Ninth National Congress in April 1969, many foreign observers concluded that the communist regime would enter a new, stable era of governance. CCP leaders at the Ninth National Congress demonstrated a show of party unity. ROC China-watchers, however, saw no prospects for a peaceful, stable era; they warned that the Cultural Revolution had not really ended but was only entering a new stage of struggle. They predicted that Peking's leaders would continue to foment revolution in other Asian countries and to quarrel among themselves on the sharing of party power.[37]

After the CCP's Tenth National Congress in August 1973, many Western experts again expected that political stability would resume and that more attention would be devoted to matters of economic development. ROC experts, however, suggested that this congress did not mean the end of internal struggle within the party but was merely the starting point for a new power struggle.[38]

ROC experts cannot discern any mechanism within the Communist Party that would provide checks and balances against the excessive accumulation of power by some leaders. Because the party supposedly represents the proletarian dictatorship over society, how can party leaders be expected to establish institutions that would curtail or limit their power? Furthermore, these experts believe that the formation of any organizations outside of party control or supervision would only be crushed by the party and the state. Therefore, they strongly assert that the only way this political system could be replaced by another would be to remove the Communist Party from power by force. There does not seem to be any mechanism within this regime that would allow a peaceful transition to a different political order.

4

Verification of Typologies

Prior to 1978 Communist China had published very little information about internal developments, and few foreigners had been allowed to visit the country for extensive travel or to take up long-term residence. Conditions dramatically changed after 1978. The regime's leaders convened important meetings and published their findings. They delegated commissions to review Communist Party history and issued revealing statements about the events of the past thirty years. Foreign journalists were allowed to travel and to live in Beijing, an opportunity that enabled the more enterprising to interview the ordinary citizen. During the years 1978–79 many Chinese intellectuals were even permitted to publish private newsletters and journals that severely criticized the Communist Party and its policies. Many of these writings were collected by foreigners and taken out of the country. All of these activities produced an unprecedented flow of new information about the behavior of the party leadership and the impact of the party's policies on both the Communist Party and the lives of the common people.

We will now consult some of this new information to try to verify which of our five descriptive typologies best characterized Communist China between 1949 and 1978. What does the new information really tell us? Three broad themes can serve as reference points for verifying which typologies were valid: (1) the admissions by party leaders of policy errors, (2) the nature of party control over society, and (3) the crippling effects of party policies on Chinese society. Let us examine each of these themes and then relate them to the typologies of the previous chapters.

COMMUNIST PARTY ERRORS

After Teng Hsiao-p'ing ousted Hua Kuo-feng, Teng and his colleagues ordered an independent inquiry to reassess party successes and failures since 1949. This inquiry committee published a report in 1981; it was circulated, revised, and finally endorsed to represent the correct party position at the sixth plenum of the Eleventh CCP Central Committee on June 27, 1981. The report, drafted by Liao Kai-lung, candidly admits a number of party errors.

First, the party's policies toward its opponents was often very wrong. When the party tried to root out so-called rightists, either inside or outside the party, its activities merely persecuted millions of innocent people and inflicted terrible punishment, frequently causing death to the victims. "The broad scope of the anti-Rightist struggle was far too broad . . . It produced unfortunate consequences."[1]

Why were the antirightist struggles over this period wrong?

> The reason for this mistake was to make the sphere of class struggle too broad. The consequences of doing that are now much clearer. The Rightists cited in statistical sources numbered around 550,000 throughout the country. The people in the countryside who had been classified as anti-socialist elements or given other labels probably exceeded that number. And others never included in such listings probably came to only a couple of million. Our investigation so far has revealed that 98 percent of the cases of the 550,000 sample were wronged incorrectly, and these have been corrected.[2]

The party, it appears, had incorrect information, persecuted the wrong people, and overlooked many in the villages who presumably strongly opposed party policies. One result of these excesses (such as the Cultural Revolution) was a breakdown in law and order and the subsequent slaughter of millions of people. According to one report, Hu Yao-pang personally admitted that 10 million people had been killed during the Cultural Revolution and another 100 million had been victimized or persecuted during that decade-long purge.[3]

Second, certain party policies were forced upon a reluctant, unenthusiastic populace that was never given the opportunity to voice an opinion about these policies. Take the example of the Three Red Banners campaign in the late 1950s. The populace was not consulted beforehand on whether they approved or disapproved of the new party policies. "In 1958, 1959, and 1960 serious and overall mistakes took place while searching for a new road of socialist construction. These errors included Party work . . . There actually occurred no great leap forward at all."[4] After admitting that the harvest failures of these years had not been produced by the "worst weather in centuries," the Liao report admitted the failure of the party's commune policy. "The people's commune in itself was a gust in the wind of Communism . . . Maybe we should not say [they were tried] too early, but even in the future these communes might not be welcomed . . . The people's communes no longer exist . . . but we still use the name."[5]

Third, the policies flowing from the Cultural Revolution also represented a failed party policy. After calling the Cultural Revolution "ten years of turbulence," the Liao report concluded that "the essence and major aspects of the Cultural Revolution were mistakes, disasters, cataclysms, and darkness."[6] Other leading figures in the party echoed this opinion. "The Cultural Revolution which lasted from May 1966 until October 1976 was responsible for the most severe setbacks and the heaviest losses ever suffered by the Party, the state, and the people since the founding of the People's Republic."[7]

In trying to identify the reasons for party errors and excesses, the Liao report alluded to the new sense of power and euphoria that had spread among the party leadership after its remarkable success in the early 1950s in eliminating private property and free markets and in replacing them with socialist organizations based on nationalized property and a collective leadership. Confident that the party could do no wrong, party leaders decided on even more radical policies to transform society. But these attitudes blinded some party leaders to the realities of Chinese society.

> With the final climax of the socialist transformation, Party leaders began to over-estimate the speed of economic development and to over-emphasize the importance of such factors as subjectively initiated political forces . . . Following the victory of the socialist transformation, our Party leaders became arrogant and imprudent, and they even began to blindly believe they could obtain quick results [from any actions they undertook]. By this time, the mistake of the so-called Great Leap Forward had already taken place.[8]

The Great Leap Forward campaign had its own peculiar momentum and characteristics that seemed to differ from previous party campaigns.

> The shortcoming of the general line for socialist construction adopted by the 2nd plenum of the 8th CCP Central Committee (November 1956) ignored objective economic laws . . . Left-wing errors and excessive targets, arbitrary directives, boastful statements, and the propagating of a "Communist" wind spread unchecked throughout the country . . . Politically, these developments undermined inner-Party democracy from the central level down to the grass roots. For the economy, they cut short the process of correcting former "Left" errors, thereby prolonging their influence.[9]

The Liao report also argued that yet another factor was responsible for party errors: the ill-advised arguments advanced by leaders, particularly by Mao Tse-tung. First, there was a close connection between the persecution of so many people by the Communist Party and Mao's ideas of class warfare. The Liao report stipulated that Mao had sidetracked the party into giving first priority to class struggle. "Our Party originated, evolved, and developed through fierce class struggle. Comrade Mao Tse-tung, in particular, stood for a long period at the center of the class struggle vortex. Protracted class struggle first led Comrade Mao, and then the Party, to attach the greatest importance to this approach and finally to entirely over-estimate the significance of class struggle."[10] By persuading the party to struggle continuously against all its critics and alleged enemies, Mao reputedly promoted those policies that produced the countrywide persecutions of many people.

Second, there was a close connection between Mao's insistence that class struggle be the centerpiece for party policy and the glorification of a single party leader. "During the period 1956–66, Mao Tse-tung's theoretical and practical mistakes concerning class struggle in a socialist society became more and more serious. His personal and arbitrary use of power gradually undermined democratic centralism in Party life, and the personality cult grew to become a grave problem. The Central Committee failed to correct these mistakes."[11] As Mao gathered greater power around him, the Central Committee of the CCP somehow failed to take appropriate action to check this new trend. Therefore, just when Mao's prestige had become enormous and his influence most widespread, his personal leadership style, his political behavior, and his policies began to have a damaging effect on the country in the form of the decade-long Cultural Revolution.

> Owing to the enormous prestige of Comrade Mao Tse-tung and the prolonged propaganda attacks against revisionist thinking promoted by Comrade Mao and the Central Committee, when the Cultural Revolution erupted hundreds of millions of people participated and supported it. In this great revolutionary movement, however, within only a few months many people and cadres, the majority of Party members and Communist Youth League members, and older workers and peasants in particular, saw that it was wrong.[12]

This final episode of party-produced errors left the country in ruin and the people sorely disillusioned. Also, by this time the party had become too large and too corrupt to give the people effective leadership. In 1980 several of the party's top leaders admitted as much. Before being removed from the political bureau of the party, Hua Kuo-feng spoke to the third meeting of the Fifth National People's Congress on September 7, 1980 and admitted that both party and state weighed too heavily on society. He revealed that bureaucrats had violated the laws and that party decisions had constantly been subverted at the middle and lower echelons of officialdom.[13] At the August 18, 1980 CCP Central Committee meeting, Teng Hsiao-p'ing complained about the bloated bureaucracy, within which officials had abused their authority, taken bribes, deceived their superiors, and, in short, demoralized their subordinates.[14] By the late 1970s this combination of party errors had produced both a serious crisis in society and a crisis of confidence within the Communist Party.

COMMUNIST PARTY CONTROL
OVER SOCIETY

By 1979 many American journalists were living in Beijing, and some American scholars were even permitted to live in the countryside for brief periods. This temporary relaxation of party-state controls gave these Americans the unusual opportunity to gather first-hand accounts from the people about what life had been like under Communism for some thirty years. A major impression to emerge from these writings was a realization of how effectively the party had controlled its citizens. The journalist Richard Bernstein, a staff member of *Time,* wrote the following description of the methods of party control over the populace.

> There is no right to privacy in this system. It is alien to its modes, to its motivating spirit. Every factory, every enterprise, school, performing arts troupe, professional association, neighborhood, or government section contains a security department (often known as the personnel department) that supervises the lives of the members of that unit, approving or disapproving travel abroad, marriage, divorce, or a change of jobs. Every person is followed around by a dossier, which that person has no right to see, containing he knows not what information about him. One important, unannounced step taken after the disorder of the Cultural Revolution was to throw out all materials in the dossiers that dated to that ten-year period—on the grounds that there was so much slander being tossed around then that it would be impossible to tell genuine materials from false.[15]

After the socialist transformation of the early 1950s, the iron hand of bureaucratic control permanently closed on the country. The regime repeatedly relied on bureaucrats to do its bidding in controlling, coordinating, mobilizing, punishing, rewarding, and so forth. Steven W. Mosher, an American anthropologist who lived in a rural commune in Kwangtung, described how the local bureaucracy worked.

> Chinese officials at all levels seek safety less in scrupulous adherence to regulations than in a cat's cradle of mutual involvement with others of their class. The essence of the Chinese bureaucratic style is to rely on informal consensus rather than, as in the West, on formal authority. This means that byzantine backroom negotiations form an intricate and essential prelude to

decision-making, as a young cadre in the Guangdong provincial department of foreign affairs revealed. 'We say that decisions are made in four stages—consideration, research, discussion, and decision,' he told me. 'The first stage, consideration, is the most important. Here we consider the issue from a personal angle. We weigh how it will affect us, how it will affect those with whom we have a personal relationship [ganging]. In this way we arrive at a personal position on the issue. This comes ahead of everything else.' He fixed me with a glance to underline this point before going on. 'The second stage is research. Here we study any rules and regulations that relate to the issue. The third stage is discussion. We discuss the content of the regulations in relation to the issue and various proposals. We also contact all other units concerned and ask for their opinion at this point in an informal way. Of course, we don't voice our personal position to anyone except maybe privately to those we are very close to. The final step is a formal meeting. The decision has already been reached by this point, so this meeting is really just a formality. The highest-ranking cadre puts forward the proposal already agreed upon and the others present approve it unanimously.'[16]

This observation reveals the importance still accorded to personal relationships in the party's bureaucratic control over society and the kinds of pressures that discouraged the use of formal rules of law. If all formal organizations in this society worked by these principles, here was a bureaucracy more corrupt than in imperial times.

THE EFFECT OF
PARTY CONTROL ON SOCIETY

American observers were astonished by the widespread practice of bribery and corruption that seemed necessary for the attainment of even the most simple amenities of ordinary life. Fox Butterfield commented on *tsou-hou-men,* a custom widespread among factory workers of "going through the back door," or exchanging favors.

Drivers of trucks, buses, and cars are valued, I learned, because there are virtually no privately-owned motor vehicles, and drivers, therefore, have an unusual ability to move around the country. Once in a noisy restaurant that stays open late and is frequented by drivers, I met a swarthy man in his late twenties who said he drove a truck for a farm machinery factory in Shandong province, east of Peking. After we exchanged a few toasts of beer and cheap white grain alcohol that stung my throat, he began recalling his adventures. It seemed that his factory often had slack periods, when there weren't enough raw materials or there was a shortage of electricity.

When these occurred, he would take off in his truck to haul coal from
another province. The scheme worked well, with him splitting the profits
with the factory Party Secretary, until one evening he fell asleep at the
wheel and crashed into another vehicle, wrecking his truck.[17]

Butterfield also related that the driver had informed him that "on Sundays I
used to be able to use the truck to take my girlfriend and some of our other
friends on picnics."[18] The use of public property for private concerns was
apparently a common practice in Chinese society.

But was bribery typical only of the citizenry or was it an endemic feature
of the Communist Party itself? From the remarks appearing in the public
media, it would seem that bribery was also clearly rooted in the party. An
editorial in *Jen-min jih-pao* on June 30, 1980 commented that cadres "tell
lies, forge reports, make false plans, rewrite history, and fabricate the
news."[19]

The well-known habit of shirking went along with bribery. Socialist organizations failed to maintain the traditional work ethic of the people.
Mosher reports that the head of a production team told him that "before
collectivization people worked hard . . . Take that piece of land you worked
on today. At the time of the land reform one person could have hoed it in six
days or so. Now it takes eight people two full days to do it. Everyone works
at the same slow pace. People have learned from collectivization to do just
enough to get by."[20] Other socialist organizations also continued to reward
people even when they were no longer needed on the production line. The
national practice of guaranteeing life-employment (the so-called "iron rice
bowl") seems to have been adhered to in the factories as well as on the
collectives. Fox Butterfield cites the following example.

In China, unless you commit a serious crime like robbery or murder, it is
virtually impossible to be fired. At the huge Lanzhou Petrochemical complex in the west, the biggest of its kind in China with 36,000 workers, a
plant official told me they had never dismissed a single employee. And
every worker has the right to pass on his post to one of his children, creating
a system of inherited jobs.[21]

The effects of such practices on innovations and productivity can easily be
imagined.

Many economic reports from conferences indicated that the Chinese economic system was plagued by sluggish or stagnating productivity. This, in
turn, led to widespread shortages of ordinary consumer goods as a way of
life. The decline of privately-produced services in commerce, entertainment,
finance, and communication greatly contributed to a drab, dull life for the

ordinary citizen. Richard Bernstein depicted the dreary life-style of the urban people in a large city of Szechwan Province.

> Too many people, cramped, stuffy living quarters, an enforced idleness—these are the conditions of daily life in most Chinese cities where the phenomenon of hitting the streets seeking a good time (*shang jie kan re nao*) lasts from late at night until early in the morning. When I got to Peking as a resident I used, in the summer, to walk after dinner down the *huting,* or narrow lanes, that wind through the residential neighborhoods. The young, the old, the middle-aged stroll through the streets. They sit on small portable chairs or on the elevated sills of the entryways smoking or talking. They play chess or read newspapers in the feeble yellow cones of light cast onto the ground by the street lamps. They cluster, like swarming bees, around the few places that sell summer refreshments—cool yogurt in returnable crockery pots, or ice on sticks.[22]

In addition to miserable living conditions, declining ethics, and the oppressive controls of party and state officialdom, there was an enormous loss of life. It is difficult to estimate how many people perished or were incarcerated during the years of the socialist transformation (1949–56). We are on firmer ground in trying to calculate the loss of life caused by the ill-fated Three Red Banners campaign of 1958–60. On April 28, 1984 the *Japan Times* reported that Judith Banister, an analyst in the U.S. Bureau of the Census, had estimated that fifteen to thirty million people might have perished during the years 1958–61. "The 30 million deaths were calculated by comparing the number of people counted in China's 1953 and 1964 censuses and drawing conclusions based on the censuses' breakdowns of population by age, sex, and other factors."[23]

Shortened life-expectancy became a fact of life under this regime. Also, fears of terrorism and the labor camp haunted daily life. In 1983 the leadership made a powerful display of its methods of dealing with corruption and crime by filming and reporting the public executions of truckloads of alleged convicted rapists, robbers, and murderers.

A VERIFICATION OF TYPOLOGIES

This new information about Communist China that became available since 1978 makes it possible to confirm the accuracy of the various descriptive typologies we used to summarize the research of American and Chinese scholars. Our typology describing American research during the 1950s is more applicable to the 1949–57 period than to the remaining years of that decade. This typology accurately stressed those new features of the Chinese communist regime that allowed it to exercise awesome power over its citizens, but it failed to detect the severe political factionalism that broke out in the ranks of the top leadership in the late 1950s. A number of China experts were dissatisfied with the conceptualization of China portrayed by the scholarship of the 1950s. In 1961 George E. Taylor (who had played a key role in instigating research on Communist China) warned his colleagues of the need to find appropriate terms to describe and characterize this new society. "The main problem, however, is a conceptual one. We have a new kind of society to comprehend and, until its main outlines are identified, most of our work will be superficial or pure fact-gathering."[24]

The second typology, termed the modernizing communist regime, also seems flawed. Although the mix of policies enacted by the party were more transformative than accommodative, it now appears that severe setbacks and difficulties occurred for both the Communist Party and society. These included an inefficient collectivized agricultural system; an inefficient, stagnating industrial sector; the frequent use of coercion and repression; low leadership morale and low cadre commitment to the polity; periodic starvation; a monumental loss of human life; corruption and the decline of traditional ethical behavior; and the loss of personal freedoms. There also seems to be little evidence that the political instability and difficulties experienced by this regime were attributable to the absence of certain values and institutions necessary for the modernization of China. Rather, acute party factionalism and the struggle for power among its top leaders seem to have accounted for China's extreme political instability.

Our third typology was termed the revolutionary socialist regime. The Communist Party and its leaders initiated very revolutionary policies that turned Chinese society upside down. But we now know that these policies created a new system of control over society that made possible the concentration of enormous power in the hands of a few leaders. These revolutionary policies also had devastating effects on society; the costs to the Chinese people appear to have enormously exceeded any of the benefits. Of the five typologies, the body of scholarship represented by our revolutionary socialist regime typology was furthest from the mark.

This leaves us with the fourth typology—the Communist regime—and the typology implicitly developed by Chinese scholars in the ROC—the Chinese communist totalitarian system. These two typologies are very similar in their characterization of Communist China, and both are strongly confirmed by the new information available since 1978. In the early years of its rule, the Chinese Communist Party was primarily concerned with consolidating its power. The party also tried to use its new power to control the thoughts and behavior of hundreds of millions of people, seeking, in this way, to rapidly transform the cultural values and norms of this traditional society. The obsessive concern with power produced fierce struggles among the leadership elite. Although differences of strategy and tactics were certainly important, these differences inevitably became struggles for power, in which one leader and his faction tried to impose their will on the Communist Party and, in turn, society. These power struggles and the unending attempts of the Communist Party to control its citizens in unexpected and undesirable ways produced incredible hardship, great loss of life, and despair for hundreds of millions of people.

Our conclusions, then, are that a small group of American scholars produced a conceptual framework or descriptive typology that captured the essential features of the Chinese communist regime. ROC scholars constructed a descriptive typology that identified the essential features of this regime. Although American scholarship on Communist China was varied and complex, a small group of American researchers shared with the scholars on Taiwan a similar general descriptive typology of Communist China.

A REMAINING PARADOX

American scholarship on Communist China has, therefore, been paradoxical. Prominent interpretations in the public media by American intellectuals typically described Communist China in terms similar to typologies two and three rather than four and five. Why has there been this notable prejudice to favorably evaluate the performance of the communist system in China?

We cite a number of examples to show that many widely publicized accounts of Communist China have been at variance with the interpretations offered by the two typologies we believe have most accurately described this society. Visitors like John Kenneth Galbraith favorably described the many successes of Communist China's planned economy without commenting on the failures.

> One has the feeling, very simply, that the economy works better than in Russia or Poland—at least as I saw those countries a few years ago. Things in China give the impression of meshing; slighted workmanship, diminished quality are much less obvious. Something depends on the easy, affable and sensitive manners of the Chinese. One transfers his reaction to this to the society. Dissidents are brought firmly into line in China, but, one suspects, with great politeness. It is a firmly authoritarian society in which those in charge smile and say please. The leadership rebukes what is called

"Commandism." And there is also the obvious willingness of the Chinese, given the opportunity, to work. But, for whatever reason, the Chinese economy appears to function very easily and well.[25]

Harvard University's distinguished sinologist John K. Fairbank wrote a similar glowing account of life in China in the fall of 1972. As is customary in so much of Fairbank's writing, however, he provided a few caveats to convey to the reader his sense of balance, sagacity, and fair play.

The big generalizations are all agreed upon: There has been a tremendous betterment of the material life and morale of the common people. Incredible hard work has produced a credible miracle reshaping both land and people . . . but China is not America. Individualism is not esteemed. Art and letters are at a mass propaganda level. The national political process remains shrouded in mystery. Higher education is slowly reviving after a four-year shutdown.[26]

On October 14, 1976 Fairbank again commented in the *New York Review of Books* that, unlike America, China "has no crisis of inflation, unemployment, crime, or corruption."[27] Harrison Salisbury, an eminent correspondent for *The New York Times*, referred to China's May 7th Schools, where party cadres were sent for thought indoctrination and severe manual labor, as a "combination of a YMCA camp and a Catholic retreat."[28] An American scholar described Mao Tse-tung as a person who "by the example of his struggle communicates the vigor of hope, the vitality of possibility, the vision of justice."[29] In 1976 Michel Oksenberg put Mao Tse-tung in the same category of historical greats as Thomas Jefferson, Winston Churchill, Charles DeGaulle, and Franklin Roosevelt.[30]

John K. Fairbank described the disagreements among the top party elite as

policy problems on which honest revolutionaries disagree. Ford vs. Carter is a more naked power struggle than anything going on in Peking . . . By calling the conflict between Peking policy factions a 'power struggle,' we . . . cut down dedicated revolutionaries and personal aggrandizement to the size of ambitious individualists of a type we know well—Chang Ch'un-ch'iao, for instance, is implied to be no more than John Connolly with chopsticks.[31]

A popular, best-selling book entitled *800,000,000: The Real China* compared the China of 1970 with that of 1964 in these terms: "But the greatest change since 1964 is a heightened sense of citizenship on the part of the ordinary people."[32] The author, Ross Terrill, of course, meant a "sense of involvement" and not political orthodoxy. But he later characterized Chinese Communist Party methods of control as light-handed, compared to those of other communist states. China was "not like Poland or Hungary, where the Communists are a blanket spread over the body social."[33] Also, the Chinese Communist Party could not encourage private pursuits of wealth, because such diversity and richness would be intolerable. "China simply could not afford to encourage the privatistic alternative. At today's economic levels, Peking could hardly permit its 800,000,000 people to build their separate individual worlds, to carve out separate career patterns and philosophies, to surround themselves with separate sets of possessions."[34] Terrill apparently failed to realize that artistic creativity and ideological diversity had developed in the densely populated Chinese communities of Hong Kong, Singapore, and Taiwan and insisted on believing that the conditions of Orwell's *1984* were appropriate for the Chinese—simply because there were so many of them.

In a striking turnabout some years later, however, this same author was to write that "for the billion who live there [in China], as distinct from the foreign tourist, businessman, or journalist, China is first and foremost a repressive regime. The unchanging key to all Peking's policies is that the nation is ruled by a Leninist dictatorship that intends to remain such."[35] Unlike many who spoke out in favor of the regime in the 1960s and 1970s, Ross Terrill came full circle and espoused a vision of China similar to that offered by the two typologies we have verified as being most accurate in describing the dynamics of the Chinese communist regime.

5

Understanding Communist China by Means of Prediction

According to Friedrich Nietzsche, "there is no way of telling what may yet become part of history. Perhaps the past is still undiscovered! So many retroactive forces are still needed!"[1] If an understanding of the future can be achieved by correctly understanding these retroactive forces in history, our five typologies may provide some clues on the accuracy with which scholars have predicted change in Communist China.

Prediction, of course, constitutes another kind of understanding; correct prediction implies that one's understanding of present conditions has some basis in truth. In this chapter we examine research that was strongly directed toward forecasting change in Communist China. We review various writings that attempted to foretell shifts in Communist Party and state policies and assess their impact on foreign affairs and Chinese society.

Because many complex events took place in China during this thirty-year period, we can only focus on a few important ones. These events were the Socialist Transformation, the Three Red Banners Campaign, and the Great Cultural Revolution. In the first two sections we consider (1) those predictions that tried to forecast the impact of the rapid socialization of China and (2) those Maoist policies that tried to catapult China into the era of communism overnight (the Three Red Banners Campaign). In the third section we examine how well experts anticipated the developments that evolved out of the policies of the Great Cultural Revolution. Finally, we relate our findings to our five typologies.

THE SOCIALIST TRANSFORMATION, 1949–57

Few American experts expected that the CCP could quickly restructure property rights in the countryside and reorganize farmers into teams and collectives so that they merely received a share of the net output of their efforts. Writing in early 1955, Richard L. Walker correctly predicted the full-scale collectivization of agriculture in China. "For the sake of an outmoded doctrine maintained by the tiny minority in power, the Chinese peasant is to be brought under a system which has proven a failure in application, as the post-Stalin Soviet leadership has itself revealed."[2] In late 1956 the regime successfully established agricultural-producer cooperatives in the villages. These organizations sold farm products to the state at a fixed price and paid farmers a wage income after deducting various expenses for operating the cooperatives.

Predicting political developments was another matter. After the Kao Kang and Jao Hsu-shih purge in 1957, Peter S. H. Tang predicted that Liu Shao-ch'i would probably succeed Mao Tse-tung and that the leadership succession in the Communist Party would be smooth and orderly. This view was widely shared by other American experts, who perceived only warm collegiality among the top party leadership. "The question remains whether the Chinese Communist regime will be able to survive the death or withdrawal of Mao Tse-tung without a disruptive struggle over the leadership succession. Although no definite answer can be given, the events of the purge suggest that if the present power balance continues, Liu Shao-ch'i will be able to succeed to the Party leadership without facing too much opposition."[3]

The predominant U.S. view was of a monolithic Chinese Communist Party without cleavages in its leadership that would experience an orderly replacement of Mao by Liu. This view persisted as late as 1967.[4] Further, American China experts predicted neither the Hundred Flowers campaign in spring 1957 nor the Three Red Banners Campaign launched by Mao and the party between 1958 and 1961. Writing in 1955, W. Rostow compared Chinese and Russian societies under communist leadership and offered the following observation about the stability of the CCP leadership: "If our view is even roughly correct, we see in Peking, for the moment, a more stable and unified form of executive command than in Moscow."[5] Rostow went on to predict that, in both communist systems, powerful nationalistic impulses would eventually erode communist leadership and ideology and make possible the transfer of power from the center back to the regions, cities, and villages. He envisaged that the Chinese communist regime would adopt "temporizing and even passive measures at some future stage, in which initiative passed for a time from Peking back to the regions, the villages, and the individual families and clans in which Chinese society is still rooted."[6] Rostow never claimed that the transition to a new political and social order would be automatic or peaceful, but he contended that in the future nationalism would play a key role in profoundly altering the Chinese communist regime. Developments during the 1980s have borne out Rostow's predictions to a remarkable degree.[7]

Still others, like A. Doak Barnett, marveled that the "top leaders have maintained a unity unparalleled by that of any other Communist Party in the world."[8] Barnett also speculated that the second generation of communist leaders would desire to make China a powerful national state.

> It is quite conceivable, in fact, that the second generation of leaders in Communist China might be equally driven by the desire to build national power as rapidly as possible, and at the same time might be even less sensitive than the present leadership in taking popular sentiment into account, less flexible in adapting their policies as new problems arise, and less restrained in the use of coercive methods of rule.[9]

Barnett did not perceive that the party's first generation of leaders would continue to rule China until the early 1980s, that violent intraparty struggles would cause the death of many top leaders, or that the party's enactment of extremely harsh policies to strengthen its control and to speed up industrialization would force the populace to pay an enormous price. At the time of this writing it is still not clear exactly how the second generation of communist leaders will rule China.

For economic trends, however, Barnett's predictions were more accurate. He pointed out that relentless population growth and the regime's failure to introduce a technological revolution in agriculture would cause serious economic problems. He also said that the "lag in agriculture will be one of the most basic and serious problems confronting the regime for a long time to come."[10] The disastrous famine of 1959–60, the huge imports of food grains (especially wheat) after 1961, and the lack of a significant rise in per capita food-grain availability during the 1960s and 1970s have confirmed this prediction.

U.S. communist-affairs experts have always been interested in Beijing's foreign policy zigzags, especially as they have related to Moscow. Writing in 1960, Donald S. Zagoria pointed out that new tensions had indeed emerged between the two communist giants. Nevertheless, he foresaw no break between them. "That the strains in the Sino-Soviet alliance are numerous and acute is, in the writer's view, no longer open to question; but that they are, or will soon become, severe enough to produce an open break is improbable."[11] Zbigniew Brzezinski echoed Zagoria's prediction later that same year. "Yet neither, given their ideology, is quite willing to precipitate an open clash by being the first to make an implicit condemnation . . . Formal unity is thus likely to be preserved, at least until such time as the more radical partner can feel that unity, which it now describes as the necessary prerequisite for victory, is no longer needed."[12]

In 1962 the Sino-Soviet alliance collapsed, and the Soviets left China. Later, A. Doak Barnett admitted that "most informed observers [in the

United States] have felt that a split was highly improbable."[13] The Moscow-Beijing split apparently made a sharp impression on Barnett, for in 1962 he counseled his readers that predicting the shifts in Beijing's foreign policy would be as difficult in the future as in the past.[14]

But Barnett also warned that "assuming that Communist China's totalitarian apparatus does not disintegrate—the result of growing domestic crises and pressures might simply be an increased tendency on the part of Communist China's leaders to seek solutions for their problems abroad."[15] There is no convincing evidence linking China's domestic troubles with expansionism, however. Beijing provided matériel and support for communist insurgents throughout Southeast Asia in the 1960s and 1970s, but, even during the turmoil of these decades, the CCP largely refrained from making incursions against neighboring states. An exception occurred between September 30 and November 20, 1962—when Chinese and Indian troops fought—and between February 17 and March 5, 1979—when PLA units briefly invaded northern Vietnam.

The record of American experts for correctly predicting events in Communist China in the 1950s was very mixed. ROC communist-affairs experts seem to have had greater success in predicting key political events and assessing their significance. Before the CCP's Eighth National Congress met (September 15–27, 1956), ROC experts suggested that Mao's occupancy of the state chairmanship would probably end and that the CCP's constitution would be revised to check any efforts by a powerful leader to establish his personal dominance over the party.[16] In fact, the congress deleted the following passage of the *General Program* of the party constitution: "The Communist Party takes the theories of Marxism-Leninism and combined principles derived from the practical experience of the Chinese revolution—the Mao Tse-tung thought—as the guiding principles of all its work." The new party constitution also stressed "collective leadership" and opposed the formation of a "personal cult." Then on November 20, 1958, the sixth plenum of the Eighth Party Congress approved Mao's proposal not to stand as a candidate for the chairmanship of the state; on April 27, 1959, the National People's Congress appointed Liu Shao-ch'i to Mao's old position. Even so, ROC experts pointed out that Mao's decision to relinquish state power was probably only a ruse to give him enough time to gather his forces for another attempt to take over the party and the state. "Mao's resignation probably is a strategy of pretending to retreat in order to advance (*i-t'ui wei-chin*). He resigned in order to soften the people's resentment for the failure of his Three Red Banners Campaign. He is only waiting for another opportunity to attack his enemies."[17] Mao would eventually do just that by creating the Red Guards, launching the Cultural Revolution, and thereby eliminating his rivals in the party.

THE THREE RED BANNERS
CAMPAIGN, 1958–61

The most remarkable event of the 1950s was the Three Red Banners Campaign, launched between 1958 and 1961 by Mao and imposed on the country by the power of the party and the state.[18] This campaign called on the populace to, first, build socialism as rapidly as possible by self-reliance, greater productivity, and a better quality of production. Second, the party appealed to the people to make an enormous effort to increase production in ten subsectors of the economy, so that China's output could surpass that of England within ten years and that of the United States within fifteen years. Finally, the party demanded that producer cooperatives be amalgamated to form rural and urban communes with common dining halls and living quarters in order to accelerate the country's conversion to communism. These communes were also intended to militarize society by providing a new vehicle for the mobilization of huge numbers of people for any task—either peaceful or warlike—the party might assign.

American experts seldom mentioned the Three Red Banners Campaign, preferring to call it the Great Leap Forward, a term that actually described only one element of the party's campaign. Also, their research never hinted that this campaign was about to take place or that it might take on the remarkable qualities it did. On March 20, 1958 Mao addressed the Cheng-tu Conference of the party's Central Committee and talked about mobilizing the masses for agricultural development. On April 29 Honan Province established the first commune, called the Sputnik Federated Cooperative. Writing in September of that year, a ROC observer stressed that the populace hated the establishment of communes and predicted that the party would not be successful in achieving its aims.

> The loss of private property, the ruin of family life, the exploitation of their labor and resources, and the severe restriction of consumer goods are hated by the farmers. There is no doubt that the farmers will try by any means possible, either directly or indirectly, to fight against the People's Commune system. The chances this regime will have any success in establishing this commune system are very remote.[19]

Some ROC experts contended that the rural commune system could not succeed because it ran counter to all previous institutional supports of country life. They believed farmers would systematically sabotage communist cadres' efforts to create the new barracks-style living quarters and the communal dining halls.[20] Others argued that the "People's communes have brought people on the China mainland into a dark period of slavery; they represent a turbulent, perverse current in the stream of history for human development."[21]

Whereas American experts refrained from making moral judgments about this new socioeconomic experiment, ROC experts were naturally outraged at the new policy being imposed on their countrymen, and they expressed their anger accordingly. Of course, the regime never established those idyllic common dining halls and living quarters for a communist society. After the regime began reversing its policies in the early 1960s, the commune merely became a new administrative unit within the county administration; it had jurisdiction over large villages (renamed brigades) and small villages or clusters of households (called production teams).

By the end of 1958 Beijing officials were already claiming that industrial and agricultural output had increased by 65 percent over that of the previous year. But ROC experts were forecasting that the second five-year plan to elevate production would not be achieved and that targets to double production output for steel and food grain could never be fulfilled.[22] In fact, after 1978 Beijing's leaders candidly admitted that the statistics for 1958 had been fabricated and that the precise amount of output increase could probably never be correctly measured.

By early 1959 ROC experts were warning that the campaign underway would soon create terrible disasters for the people and would even jeopardize Mao Tse-tung's dominance over the party.[23] At summer's end of 1959, some ROC China-watchers were already describing the severe economic crisis that was taking place and predicting that conditions would become even worse.[24]

Looking back, we can say that ROC experts accurately charted the evolution of the severe economic crisis that overtook the CCP by 1960–61, but they were incorrect in their assessment of the extent of popular resistance and of the regime's capability to execute a quick retreat and revive a stricken society. Certainly, most American experts did not correctly evaluate the enormous damage of the Three Red Banners Campaign—particularly the demoralization of the party leadership. It would not be until the 1980s, when new information began to emerge, that many in the American scholarly community would realize that famine had been widespread and that the social and psychological effects of this campaign had been devastating.[25]

THE GREAT PROLETARIAN CULTURAL REVOLUTION, 1966–76

For the decade of the 1960s, American China-watchers' predictions were mixed; there were many more failures than successes. First, some modest successes. Writing in June 1966, Robert F. Emery pointed out that "total agricultural output is expected to grow only moderately in the next few years."[26] Emery was correct—in part because modern inputs like fertilizer were still in limited supply. But he never mentioned the existence of a very inefficient farming system that lacked incentives to spur managers to use their resources efficiently and to encourage team members not to shirk and to work harder.

In the prediction of political developments, the story was very different. Writing in early 1966, Michel Oksenberg reviewed conditions in 1965 and concluded that the leadership was "facing a quiet crisis in its attempts to keep the revolutionary fires burning."[27] Oksenberg saw the crisis this way: The party had long resorted to using the campaign, or *yun-tung*, to enforce and accelerate political and ideological change, but such actions had produced disasters like those of the late 1950s. If the party failed to accelerate the pace of change, however, it invited "bureaucratic calcification." The party was therefore at a crossroads—reluctant to initiate massive campaigns but blocked by the state's huge bureaucracy.

This interpretation entirely ignored the massive power struggle that was already building at the top of the CCP and would burst forth in mid-1966. Oksenberg commented that "within the Party, the problem of succession appears to be settled."[28] Mao would indeed settle the succession issue by deposing Liu Shao-sh'i that same year. In another essay, written in late 1967, however, Oksenberg changed his assessment of the political situation in China. He predicted continuing political turmoil for the country and struggles that would continue for another decade. He also correctly speculated that the newly-created Red Guards would adversely influence ongoing economic progress and even become alienated from Mao's regime.[29]

Writing in 1967 at the height of the Cultural Revolution, A. Doak Barnett conjectured that in the future Mao's successors would not use "Yenan-type measures to preserve outdated revolutionary traditions" and that "heroic proselytizing for 'people's wars' abroad will not adequately serve the needs and interests of a modernizing great power."[30] In the 1980s Communist China under Teng Hsiao-p'ing's leadership pursues the moderate course predicted by Barnett in 1967. But in 1967 more than another decade of intense intraparty struggle had to pass before a new group of leaders (and they were still of Mao's generation) would be able to initiate a different course of economic development for the country. It is evident that experts like Barnett continued to ignore the ongoing struggle for power within the party, because they did not predict that these activities would shape future political events. For instance, power struggles did not feature in Barnett's speculation about China's future.

The uncertainties about the future arise in part from fundamental ideological and policy dilemmas, and from the prospect of mounting pressures to solve basic problems, such as how best to push forward the developmental process in China, to sustain a sense of revolutionary momentum, to adapt revolutionary techniques of social mobilization to a society striving for modernization, and to apply Maoist principles under conditions very different from those out of which they evolved.[31]

Barnett thought that problems would arise from policy dilemmas rather than from the effects of intraparty struggles among the top party leaders and their factions. In one regard, however, Barnett appears to have been correct about the relative roles of domestic and external forces in affecting the future dynamics of this regime. "In the future competition of forces and influences affecting Chinese policies, domestic factors are likely to be crucial. Probably external influences, exerted by the United States or any other nation, can at most have only a marginal effect on the outcome."[32]

In 1969 Parris H. Chang described how Mao's policy failures of the late 1950s had galvanized strong opposition and had culminated in a dramatic struggle for power between Mao and his opposition. Chang speculated that in coming years the CCP leadership "seems likely to be focused more on internal problems and the building of 'socialism in China.'" China's relations with the two superpowers would "become much more fluid after Mao is gone."[33] This prediction, like those cited above, failed to foresee that intraparty factionalism would dominate for the next decade—lasting until Teng Hsiao-p'ing consolidated his power in 1979. It also failed to take into account Beijing's new outward-reaching policy toward the United States, which commenced in the early 1970s and was engineered by both Mao and Chou En-lai. It did, however, accurately describe political behavior after 1979.

As early as 1965 Tang Tsou and Morton H. Halperin correctly predicted the adverse effects of Mao's advocacy of revolutionary-guerrilla warfare by insurrectionist groups abroad. "Mao's revolutionary strategy will tend to make Communist China a disruptive influence in world politics for some time to come and will delay its adjustment to the established norms of international behavior. In the meantime, Communist China will be a formidable force to reckon with, and Mao's strategy will pose a serious challenge to the stability and peace of the world."[34] As is well known, in the late 1960s and 1970s an upsurge of guerrilla activity in Southeast Asia occurred, often fomented by material and spiritual support from Beijing.[35]

Except for occasional insights of this sort, however, during the 1960s and 1970s American Pekingologists were unsuccessful in accurately predicting future events in Communist China. In contrast, after some initial mistakes, the predictions of ROC experts were remarkably successful. In the early months of 1966 ROC China-watchers merely interpreted the political policies of the party as another "thought reform" or "literary rectification" campaign. Experts like Tsai Hsuan, K'ung Teh-liang, and Chou Chia-tung described the new debates raging in the communist press in just these terms, failing to realize that, in fact, an enormous power struggle was imminent.[36] On November 10, 1965 Yao Wen-yuan denounced Wu Han's historical drama "The Dismissal of Hai Rui" on the front page of the *Shanghai Wen-hui-pao* as an "anti-Party poisonous weed." The subsequent attacks on this play appeared to be but another rectification campaign against errant intellectuals. Then, on April 14, 1966, the New China News Agency referred to this new development as a "Socialist Cultural Revolution" (as these literary attacks on Wu Han and his defenders were euphemistically termed). The *Liberation Army Daily* used this same expression in its editorial on April 18, 1966, and on June 6 the same daily introduced another new gloss—the "Proletarian Cultural Revolution." Finally, on August 8, 1966, the eleventh plenum of the Eighth CCP Central Committee adopted its "Decision of the CCP Central Committee Concerning the Great Proletarian Cultural Revolution " (the so-called "sixteen points"). Thereafter, the "Great Proletarian Cultural Revolution" became the formal term used to describe the extraordinary events that took place that year and during the next decade.

Although early in 1966 ROC experts were briefly misled, by May 1966 Li Ping-hsüeh made a correct appraisal of events. "On the other hand, the current purge campaign has turned out to be a severe power struggle . . . It will no doubt be but the prelude to a power struggle for leadership [over the party and state]."[37] In June Chen Yu-ch'ang predicted that "the thought-purge campaign will soon become a harsh intra-Party struggle for leadership."[38] He further predicted that the power struggle would be between Mao Tse-tung and Liu Shao-ch'i and that Chou En-lai would side with Mao. Chen also correctly predicted that "Liu will probably lose his position [as chairman of the party and state] . . . The PLA has become involved in this power struggle . . . Mao will pull the entire country into the orbit of his dark and harsh control."[39]

Although a month previously the chief organs of the party and state had criticized Teng T'o, the secretary of the CCP Beijing Municipal Commission and editor-in-chief of the Beijing party organ (*Ch'ien-chien* magazine), and the cadres of the CCP Beijing Municipal Commission, other ROC experts were not misled. They identified (but did not name) the real targets of these vicious attacks as Teng T'o's backstage bosses (*hou-t'ai lao-pan*)—men like P'eng Chen and Liu Shao-ch'i. They also claimed that the "PLA has become a vital element in this internal struggle" and "the struggle is probably related to Lin Piao's ambition to be Mao's heir apparent."[40]

By early June 1966 many ROC experts had formulated a fairly clear picture of the developments taking place on the mainland and had summed the situation up in a number of articles.[41] First, the Cultural Revolution was not simply a literary rectification campaign; a major political power struggle had broken out in the party. Second, not only party literary cadres like Teng T'o, Chou Yang, and Lu Ting-i would be purged; P'eng Chen and others belonging to the Liu-P'eng faction would also soon fall from grace. Third, the party purge would not be confined only to the party; it would spread throughout the society and involve the military and state organs. Fourth, this power struggle had originated in a sharp contest among key leaders to acquire absolute control of the party and become Mao's heir. Finally, Mao and Lin Piao had gained the upper hand in mid-1966, and Liu and his supporters would encounter enormous difficulties in meeting their challenge. In fact, the ROC experts correctly deduced that Lin Piao had already become the number-two man in the party leadership hierarchy.

In July 1966 Tseng Yung-hsien also correctly predicted that the political struggle for power in Communist China would be "the most severe intra-Party struggle since the founding of the People's Republic of China" and the chief individuals soon to be purged would be those "belonging to the Liu Shao-ch'i clique."[42] In August 1966 Li T'ien-min predicted that resistance to Mao's political purge would be great; the CCP would find it enormously difficult to control the Red Guards; and the inefficient commune system would become largely responsible for the disputes among party leaders and their factions.[43] As we now know, many old party cadres gathered at Huai-jen Hall to oppose Mao and Chiang Ch'ing on February 18, 1967. Other examples of party members fighting to resist Mao's new policies could also be cited. In the same year, Mao had to call in the PLA to control and disband the Red Guards.[44] To what extent the socioeconomic dysfunctions in the countryside brought about by the commune system were responsible for leadership debate and acrimony is not clearly known, but agricultural problems remained serious throughout this entire period; in 1980 leaders like Teng Hsiao-p'ing would argue for reforming the rural socialist system once again.

Although American China experts did not fare well in predicting future elite political behavior on the mainland in the 1960s, their record improved somewhat in the 1970s. Because the power struggle between party factions continued to drag on year after year, it became perhaps less difficult to err in predicting more of the same. American experts became more sensitive to party factionalism and the issues dividing groups and some demonstrated remarkable clairvoyance about the near future.

In early January 1970 Gordon A. Bennett astutely sized up the current struggles in the CCP, noting that "the political initiative has been recovered by Mao-oriented socialists. They may share power in given organs and given localities with leaders of somewhat different persuasions; nevertheless the 'revolution' will go on."[45]

In early January 1971 Harry Harding, Jr., characterized the policies of the new leadership in Beijing as "revolutionary pragmatism," which included trying to rebuild the shattered CCP, reviving the ruined educational system, and initiating economic growth.[46]

Daniel Tretiak, taking a lead from Morton H. Halperin's hypothesis that China's foreign policy would eventually turn outward again, noted many indications of this trend in the late 1960s. As of March 1971 he foresaw that China would begin to display less hostility in its relations with other Asian states and even try to improve ties with some neighboring countries.[47] As it happened, China did just that in its relationship with Japan during the next six years.

In early 1972 Harding again correctly noted that although Chou En-lai appeared to be on the ascendency in the party, "his position is tenuous" and many leaders strongly opposed his ideas and grand foreign-policy design.[48] Writing in December 1972, Parris Chang saw China entering a "period of transition in which the leadership will face a succession crisis marked by instability and abrupt changes."[49] Several months earlier Chang had noted that "over the long run, it seems doubtful that Peking can significantly reverse the present state of decentralization" in the country because (1) provincial leaders already exercised considerable power in politics, (2) Mao's successor was not likely to make these leaders toe the line, and (3) after Mao died, the leadership would still be split over which policies to adopt.[50]

The staying power of Mao during the 1970s (especially after the bloody years of 1966–67) led some American experts to speculate that other cultural revolutions would erupt after Mao's demise—a contention still held by many U.S. China-watchers in the 1980s.[51] Because Mao's radical policies of the late 1960s continued to compete with the moderate communist policies of his rivals, other experts perceived no resolution of these conflicting policies in the foreseeable future. In mid-1974 Richard Wich offered the following comment on China's future in the next five or ten years.

The question arises, then, whether the familiar polarization of interests that has shaped the dialectic of Maoist China's development will again form along a line of conflict, a line passing between the pragmatic and the ideological, between the trend towards consolidation and the impulse toward radical change, and, in the new circumstances, between a veteran generation of administrators and a new generation which the Chairman may propel into a new pursuit of the Maoist vision.[52]

As we now know, Communist China vacillated between these two broad alternatives until 1979–80, when it finally began to veer toward the more moderate path. Writing in late 1974, Alan P. L. Liu saw only crisis looming, because the radical Maoist faction was locked in a bitter struggle with the more techno-bureaucratic party leaders. According to Liu, "the national mood in China is not conducive to cosmopolitanism," implying that a free flow of information from the outside world could not yet occur under these political circumstances.[53]

By late 1976 American China experts had already witnessed ten years of intense intraparty leadership struggle. It was natural that Parris H. Chang, commenting on Mao's legacy to the Communist Party, would offer this forecast: "It seems certain that the Maoist cult and the thought of Mao Tse-tung will survive Mao. Long after Mao's departure from China's political scene, the Maoist ideological tenets will continue to structure the policy alternatives to be mapped out by the post-Mao Chinese leaders and affect the parameters within which they tackle problems."[54] This forecast proved accurate as long as Hua Kuo-feng's faction remained in the CCP's Central Committee; Mao's ideological influence has also resurfaced since the takeover of the Central Committee by Teng and his faction in 1978–79.

The arrest of four top radical party leaders, the ascendency of an unknown named Hua Kuo-feng to power, and the sudden return of Teng Hsiao-p'ing to the top leadership stunned American observers. As Allen S. Whiting wrote in November 1977, "no foreign analyst or novelist could have credibly written this dramatic scenario in anticipation of how China would enter the post-Mao era."[55] Because of these events, American experts refrained from making any predictions at all in 1976.

Writing in the spring of 1977, Harry Harding, Jr., charted the intraparty power struggle between 1973 and 1976, but he offered no speculations on how the post-Mao leadership struggle would turn out.[56] In late 1977 Maurice Meisner foresaw China as stalled on the Maoist road and unlikely to go forward. Meisner thought that a reversion to a pre-1949 China was highly unlikely. Mao's successors would not push radical change "for they are cautious men who are essentially the managers of a powerful Party-state bureaucratic apparatus which has a strong interest in its own self-preservation, and thus a vested interest in the political apathy of the masses."[57]

As the Hua-Teng struggle for control intensified during 1977–78, American observers usually predicted "an equilibrium and sharing of power" without any clear indication of which leader would eventually emerge supreme.[58] In sum, except for the work of a very few American specialists, predictions about political events in Communist China of the 1970s were unenlightening and often off the mark.

On nonpolitical issues, U.S. China-watchers produced mixed forecasts, some accurate and some inaccurate. In late 1973 Robert Michael Field surmised that China might be able to produce nearly 300 million metric tons of food grain in 1980 if the output trend of the early 1970s held firm and if the northern provinces continued to expand their production as they had in the recent past.[59] But even if China attained the 1980 target of 300 million tons, the country would still have to import substantial amounts of grain every year. In late 1976 Kuan-I Chen and Robert T. Tsuchigane estimated that China would produce 308 to 314 million metric tons of food grain in 1980.[60] The farming incentive system greatly constrained production during the 1970s, but by 1979–80 the regime began allowing production teams more freedom to allocate their resources and use markets. Food grain output jumped to 320 million metric tons in 1980, 325 in 1981, and 344 in 1982— much greater amounts than U.S. experts had believed possible. Our conjecture is that they erred because they did not realize how inefficient the team-farming system had been even with the help of modern inputs like fertilizer.

In an appraisal of Communist China's first twenty years of economic development, the late Alexander Eckstein offered an interesting futuristic reading that was fundamentally correct. He contended that there would be a "different course of economic development in China after Mao's death; one which will follow neither the pattern of the first nor of the second decade."[61] He did not specify the steps by which the party would initiate this new pattern, but after 1979 China did adopt a new open-door policy toward foreign trade and foreign investment; it even established new economic zones to welcome foreign investors. We do not know whether or not the economic reforms being introduced in the 1980s within the framework of a central planned economy will produce an economic development pattern different from that of the 1950s and 1960s. Our sample of China-studies materials makes no predictions about social and cultural behavior.

We now turn to ROC predictions about China. Instead of attempting to predict economic trends using data they regarded as unreliable, ROC experts focused on political trends, which they believed were fundamental for understanding future change. The CCP's Ninth National Congress, convened during April 1–24, 1969 and concluded with a resolution to use Marxism-Leninism and Mao Tse-tung's thought as the theoretical basis for guiding the CCP. Chang Ching-wen has examined the characteristics of 170 members of the CCP Central Committee, including those in the political bureau and its standing committee. He noted that PLA cadres predominated in the Central Committee and that Mao was trying to control the political bureau's standing committee.

What hitherto has been identified as a struggle between anti- and pro-Maoists will soon turn into a conflict within the pro-Maoist ranks. This conflict will be a triangular contest between groups represented by Lin Piao, Chou En-lai, and Chiang Ch'ing. Chou will probably be an underdog. Mao will continue to rely on Lin Piao to tighten his grip on the military and at the same time he will groom the Cultural Revolutionists under Chiang Ch'ing to replace very gradually the first-generation cadres of Chou's group. In trying to bring about a new power alignment, Mao will encounter two critical problems: to maintain the unity within the PLA itself and to prevent rivalry between the PLA and the Cultural Revolutionaries.[62]

Chang accurately identified the key factions that would compete during the next eight years, and he correctly forecasted the difficulties Mao would have with the military—especially with its principal leader, Lin Piao. Other China-watchers began to endorse these predictions and refine them.

On May 15, 1969 a conference at the Institute of International Relations offered three predictions of future developments in Communist China.[63] First, the turmoil associated with the Cultural Revolution would become even more intense, and the party would try to export Mao's theory of "continued revolution" to other countries. Second, the new role played by the military would produce a power struggle between the top leaders of the military and the party—namely, between Lin Piao and Mao. Finally, Mao would press for the widespread adoption of his radical policies, but, even if these policies were adopted, they would not improve living standards either in the cities or in the communes. Mao would probably speed up his "rustication policy," but this would only intensify the bitterness of the students and intellectuals already sent to the villages and anger the rural people who had to receive them. Moreover, this bitterness would be directed only toward Mao and his policies. All of these predictions were eventually vindicated.

In late 1970 Li T'ien-min argued that the rivalry between Mao and Lin Piao was already becoming acrimonious and that both would soon be competing for the necessary political power to eliminate the other.[64] We now know that Lin did try to physically eliminate Mao, but he failed and perished himself. After the fall of Lin Piao in late 1971, ROC experts shifted their predictive analysis from a three-factional struggle to a two-factional one. Their predictive success would prove to be as remarkable for the 1970s as for the late 1960s. Some ROC China-watchers perceived that the struggle would be between Chou En-lai and Chiang Ch'ing and their followers. In early 1973 one expert commented that "both [party leaders and their supporters] are feverishly at work behind the scenes organizing their respective backing in the Party and in the military to amass the leverage needed in future struggles . . . Right now the struggle between the two is a clandestine one, and any internal or outward change will bring that conflict into the open."[65] Within the context of this new factional struggle, both sides naturally maneuvered to expand their faction's influence. But according to ROC observers, neither side reckoned with the skillful abilities of Mao to manipulate this power struggle to his benefit and satisfaction.

In summer 1971, before the Lin Piao incident was made public, ROC experts noted Mao's inspection tour of several regions and his criticism of Liu Shao-ch'i, P'eng Teh-huai, P'eng Chen, Lu Ting-i, Lo Jui-ch'ing, and Yang Shang-k'un, and they insightfully pointed out that Mao had omitted any reference to Teng Hsiao-p'ing. Taking a clue from this event, they predicted that Teng would soon be reinstated. In fact, in early 1973 Teng returned to the State Council, and his power again grew rapidly. Other ROC experts, like Chung Tao, predicted Teng's return and his powerful influence. "Teng's experience and capability will no doubt be of great help to Chou En-lai . . . Teng is also a chess piece, manipulated by Mao in order to pacify the resentment of the many former cadres who had been purged by Mao and to set the stage for the power-grabbing Chiang Ch'ing and her cohorts."[66] Chang Cheng-pang also described Teng's return as "a trick played by Mao in order to reduce any obstacles for his cultivation of the cultural revolutionaries who are now in the process of trying to grab power."[67] We do not know whether or not Mao truly engineered Teng's return, but Mao definitely endorsed the decision that allowed Teng to retrieve his former position of power. And ROC experts correctly predicted Teng's return before it actually occurred.

After Chou died in January 1976, some Western observers believed that Teng would quickly assume Chou's premiership. ROC observers, however, had always contended that Teng could not count on Mao's backing and that Mao did not trust Teng. Therefore, they strongly doubted that Mao would allow Teng to replace Chou. Moreover, they recognized that Teng had become the target of a campaign launched by Mao in early 1976, called "Counter-attacking the Right-deviationist Wind." Hence, they predicted that Teng would soon be in deep trouble.[68] In fact, within three months of Chou's death, Teng was again purged, dismissed from all party and state posts. ROC experts correctly foresaw Teng's rapid eclipse, but they failed to predict the sudden emergence of the unknown Hua Kuo-feng.

ROC experts therefore accurately predicted the major shifts in the party power struggle between the outbreak of the Cultural Revolution and the comeback of Teng Hsiao-p'ing; they also accurately predicted the eventual defeat of the cultural revolutionary faction (later known as the Gang of Four). Writing in fall 1974, Chang Cheng-pang pointed out that after the CCP's

Ninth National Congress, Mao decided to promote the cultural revolutionary faction as his successors in the domination of party and state.[69] Chang noted that, although the cultural revolutionary faction had Mao's strong backing and exercised some control over the party's Central Committee, this faction was still enormously handicapped. He offered the following explanation of this situation.

First, the cultural revolutionary faction had made too many enemies, especially among the old powerful cadres of the party and in the military establishment. Second, this faction and its leaders lacked sufficient experience in statecraft and in outmaneuvering their enemies. Third, their status in the party was not very high, and they lacked credibility with most party comrades. For these reasons, Chang concluded, Mao and the cultural revolutionary faction would first have to eliminate their foremost rival, Chou En-lai, from the State Council, but they would have to do this before Mao died. If they failed to accomplish this goal and to arrange for an appropriate successor prior to Mao's death, their future success was most unlikely.

During 1975 ROC experts became more and more aware of the weaknesses of the cultural revolutionary faction. "After Mao's death, there is a distinct possibility of a transitional collective leadership in the Chinese Communist Party. But a bitter power struggle will take place at the same time. The most likely way this will happen is through either a conspiratorial *coup d'état* or a mass movement."[70] ROC experts repeatedly stressed that the cultural revolutionary faction had never successfully brought the military under their control. Li T'ien-min forecasted the following developments. "The military will become the base or seeding ground for a gradual and powerful opposition against the Chiang Ch'ing faction . . . The old Party cadres detest Chiang Ch'ing, and even those cadres who have not been disgraced hardly respect her. Once this long, suppressed resentment boils over, we will see the elimination of Chiang Ch'ing and the desecration of Mao."[71] Within a month of Mao's death Chiang Ch'ing and her associates were arrested; within a few years, de-Maoification began in earnest.

Perhaps the most impressive forecast of 1976 was made by Warren Kuo, one of the most knowledgeable and insightful China-watchers in the ROC. On September 30, 1976—three weeks after Mao died—Kuo predicted that the transition would depend on how three groups competed with each other: the cultural revolutionaries (or Chiang Ch'ing and her cohorts); the pragmatist communist faction of Teng Hsiao-p'ing and the many purged cadres; and the neutralist communist faction made up of senior party cadres and top military leaders like Yeh Chien-ying, Li Hsien-nien, Ch'en Yun, and others. Kuo offered a specific scenario of how this three-factioned power struggle would evolve.

The Cultural Revolutionaries must take the bold risk of being eliminated if
the pragmatists and the neutralist factions form an alliance to oppose them
at the 3rd Plenum. If this alliance does occur, the purge of Chiang Ch'ing
and the end of Maoism will be inevitable. Stalin was denounced in Russia
only three years after his death. Mao very possibly could be subject to the
same kind of treatment in even a shorter period of time.[72]

Kuo further predicted that "a severe power struggle within the Chinese Communist Party is expected to take place within one month after Mao's death."[73]
On September 9 at 12:10 A.M., Mao died in Beijing at the age of 82.
On October 6 Chang Ch'un-ch'iao, Wang Hung-wen, Yao Wen-yuan, and
Chiang Ch'ing were arrested, and on October 7 the three former power-
holders were dismissed from all posts in Shanghai. Kuo's extraordinary prediction was correct almost to the day.

Only eight days after Mao's death Cheng Hsüeh-chia also wrote that
Chiang Ch'ing and her faction did not have enough real power in the party
and military and that her followers simply did not have the experience and
connections to deal with the top military leaders and the older party cadres.
Cheng offered this observation about some of the well-known military leaders who were thought to be Maoist. "Will Wang Tung-hsin support Chiang?
It is very doubtful. Since Mao has died, Wang is not likely to be stupid
enough to support Mao's widow, who has so many enemies in and outside
the party."[74] Cheng further predicted that "once the power struggle erupts,
the Chiang Ch'ing faction will become the underdogs and will be ignomin-
iously defeated."[75] On October 6, the day of the coup, Wang Tung-hsin fully
cooperated with Hua, even supplying private documents incriminating
Chiang Ch'ing.

Other ROC experts also foresaw the speedy end of Chiang Ch'ing's
power in the party. In July 1976 Li T'ien-min remarked that the cultural
revolutionary faction, which was younger and had been nurtured in the hot-
house environment of special privileges, possessed little experience for political struggle. Mao hoped to manipulate party affairs and direct party activities to a new stage by promoting the cultural revolutionary faction to succeed
him in power. But according to Li, this long-cherished hope would not be
realized and would probably be crushed like "the spring storm of the Tienanmen Incident."[76] Li went on to say that Hua Kuo-feng was incapable of
shouldering the responsibilities of the premiership and was simply too inept
to lead both the party and the military.[77]

After Hua Kuo-feng ordered the capture of the Gang of Four and routed
the top leadership of Chiang Ch'ing's faction in Shanghai and other cities,
ROC experts emphatically asserted that Hua's position was very insecure.
They charged that he lacked the basic qualities needed to rule the Communist
Party; that is, he had no close connections with top military leaders, and he

lacked prestige either within the party or in the state bureaucracy. These experts predicted that Hua could survive only by quickly consolidating his power; this would entail blocking, by any means possible, the return of Teng Hsiao-p'ing to power. Teng was far superior to Hua in political skills and had a higher standing within the party; he was Hua's most serious threat. Li Chiu-i described how the party leadership would change if Hua could not handle Teng. "If Hua cannot successfully stonewall the demands from the old cadres and the military for Teng's return, he would have to cease making any criticism of Teng or even go as far as to rehabilitate him. If that takes place, the entire character of the competition for power in China will then change."[78]

In a November 1976 editorial in *Chung-kung yen-chiu,* ROC China-watchers pointed out that Hua Kuo-feng had been invited into the top leadership of the CCP either because of a cooperative effort or because of a compromise agreement by military leaders and the old party cadres. They also stated that "Hua can neither maintain his control over the Central Committee nor even his own position . . . The final showdown will take place at the 3rd Plenum of the 10th Party Central Committee meeting."[79] As we now know, at the third plenum of the Tenth CCP Central Committee held in July 1977, Teng was indeed restored to prominent membership in the party. He was allowed to return to the political bureau and even to the standing committee of that body and to hold the posts of deputy chairman of the party and of the military commission.

Writing in early January 1977, Ch'iu K'ung-yuan offered the standard interpretation of why Hua and his followers could not survive for long in the party.[80] He also pointed out that the various military leaders had strengthened their own power by supporting Hua in the October 1976 coup that destroyed the cultural revolutionary faction. He stressed that Hua could not really be expected to carry Mao's banner forward if he relinquished power to the military and party elite who had borne the wrath of Mao (who had, in fact, even been purged). Ch'iu predicted that ideological confusion within the party would be rife as a result of these recent developments. Further, he contended that this confusion would produce demands for more free expression and debate both inside and outside the party and that these pressures would pose new and serious difficulties for the party leadership.

During the next few years the Democracy Wall Movement took place, and in many provinces demonstrations criticizing Communist Party-style politics occurred. ROC experts made quite accurate forecasts of many of the major shifts in Chinese communist politics. They correctly predicted that Hua's days were numbered, explained why he would not survive for long, and accurately described the conditions by which Hua could keep or regain his power.

CONCLUSIONS

This brief survey of predictions by American and ROC Communist China experts naturally contains some omissions; we are dealing with a large and complex literature. Even so, one cannot fail to be impressed with the remarkable abilities of ROC experts to predict the behavior of the CCP elite and to identify which leaders and factions would dominate the party and state. U.S. experts enjoyed fewer predictive successes, particularly in keeping track of the CCP's intraparty struggles and changes in policies. Why was this?

First, we would argue that the ROC China-watchers implicitly used a typology to analyze political change on the mainland that was more accurate than some of the typologies that were guiding American China-watchers. The ROC typology stressed that the motive to hold, consolidate, and wield power governed all political behavior in China. Because of this overriding motive, power struggles became endemic in this system. The U.S. experts who implicitly used the totalitarian or communist authoritarian typologies also seemed to have correctly predicted certain developments in this system. The use of an appropriate descriptive typology therefore appears to be an important prerequisite for understanding how current behavior and activities will shape future political outcomes in Communist China.

Perhaps a second reason for the superior predictive abilities of ROC experts is their extraordinary capacity to understand the thinking and behavior of the Chinese communist cadres—especially the top leaders. Some of these experts were former members of the Communist Party, and they understood Communist Party politics and the ways in which party cadres maneuvered, relied upon personal networks, and plotted to seize power. Because of their intimate understanding of Chinese culture and social behavior, they could closely empathize with popular reactions to communist policies and conflicts. They could therefore correctly gauge whether the populace would conform to or resist party policies.

A third factor to be emphasized is the ability of ROC researchers to examine large quantities of Chinese records and publications and understand their true meaning. ROC experts were especially sensitive to, and could extract the real meaning from, the written record and the vocal statements of the Communist Party leadership. Only a few American experts have possessed the ability to do this, and there is no substitute for the native reader who is at home with the language and understands the nuances of every word or statement.

Finally, we would strongly emphasize that a superior method of analysis is no substitute for missing information about the origins of policies and the behavior of people in a closed society like Communist China. Access to relevant facts is necessary and important. The ROC China-watchers were extremely fortunate in having access to a vast storehouse of intelligence information. They were privy to many CCP Central Committee documents and other records, which revealed intraparty debates and high-level political maneuvering among the leadership. Even though institutions in the ROC made these documents available to researchers in Taipei (some documents were translated into English), a careful reading of our sample of U.S. research findings on China suggests that less than 15 or 20 percent of this literature ever referred to these intraparty documents available in the ROC. We find this rather odd, because the paucity of information on Communist China should have inspired greater usage of these research findings and original documents. This finding strongly suggests that many U.S. experts had prejudices that discouraged their use of this source of information. The most common prejudice was probably the belief that ROC China-watching experts could not be trusted to produce objective research because they were committed to supporting their government—a government that had been engaged in bitter conflict with the Chinese Communist Party for more than a quarter-century. Many American China-watchers also charged that ROC scholars implicitly hoped the Chinese communist regime would collapse and they too often focused on the negative, dark side of the socioeconomic and cultural conditions in mainland China. Therefore, how could ROC documents and scholarship be trusted? We believe these observations largely explain why the predictive powers of U.S. and ROC China-watchers differed greatly. We will now consider another dimension of understanding Communist China: attempts to explain events and to accurately identify the trends or processes of change that are closely related to these events.

6

Understanding by Means of
Interpretation of the Event

Interpreting unusual events in a foreign society is another way of trying to understand behavior and activity in that society. If we can understand why certain events occurred and what meaning they had for different participants, we can achieve new insights about a foreign society. Understanding unique events in Communist China has been particularly difficult, however, because of the fragmentary evidence available on the origins and evolution of these events. In this chapter we will examine research related to three major events that greatly transformed Chinese society from what it was prior to 1949: the Socialist Transformation movement of 1949–56, the Three Red Banners Campaign of 1958–61, and the Great Cultural Revolution of 1966–76.

THE SOCIALIST
TRANSFORMATION

How the Communist Party successfully collectivized agriculture in 1955–56 with so little resistance from the peasantry is a puzzling question. In September 1967 Thomas P. Bernstein provided an answer with his comparative analysis of the collectivization campaigns in the USSR (1929–30) and the PRC (1955–56).[1]

In the Soviet Union Stalin had to complete two difficult tasks at the same time. He had to eliminate the leaders of the rural elite so he could impose party control over the villages, and he had to extract a large economic surplus from the peasantry so he could industrialize the country. Elite opposition to collectivization forced Stalin to resort to draconian measures to remove them from power. But this was done at the regime's expense, because peasants slaughtered their livestock and burned their grain. In China, the party had already destroyed the rural elite during the land-reform years (1946–52) and substituted party-dominated peasant associations to govern villages. Therefore, when Mao urged rapid collectivization, "the upsurge of 1955–56 could be successfully carried out on the basis of a tightening of these already established controls."[2] Unlike its counterpart in the Soviet Union (which had to create new controls overnight and at great cost), the CCP already had an apparatus of control in the villages; peasants simply could not organize effective resistance to collectivization. Bernstein's comparative analysis illuminated the importance of the relationship between the party and the local elite. It showed how land reform operated differently in China and the USSR. In China, land reform entailed destroying the local elite and distributing land to the poor; in the USSR, land reform allowed the rural elite to control their villages.

In 1953 three American experts presented a very perceptive interpretation of Soviet reactions to Maoist theoretical writing on the Chinese revolution.[3] Their interpretation suggested that as early as 1950–52 significant tensions were building between the two communist giants over the theoretical importance of the rise of the CCP to power in China, the subsequent socialist transformation of China, and the implications of these events for revolution elsewhere in the world.

In late 1950 Soviet propagandists praised Chairman Mao's contributions, but they insisted on characterizing his writings as "filling out" or "advancing" Lenin's and Stalin's theoretical statements.[4] In 1951 Chinese theoreticians responded by stressing that Mao had made new theoretical contributions to the revolutionary struggle. In January 1952 Kuan Meng-chüeh described Mao's "Strategic Problems of China's Revolutionary War" as a Marxist classic.[5] Using a narrative approach, the American authors traced the various exchanges between Moscow and Beijing propagandists on the significance to be attached to Mao's writings. They concluded that by the end of 1952 the Soviets had refused to admit Mao into the pantheon of Marxist giants (Marx, Lenin, and Stalin); the Soviets preferred to regard Mao's thought as merely an application of their principles to the special conditions of China. The Chinese side did not press the issue at the time, thus avoiding a conflict with the Soviets. But there was already a "real, albeit latent, area of disagreement between the Chinese and Soviets which the Chinese, presumably, could exploit in the future."[6]

Chao Yu-shen described three important developments in the early 1950s that he contended probably influenced Mao's views on how China should be ruled and transformed.[7] ROC China-watchers often stressed the importance of understanding leadership motivation and psychology. They believed that unless one understood the true motives of powerful leaders who tried to impose their policies, important political events could not be understood in their entirety. The question of why Mao believed the party could establish a communist society in a matter of a few years has not been fully explored or answered. Chao Yu-shen's argument was that Mao's decision to have the party carry out the Three Red Banners Campaign was probably influenced by the remarkable successes the party had achieved a few years earlier in carrying out the socialist transformation of China so quickly.[8]

Seeking to avoid the mistakes of the Soviet Communist Party in the 1920s and 1930s, the CCP set out to eliminate both the rural and urban ruling elites in the private sector by means of a series of political campaigns. These nationwide movements—first in the countryside by means of land reform, and subsequently in the cities by means of campaigns to eliminate corruption in private enterprise—were synchronized with a massive effort to suppress all enemies of the new regime. By simultaneously operating on a number of fronts, the party was able to successfully appeal to nationalistic sentiments when faced with the American military threat in the Korean War. After having effectively quelled their opposition, the party quickly organized the farmers into new collective organizations linked to the state and party control apparatus, which brought the entire rural sector under the control of a planned economy. Remarkably, aggregate production did not decline during these years but steadily rose; even consumption modestly improved.

Chao contends that these achievements probably made Mao supremely confident; with the party carrying out his policies, anything was possible. Instead of abiding by the original leadership schedule set in 1953 to bring society under state control within fifteen years, Mao and the party achieved their aim by 1956. But instead of consolidating the gains and institutionalizing the organizations that the party had just established, Mao hastily set about transforming China into the final stage—Communism—by launching the Three Red Banners Campaign in 1958.

THE THREE RED BANNERS CAMPAIGN

Referred to as the Three Red Banners Campaign by ROC experts, and as the Great Leap Forward by American experts, the events of 1958–61 constituted important developments for the CCP and Chinese society. For an unusually long time the Chinese Communist Party had avoided the sort of fratricidal conflict in which top leaders purge and ultimately liquidate their colleagues and followers. But, eventually, unbearable tensions forced Mao to turn against old comrades. One aspect of these tensions, examined by American scholar Frederick C. Teiwes, consisted of Communist Party political norms.[9] According to Teiwes, the party had developed formal codes of leadership behavior: subordinate organs implemented higher-level directives; the majority made decisions; minority groups could dissent; members were encouraged to revise their thinking and behavior (rectification) or be purged;

and disciplinary problems were handled by the party with minimal mass participation.[10]

These practices had become procedural, and members expected that the "rules of the game" would be honored no matter what troubles engulfed the party. Teiwes argued that factional conflict was inhibited by the strength of these party norms in the 1949–57 period but that various events in the mid- to late 1950s began to undermine them. The dismissal of P'eng Teh-huai after the Lushan meeting in 1958 proved to be a watershed for the party leadership; thereafter, neither leaders nor members were ever certain which "rules of the game" existed or would be honored.[11] The dismissal of Ch'en Yun added to the apprehension of the party membership; finally, the Cultural Revolution destroyed the old party political behavioral norms altogether.

By 1956 the CCP had greatly reduced private property rights and destroyed private associations for business or social-cultural affairs. Simultaneously, the CCP had begun to create a huge state bureaucracy, much of it supervised by party cadres, to impose certain imperatives on behavior. After investigating how many CCP bureaucrats had terminated their careers in this bureaucracy, Michel Oksenberg found that by 1976 CCP members had a high probability of "ending their careers in disgrace rather than in peaceful death."[12] This was particularly true of members who had led the struggle to unify China under party control. Oksenberg pointed out that most party careers ended "either through death or dismiss[al] in disgrace" and suggested that this bureaucratic "exit pattern" was bound to make bureaucrats very cautious in their behavior. This exit pattern probably also intensified tensions between those demoted or dismissed and those still in power. According to Oksenberg, the tension-producing consequences strongly suggested an "accumulation of grievances within bureaucratic units."[13]

As new tensions spread through the party and state organizations in the late 1950s, a serious split developed between the two top leaders of the CCP—Mao Tse-tung and Liu Shao-ch'i. ROC experts explained this split by describing how political meetings unfolded, quarrels erupted, and factions maneuvered to get their policies endorsed and implemented by the party.

After the failure of the Three Red Banners Campaign, Mao was forced to retreat before the onslaught of criticisms voiced at the sixth plenum of the Eighth CCP Central Committee in November 1958. Stung by these criticisms, which detailed the damage inflicted on the country by his policies, Mao agreed to a reorganization of the People's Communes and a suspension of communes within the cities. To further mollify his critics, Mao announced that he would not seek the chairmanship of the State Council. In effect, Mao signaled to his colleagues that he was now willing to share more power with other leaders like Liu Shao-ch'i, Chou En-lai, Teng Hsiao-p'ing, and P'eng Chen. In 1971 K'ung Teh-liang carefully pointed out that Mao had publicly admitted that the party had two headquarters (*liang-ke ssu-ling-pu*), a figure of speech that signified his loss of power.[14]

K'ung suggested that Mao was not and could not be reconciled to sharing political power with others, particularly when he saw Liu Shao-ch'i enlarging his sphere of influence in the party. Furthermore, Mao grew increasingly unhappy and restless as he observed Liu and his followers introducing policies to dismantle his own efforts to convert China to communism. In K'ung's estimation, Liu's arguments that his policies were sorely needed to solve the political and economic crises caused by the Three Red Banners Campaign also must have grated on Mao. He probably became furious as reports trickled back to him about what the party was doing throughout the country. Mao naturally considered that these new steps were only leading the country back to capitalism; he also recognized that there was enormous discontent within the party and among the population with the policies of his rivals Liu and Teng. Therefore, said K'ung, Mao felt increasingly frustrated. His power had steadily declined; his policies were being ridiculed; policies he abhorred were widely rampant; and party cadres and ordinary people were unhappy and resentful about party policies. "Fearing a 'capitalist comeback' and also a 'palace *coup* of the Khrushchev type' in the Party and a 'revolutionary movement of the Hungarian type' outside the Party, Mao decided to launch the Cultural Revolution in an attempt to get out of a precarious position."[15]

In a deeper exploration of the growing antagonism between Mao and Liu, Wang Hsüeh-wan stated in 1968 that both leaders had gradually come to have very different views of the meaning of the Marxist concept of class struggle.[16] Wang argued that Liu believed that after the bourgeoisie had been dispossessed of property and power, class no longer existed (although he did not say exactly when Liu had articulated this viewpoint). In the eyes of the party and state, every citizen was now a proletarian; without the means of production and working for a wage. Liu also believed that the party should make economic development its top priority. In contrast, Mao believed that ideas were primary. In other words, even if rich men were deposed and their property confiscated, they could still be reactionary in heart and mind. These types of people were clever and imaginative and could plot to acquire power and influence again—even in the party and state. Because of these convictions, Mao stressed the need to begin an urgent transformation of ideology and behavior. For Mao, class struggle was still important. These very different perceptions of the meaning of class struggle made it impossible for Mao and Liu to ever again see eye-to-eye.

ROC experts generally tried to describe a chain of events in some order of cause and effect to understand the political dynamics of the Chinese communist regime. Much of their research focused on isolating a particular political event that allegedly set the stage for even more important events. One event that received their close scrutiny was the removal of P'eng Teh-huai and Huang K'e-ch'eng from their government posts. These dismissals were carefully examined by Tsen Yung-hśien.[17]

The CCP's Political Bureau meeting in July 1959 and the eighth plenum of the CCP's Central Committee in August 1959 were bitter affairs. Before these meetings, P'eng was a member of the CCP Political Bureau, and served as vice premier and minister of defense of the State Council and vice chairman of the CCP Military Commission. Huang had served as secretary of the CCP Secretariat, chief of the general staff of the PLA, and vice premier of the State Council. At the plenum both men vigorously opposed Mao's Three Red Banners strategy and criticized arguments presented in support of Mao's policies. After an incredibly bitter struggle, both P'eng and Huang were removed from their government positions. Chang Wen-t'ien (minister of foreign affairs), Chou Hsiao-chou (first secretary of the CCP Hunan Provincial Commission), and several other senior cadres who had opposed Mao's Three Red Banners campaign also lost their jobs. They managed to retain their positions in the party only because of the intervention of Liu Shao-ch'i. Tsen concludes his analysis of this bitter factional struggle by stating that the "P'eng-Huang incident was the first round of the Mao-Liu struggle and the prelude to the Cultural Revolution."[18] According to Tsen, this was the first time since 1949 that Mao's authority had been seriously challenged; afterwards, the lines were clearly drawn between Liu and Mao within the party. Tsen argues that if the eighth plenum is interpreted in this way, the Cultural Revolution need not be regarded as an inexplicable event.

THE GREAT PROLETARIAN CULTURAL REVOLUTION

We now turn our attention to the most extraordinary event of the three decades of communist rule—the Great Proletarian Cultural Revolution. We first examine explanations of the origins of the Cultural Revolution; we then compare some different interpretations of how the Cultural Revolution evolved between 1966 and 1976. Finally, we will cite some explanations of how this event influenced the political system.

Origins of the Cultural Revolution

Defining the precise moment that the Cultural Revolution started is not easy. Consider the following chronology of events: On November 10, 1965 Mao took the offensive against those who had criticized him in literary magazines in previous years by having Yao Wen-yuan criticize Wu Han's play

Dismissal of Hai Jui. In early December 1965 Mao persuaded the PLA military commanders to assist him in his bid to oust his rivals. On April 16,
1966 Mao organized criticism of works that had been extremely critical of
him in recent years: *Notes of the Three-Family Village* and *Evening Conver-
sations at Yen Mountain.* At a Political Bureau meeting on May 16, 1966 Lin
Piao threatened Mao's rivals, Liu and Teng, saying, "whoever opposes Mao
Tse-tung will perish." Between Liu's political blunders and Mao's influence,
Mao and Lin won the day; the Central Committee ordered veteran cadres like
P'eng Chen removed from office. Mao immediately left for Hangchow, but
returned (on July 18, 1966) after Lin's troops had occupied the capital and
seized the public media. On August 12, 1966 Mao removed Liu from the
party, and on August 18, 1966 he assembled one million Red Guards at
Tienanmen Square.

Between November 10, 1965 and July 18, 1966 Mao gradually set the
stage for imposing his control on the party and state. Thereafter, he un-
leashed the Red Guards all over the country, purged his rivals, and then
requested the PLA to restore order and occupy provincial party-state administrative posts. Until his death on September 9, 1976 Mao was dominant in
both party and spirit throughout the country. The decade 1966–76 was called
the Cultural Revolution because of the new policies and organizations that
Mao and his followers tried to impose on China.

For purposes of discussion, we refer to the events between November
10, 1965 and July 18, 1966 as the actual beginning of the Cultural Revolution. This phase constitutes Mao's step-by-step return to power. What sort of
explanations have American China experts offered for the beginning of the
Cultural Revolution?

First we will disregard the studies that deal primarily with the social
origins of the Cultural Revolution—that is, the motives behind and processes by which popular participation in the Red Guard movement spread
throughout the cities.[19] We have adopted a three-fold classification of explanations of Mao's behavior between November 10, 1965 and July 18, 1966.
These include (1) power struggles, (2) policy differences, and (3) eclectic
reasons.

Proponents of the power struggle thesis have argued that Mao sought
political power to guide China along what he perceived as the correct path
toward socialism. Writing in spring 1967, Franz Michael admitted that, originally, "two divergent communist lines" existed, but, beginning in 1962,
Mao plotted to try to recover the power he had lost after the August 1959
Lushan plenum.[20] According to Michael, Mao's failed policies of the late
1950s cost him considerable party power and prestige. Fearing a decline in
influence, he began a careful campaign to take over the party and reimpose
his policies on the country. Gene T. Hsiao also endorses this thesis, but he

stresses that both Mao's disagreement with Liuist policies and his fear of Khrushchev's de-Stalinization in the Soviet Union convinced him that the party would soon abandon his policies if he did not act quickly.[21] Charles Neuhauser points out that in the early 1960s party cadres had become more corrupt and inept, party organizations more bureaucratic, and party campaigns increasingly ineffective; Mao tried to seize the reins of power to reverse these trends.

> Indeed, the history of the CCP from mid-1964 and particularly since the start of the Cultural Revolution itself can be seen as an attempt on the part of Mao Tse-tung to re-assert his personal authority over all aspects of Party policy and over all levels of Party organization. But as the pressures toward this end grew, personal animosities were exacerbated and philosophic and policy differences personalized. The ultimate result of this trend was the explosion that has convulsed China since mid-1966.[22]

In late 1966 Harry Gelman described the conflict between Mao and the writers of the party's propaganda establishment.[23] Writers like Wu Han and Teng T'o were severely critical of Mao's policies of the late 1950s and of his demotion of P'eng Teh-huai. According to Gelman, Mao had been fighting the party and nonparty intelligentsia since 1962; in 1966, with the help of the PLA, he was finally able to purge these intellectuals and dominate the party.

Other experts, however, see the origins of the Cultural Revolution differently. Richard D. Baum pinpoints fall and winter 1963–64 as the beginning of a party campaign to "rekindle the sputtering flame of China's revolution and to immunize the Chinese people against the pernicious virus of Khrushchev's apostate 'revisionism.'"[24] Because of deteriorating conditions both inside and outside of China, Mao and others launched the Socialist Education campaign and the *Hsia-fang* (rustication) campaign to force urban intellectuals to give up their nonsocialist ideas. Baum sees the events of late 1965–66 as merely a speeding up of existing policies to spiritually regenerate the country. Naturally, this new momentum of Mao's policies pulverized his opposition; many were arrested and purged.

Both Baum and Philip Bridgham noted that by fall 1965 Mao was unhappy with the lack of success of the Socialist Education campaign. Bridgham contended that the Cultural Revolution was really a continuation of this campaign, complete with new methods of terrorism and violence.[25]

Richard M. Pfeffer described the polarization of two elite factions after 1959. One group "concentrated their attention primarily on organization-building, regularity, and modernization"; the other group, "headed by Mao, was more radical and increasingly lost faith in the bureaucratic procedures and in the Marxist notion that economic development would lead to the good society."[26] These groups had differing views on the type of socialist course China should adopt, and the struggle between them "became more and more a struggle for power—for the power to determine the course of China's development."[27] By seeking and receiving support from the PLA, Mao was able to overwhelm his opposition in the Peking party organization and subsequently to impose his policies on his rivals.[28]

By eclectic arguments, we mean any approach that considers the complex interplay of Mao's ideological differences with his rivals and his efforts to recapture power. Not all experts presented their case in this balanced way, but we cite several we believe were sensitive to such interactions. Writing in mid-1969, Chalmers Johnson considered ideology a powerful factor in the shaping of CCP policies in the 1950s and 1960s, but he also maintained that Mao had lost power in the early 1960s and feared the party might backslide down the road of revisionism. Mao launched the Cultural Revolution to regain his power and carry out the policies he believed to be correct.[29] Tang Tsou also linked Mao's vision of altering social norms and values to his dependency on the PLA and Red Guards to challenge an established totalitarian system. Both factors, he said, were essential for launching the Cultural Revolution.[30]

More recently, Paul J. Hiniker has offered a different explanation of the origins of the Cultural Revolution.[31] Hiniker suggests that Mao and his followers were extremely frustrated by the failures of the late 1950s and early 1960s and worried that their policies had been subverted by opponents. To compensate for previous failures and to deal with potential subversion, Mao became more oblivious to criticism and advice and more obsessed with a desire to impose his will on others. Meanwhile, Mao's opponents continued to distance themselves from him and became more skeptical of his views. Disagreements between the two sides intensified, producing more polarization and conflict; Mao disparaged his critics and, finally, saw that the only course open was to physically remove them.

ROC experts were also divided in their interpretations of the origins of the Cultural Revolution. Some held that ideology and policy differences separated Mao and Liu; others cited a combination of a struggle for power and ideological differences. The majority, however, opted for the power-struggle thesis. After detailing the step-by-step process leading up to the beginnings of the Cultural Revolution, Li Min-hua concluded: "Ideological struggle or line struggle is merely a flag-sign used to dazzle the populace, or only a minor ingredient to the power struggle. The Cultural Revolution is a 100 percent struggle for power."[32]

Some ROC experts believed the struggle between Mao and Liu for party power began as early as 1954 at the fourth plenum of the Seventh CCP Central Committee, when Liu referred to Mao as arrogant and egocentric.[33] But most ROC experts believe that the real beginning of the leadership struggle dates to 1959, when party leaders criticized Mao so severely that he decided not to seek the chairmanship of the State Council again. As a result of relinquishing this position, Mao had to share power with Liu and Teng.[34] Because Liu could retain P'eng Teh-huai and Huang K'e-ch'eng in their state positions, Liu gained considerable political power.[35] In this first struggle, Mao and Liu came off even.

In the second phase, Mao began to cultivate Lin Piao by having him organize a PLA campaign "to learn Mao's thoughts," but Liu tried to counter this by having Lo Jui-ch'ing, chief of the general staff, initiate a campaign to "give first place to military training."[36] At the ninth plenum of the Ninth CCP Central Committee in January 1961, Liu gained the upper hand by obtaining Central Committee support for his modification policies for the organizations established during the Three Red Banners campaign. During the next few years Mao was humiliated, with Liu's blessing, in a series of satirical literary pieces—such as *Notes of the Three-Family Village*.

The reader must appreciate the flavor of these essays to realize their likely psychological impact on Mao. In an essay written by Teng T'o, entitled "Antidote for Amnesia" [*Chuan-chi chien-wang-cheng*], a passage refers to Mao Tse-tung as a bungling leader. "A person suffering from amnesia does not even recognize his own home or his wife. He always stumbles in his statements and simply does not know how to behave himself . . . How to deal with such a person? There are two ways: first, spray his head with some dog's blood; second, hit him right on the head with a big stick."[37] In another essay, entitled "The Great Empty Talk," the author made fun of Mao's political clichés. "There is a kid in our neighborhood who always likes to copy the great poets when he tries to write a poem. Here is one of his masterpieces: 'The sky is my father, the earth is my mother, and the sun is my nursemaid; the east wind is my benefactor, and the west wind is my enemy.' "[38] This satirical passage refers to Mao's slogan "The Last Wind Suppresses the West Wind" and Mao's former dependency on the Soviet Union.

After careful study, ROC experts concluded that the personal antagonisms and distrust between Mao and his rivals must have been intensified enormously by these literary essays. The struggle-for-power proponents suggested the following outline of the evolution of the drama of the 1960s. Mao, stung by attempts to discredit him and usurp his power, managed to persuade the Central Committee to initiate the Socialist Education campaign and to reemphasize class struggle throughout the country. (This happened at the tenth plenum of the Eighth CCP Central Committee in September 1962.) Liu and his followers, however, manipulated this movement to their own purposes; they replaced Maoist cadres in the countryside and expanded their own influence in the party. According to ROC experts, the final stage began in 1964 when Mao initiated the campaign to "learn from the PLA," an attempt to extend his influence in the party and state hierarchy. Liu and his faction opposed this move, and the struggle intensified until Mao gained the upper hand in summer 1966.

Like some American scholars, a few ROC experts believed that the Cultural Revolution had roots in the ideological differences between Mao and Liu.[39] Mao and Liu viewed class struggle and the proletarian dictatorship very differently. Liu favored balanced economic growth; Mao preferred unbalanced growth and a strengthening of the collective sector by means of class struggle. Liu favored mechanization of agriculture by gradual industrial development, followed by collectivization. Mao believed communes could be built overnight; Liu thought it would take time. Liu urged monetary incentives; Mao pressed for continuous political struggle.[40]

Finally, a few ROC experts adopted an eclectic position on the origin of the Cultural Revolution. Chen Li-sheng pointed out that "Mao launched the Cultural Revolution for two purposes: to restore his supreme power and to insist on the adoption of a leftist line."[41] The above sample of writings should sufficiently describe the varying ways in which U.S. and ROC Pekingologists explained the origins of the Cultural Revolution. We will now examine how this extraordinary event unfolded.

The Cultural Revolution as a Process

Because of the complexity of the decade of the Cultural Revolution, we have divided it into two main periods: (1) the beginning period (described above) to April 1, 1969; and (2) the subsequent years until the demise of the Gang of Four. The first phase encompasses Mao's destruction of his rivals and his takeover of the party and state. The following key events should be kept in mind during our discussion of various interpretations of the changes that occurred during these years.

In fall 1966 Red Guards attacked party officials throughout the country; they vented their anger especially on Liu, Teng, and their families. On February 19, 1967 various prominent vice-premiers (like T'ang Chen-lin, Ch'en I, and Yeh Chien-ying) and other notables gathered at Hui Jen Hall to voice their anger and opposition to the Cultural Revolution and Chiang Ch'ing's attacks on veteran cadres. Their protests were ignored, and in the following weeks and months they and others were arrested and purged. Meanwhile, there was great turmoil in the provinces. On July 20, 1967 nearly a million Red Guards converged on Wuhan city and mistreated key Cultural Revolution leaders like Wang Li and Hsieh Fu-chih. On October 14, 1967 the Central Committee ordered students to return to school, but few obeyed. Violence and turmoil continued, and some high-ranking officers in the PLA were purged in late March 1968. These last two events were indications of increased fighting among Mao-, Lin-, and Liu-led groups. By summer's end the PLA disbanded the Red Guards, and many of them realized they had merely been used by their political leaders. Lin tried to assassinate Mao on September 12, 1971, but he himself perished the next day on an airplane that crashed in Outer Mongolia. These events were followed by campaigns to criticize Lin and Confucius during 1973–74. Teng was again dismissed on April 7, 1976, and, finally, the Gang of Four were captured on October 6, 1976. Our discussion of the various explanations of these events is organized around these themes: (1) the conflict over political power, (2) the distribution and use of political power, and (3) the creation of new organizations and their functions.

In early 1968 Chalmers Johnson divided American China-watchers who had commented on the Cultural Revolution into two schools. One school had emphasized that China was slowly slipping into chaos; the other had maintained that Mao was still in control but was not aware of the mounting chaos around him.[42] Johnson took the position that "Mao indeed began by exercising the controlling initiative in the Cultural Revolution, but unintended consequences of his initiatives had increasingly diverted the Maoist forces from their long-term goals into emergency salvage operations."[43]

Lowell Dittmer interpreted the process of events differently. By refining the techniques of mass mobilization and self-criticism developed during the Yenan period, Mao mobilized the masses to criticize those in the party and state who were supposedly undermining socialism and did not understand how to build communism. By using mass rallies and self-criticism sessions, Mao and his followers constantly contrasted the ongoing behavior of their enemies with Mao's ideals.[44] Mao also mobilized the populace because of immense discontent throughout the country. Dittmer asserts that "the mobilization of mass grievances (class struggle) came to coincide with a cleavage between radical favourites and career bureaucrats (power struggle, struggle between headquarters) over a decision Mao chose to exemplify as the general policy issue of mass-elite relations (struggle between two roads)."[45] When looked at in this way, the first phase of the Cultural Revolution appears to have been both a struggle between Mao and his followers and their rivals in the party and state apparatus and a mass movement of popular discontent aimed at individuals and groups alleged to be responsible for subverting socialism. In addition, Dittmer's interpretation cites the process by which Mao and his followers tried to inculcate new values and social norms of behavior in the masses, and even in their enemies. If these enemies were not ready to comply, they were forced out of power and sent to the countryside for punishment and thought reform.

Somewhat later, Hong Yung Lee focused on seven principal actors (including individuals, groups, and organizations) and examined their relationships in situations in which (1) conflict was dominant, (2) conflict and co-operation co-existed, and (3) cooperation was dominant. Lee analyzed the issues that divided his seven principal actors to show that "the radical mass organizations were largely composed of underprivileged social groups, whereas the conservatives were heavily drawn from the better-off social groups. The radicals attempted to change the political status quo as much as possible, whereas the conservatives strenuously defended the status quo."[46] To test his thesis, Lee conceptualized four time-periods of political action: (1) October 1965 to August 1966, or the politics of bureaucracy, when intraelite conflict deepened; (2) August 1966 to December 1966, or the politics of manipulation, when Mao began introducing his Cultural Revolution by employing the Red Guards and using this movement to attack his enemies; (3) January 1967 to August 1967, or the politics of the masses, when the elite began losing control and the masses began acting on their own, and (4) after September 1967, or the politics of factionalism, when Mao began backing a policy of retrenchment to avert "a direct confrontation between the Small Group and the radical mass organizations, on the one hand, and the Army, the government functionaries, and the conservative mass organizations, on the other."[47] Lee's detailed analysis of these four periods of political action describes the behavior of his seven actors, the issues that joined or separated them, and the ways in which political conflict was intensified and then resolved.

Other studies of this first phase of the Cultural Revolution focused on specific events and trends. Barry Burton examined the famous May 16, 1966 Central Committee circular and concluded that it was drafted by several top-level party cadres, unconnected with Liu, who were attempting to expel certain "capitalist-roaders" from the CCP.[48] Juliana Pennington Heaslet described the activities of the Red Guards and pointed out that they destroyed twenty-nine provincial party committees and discredited 80 percent of the Central Committee membership.[49] Because the Red Guards did not follow specific political guidelines, and because so many of their units acted on their own, they failed to rebuild a provincial political structure that could be tightly coordinated by the center.

Writing on Heilungkiang and Hopei provinces during 1966–68, Gardel Feurtado described how a new coalition evolved among Red Guards, local military units, and revolutionary cadres, which culminated in the disbanding of the Red Guards. Citing the ad hoc character of these new provincial revolutionary committees, Feurtado concluded that "a major political problem facing China in the 1970s is that of keeping the provincial revolutionary committees responsive to Central initiatives."[50] Other Pekingologists agreed.

In 1969 Parris H. Chang summed up what had happened in China in the late 1960s: Mao had purged his opponents from top to bottom; he had created a new relationship between the center and the provinces built on negotiation, bargaining, and compromise "rather than one [built on] command subordination"; political loyalty now meant adherence to Mao's ideas.[51] Several years later Chang pointed out the new role of the PLA in provincial leadership and suggested that China had become more polycentrist.[52] In late 1972 Chang noted that the party was trying "to downgrade the role of the military and to reassert Party control over the military, the RCs (Revolutionary Councils) in the provinces and lower levels, and all spheres of life in Chinese society."[53]

Some China-watchers, however, saw a new trend emerging after the Lin Piao affair. In an examination of a sample of 168 provincial municipal party secretaries, Robert A. Scalapino found that in 1976 military professionals still held 40–50 percent of these positions but that their share had declined during the 1970s. The incidence of civilian secretaries was on the rise; many were even coming from the ranks of the formerly purged. Scalapino was careful to note that turnover was high and that factionalism and the dominance of strong personalities would continue to characterize provincial and subprovincial party leadership.[54]

In 1972 Harvey Nelsen investigated the extent of the military's political power. He found that, although it had indeed carried out assigned missions and had thereby influenced the course of political behavior in the provinces, the military was still under the direct control of the Central Military Commission in Beijing, which was, in turn, still under party control.[55] Victor C. Falkenheim examined Fukien province and found that "while the Cultural Revolution severely damaged the Party organization, the systems of administrative, fiscal, and legal controls remained largely intact."[56]

Other experts observed a new redistribution of power at the center after the demise of Liu and Lin and their followers. In early 1972 Harry Harding, Jr. noted the existence of a new faction, composed of Chou En-lai and other state bureaucrats, in opposition to the revolutionary radical faction. Mao remained in the background and merely attempted to manipulate and maintain a power balance between the two.[57] Under this new sharing of power, provinces resisted Beijing, Mao's cult of personality slowly eroded, and mass participation in the new organizations of the late 1960s continued.

It was precisely this new development (the participation of the masses in new organizations), along with the policy of forcing the elite to learn how to work with their hands and mix with the masses (May 7th Cadres Schools and the rustication of urban youth campaign), that attracted the attention of many U.S. China-watchers. Richard M. Pfeffer, for example, saw this mass participation as "an organized technique that enabled the Chinese Communists to gain the support of the masses without at the same time giving very much in exchange."[58] The main concern of scholars like Pfeffer was not the human cost that might be associated with these new organizations and policies but whether or not these reforms could really be institutionalized in China and made to work in the long run.[59]

Some U.S. experts, however, foresaw great difficulties for the efforts of Mao and his followers to change the Chinese by political indoctrination and to build a new economic base for socialism by means of the organizations and procedures introduced in the late 1960s. Philip Bridgham pointed out that although "the Maoist leadership intends to persevere in the face of great odds towards the achievements of the original goals of the Cultural Revolution," it had been relatively easy to remove those responsible for "revisionist" policies. Institutionalizing the new order that Mao envisaged for China would, however, be very difficult.[60]

The new redistribution of power after the fall of Liu quickly produced a remarkable chain of events. These events were so baffling that experts were hard put to explain them. Philip Bridgham argued that although Mao had joined with Lin to oust Liu, Mao found it necessary to remove his designated successor to regain effective control over the reins of power.[61] Mao was increasingly unhappy with Lin and his leftist supporters, like Ch'en Po-ta. Moreover, Mao's anger at Lin's criticism of Chou, which he regarded as being aimed at himself, set the stage for a new power struggle between the two. Ying-mao Kau and Pierre M. Perrolle carefully described the events from the Lushan plenum (August 2–16, 1959) until Lin's death to determine why the Lin-Mao struggle took place.

> In the absence of a well-defined and accepted process of political succession, the successor-designate was forced to consolidate his power base and these attempts at consolidation ran counter to Mao's basic political principle of maintaining a diffuse power distribution, or, as Lin came to see it, a policy of "divide and rule." Having aroused Mao's suspicions with regard to his loyalty, the successor-designate saw no alternative but to attempt, by force and conspiracy, to seize power and victory from the jaws of the tiger.[62]

After Lin's demise the anti–Lin Piao movement—later combined with the anti-Confucius (p'i-Lin p'i-K'ung) campaign—spread throughout the country. This campaign greatly confused some China-watchers, and many disagreed over what the campaign was really about. Reviewing the state of affairs in China during 1974, John Bryan Starr admitted that this campaign was "difficult to fathom," but he speculated that it might be a means of ascertaining which elements of China's old culture should be discarded to make way for a new culture.[63]

Merle Goldman interpreted the campaign as an attempt by the radicals to eradicate traditional habits and attitudes; she opined that it could lead to another Cultural Revolution of more lasting impact.[64] She also interpreted the campaign as a method by which the radical faction tried to centralize power, institutionalize the gains of the Cultural Revolution, reassert ideological conformity, and emphasize economic growth—goals that had been partially abandoned during the halcyon months of 1966–67. Parris H. Chang analyzed this campaign in the context of a new, three-group power struggle in the early 1970s among revolutionary radicals, Chou and his followers, and followers of Lin Piao. Although Mao placed himself above this struggle, he nevertheless attemped to use this new campaign to curb PLA influence in the provinces and to express his unhappiness with Chou and his faction.[65] In addition, Mao used this campaign to reassert the cultural goals set forth in the late 1960s—goals he believed needed constant reemphasis. A. James Gregor and Maria Hsia Chang saw this campaign as an attempt to continue the struggles of the Cultural Revolution by inculcating new values in the Chinese people and as a "hardening of the Maoist position with respect to the Confucian tradition."[66] For Gregor and Chang, this campaign signified a struggle against the new Confucianists in the party—Liu, Lin, Ch'en Po-ta, and others.

The return and subsequent second fall of Teng Hsiao-p'ing followed this campaign—events that also puzzled many in China-watching circles. Edward E. Rice suggested that Mao had deliberately manipulated Teng.[67] By allowing Chou to rehabilitate Teng, Mao could use Teng to help Mao rebuild the Communist Party. But when Chou died, Mao decided he would have to eliminate Teng, and he did so. Therefore, although appearances suggested that Teng was in command, he was not; shortly after delivering a eulogy to commemorate Chou En-lai, he fell from grace. As can be seen, scholars were sharply divided on how to explain the key events and changes that took place during the period of the Cultural Revolution. We will now turn to the explanations offered by ROC China-watchers.

Most ROC experts concentrated their attention on the relationships among the party's dominant leaders and the ways these relationships changed over time. For them, the key question was: How had Mao been able to purge major figures such as P'eng Chen, Chou Yang, Lu Ting-i, Lo Jui-ch'ing, and even Liu Shao-ch'i when he could not even obtain a majority vote in the party's Central Committee? Chen Li-sheng offered the following explanation.

Personal prestige and the support of the PLA were Mao's most important political assets. Mao had gradually lost his position of Party dominance ever since the failures of the Three Red Banners Campaign, but he was still the Party's chairman, and Mao Tse-tung 'thought', in name at least, still served as the guiding principle for the Communist Party and the PLA. Moreover, the military became Mao's most important tool in the emerging political struggle. Without the support of the PLA, the Cultural Revolution would only have been just a 'cultural' revolution in name only, or merely another literary rectification campaign.[68]

Liu had been in power for many years, and he controlled the Central Committee. Mao charged Liu with having made Beijing his "independent kingdom" (*tu-li wang-kuo*). Why then, should Liu have lost this battle? According to Cheng Hsüeh-chia, he lost because Mao's tactics were superior. "Mao had shrewdly adopted the tactics of making his opponents believe he was going to do one thing while he instead did another. The Cultural Revolution began as an ideological debate, but only as a foil to deceive his enemies who were lulled into thinking no measures were necessary to regroup and attack Mao."[69]

Other ROC experts also attributed Liu's final fall to his inability to recognize Mao's real goal—to oust him from power—and the tactics Mao was using to realize that goal. Chen Li-sheng described in detail the strategy Mao used to dethrone Liu.

> Mao adopted the strategy of doing one thing at a time. First he criticized P'eng Chen's subordinate, Wu Han, through the tactic of literary debate. Then he attacked the Three-Family Village Group of literary critics in the same way, thus removing P'eng Chen and Lu Ting-i who controlled the propaganda apparatus. Next he ordered the Red Guards to attack Liu and Teng, and finally at the 11th Plenum of the 8th CCP Central Committee he smashed Liu, thus regaining his dominance over the Central Committee to a major extent . . . On the other hand, Liu appeared to be misled entirely by Mao's tactics of swerving from one side and then to another. Liu never realized that he himself might be the target of these campaigns. From the very beginning, Liu adopted only the most passive of measures, hoping that Mao would terminate the contest with him if some sort of compromise could only be struck. Liu failed to take any decisive, strong measures to suppress Mao in the CCP Central Committee. Instead, he committed a series of mistakes which step-by-step led him into Mao's trap . . . After the 11th Plenum, Liu already had been trapped by Mao; he was like a fish in Mao's net.[70]

Only one week after the eleventh plenum, at which Mao had won a major victory, the Red Guards appeared. ROC China-watchers pointed out that, by relying on the Red Guards to do his bidding, Mao had violated one of the most sacred party principles: A member should never go outside the party for forces to impose his will on the party leadership. Mao used the Red Guards to mobilize the masses and attack Liu and all of his supporters. Why did Mao choose these means instead of using the Central Committee or the Political Bureau to eliminte his chief rivals? Why did Mao smash the party and the Young Communist League?

ROC experts offered the following explanations. First, the Central Committee had long been controlled by Liu. Although Liu's power had waned somewhat since the eleventh plenum, held on August 12, 1966, Mao's power in the Central Committee was still not supreme. Second, Liu's supporters, located at various levels in the party-state bureaucracy throughout the country, were still capable of subverting Mao's policies.[71] Third, in spite of Lin Piao's cooperation, Mao was not sufficiently confident to allow the PLA to help seize political power. Mao therefore initiated the Red Guard Movement and charged these young tormentors with the task of criticizing, humiliating, and removing party officials from their offices at all levels of the party-state bureaucracy; his intention was to entirely eliminate Liu and his supporters from the political system.[72] As we now know, the Red Guards were remarkably successful in removing Liu and his faction from power (even though they later had to be disbanded because of the chaos they were creating in society).

ROC China experts were also intrigued by Mao's ability to mobilize hundreds of thousands of Red Guards, but they were quick to explain why this was possible. Cheng Hsüeh-chia offered the following insight:

> It would be a terrible mistake to regard the Red Guards and the Chinese masses as Mao's followers. After eighteen years of Communist rule, the Chinese people held many different views about their society. They naturally participated in the Cultural Revolution because of many different motives. Some took this opportunity to grab political power for themselves; some joined the movement simply for the fun of it; others took this opportunity to overthrow the system of Chinese Communist rule.[73]

Other ROC China-watchers interpreted the fanaticism and mass enthusiasm displayed in the Cultural Revolution as a massive eruption of frustration, resentment, and bitterness toward the communist bureaucracy. All of these feelings stemmed from many years of economic deprivation, party cadres' corruption, and declining opportunity for education and social advancement. In 1966 China was therefore in a state of extreme crisis. These experts generally agreed that Mao struck at the right time and that he cleverly and brilliantly manipulated these mass grievances to his own ends; he managed to channel much popular discontent against his own enemies and rivals. As Wang Chang-ling put it:

The masses had long been dissatisfied with their conditions. They hated Communist rule, and they hated the Communist bureaucracy. Therefore, the masses welcomed any movement initiated by someone else: a Maoist or anti-Maoist movement to smash the Communist bureaucracy. This is the reason why the Red Guards, in spite of Mao's order to attack only the "capitalists," criticized and beat all who held power or appeared to belong to any of the cliques. Instead of behaving as a tool for Mao's political struggle, the Red Guards turned out to be a worrisome burden for Mao . . .
The widespread atmosphere of despair and anarchy that now prevails is really the manifestation of popular resentment and discontent.[74]

By analyzing the power struggle in the context of extremely strained social conditions and identifying Mao's tactical methods (first, literary campaigns; then, Central Committee political maneuvering; and finally, instruments of mass persuasion—the Red Guards), ROC experts sought to explain how Mao regained his power by 1969.

By April 1969, when the Ninth National Congress of the CCP met in Beijing, Mao had eliminated his rival Liu, destroyed the party, and reclaimed power. China was now ruled by revolutionary committees composed of military officers, revolutionary cadres, and new revolutionary leaders who had risen from the ranks. This congress approved a new party constitution that extolled Mao as the supreme leader of the party, recognized Lin as Mao's "close comrade-in-arms and successor," and established Mao's thought as the "theoretical foundation for CCP thinking." The new Central Committee listed 170 members and 109 alternates, including only 53 members from former Central Committees (70 percent of the Eighth CCP Congress Central Committee's membership had been purged); 45 percent of the new membership came from the military alone.

In light of this new leadership make-up, ROC experts interpreted the new political situation as follows: First, the military was now conspicuous in party ruling circles, and this indicated a possible "ominous contradiction between the military and the Party."[75] Second, all was not harmonious within the party itself.

Having seized considerable power, the army cadres have treated other cadres with disdain. Many leading revolutionary cadres, fearing possible reprisal, have wanted to stop the flow of reinstated cadres, those older cadres who had been the target of their criticism-struggle campaigns of the past. Therefore, they have adopted an antagonistic attitude toward the new cadres in power . . . Factional prejudice and dissension exist between the revolutionary committees and the masses and, of course, within the revolutionary committees themselves.[76]

Third, Hsuan Mo pointed out that the new revolutionary cadres could not be expected to govern, because they lacked education, experience, and the personal connections necessary for their jobs. "The Communist Party's cadres, who once were a crucial asset for the CCP and had helped to control over seven hundred million people, have been purged in large number during the Cultural Revolution. The old Party apparatus has been completely smashed. The young, less-experienced, less-educated, new cadres who replaced them are neither capable of reforming the Party nor of governing the state."[77]

Other ROC China-watchers also observed that the new Maoist cadres would be unable to fulfill the needs and desires of the people. Chang Ching-wen expressed this doubt most succinctly. "Liu Shao-ch'i's revisionist economic line has been destroyed. The key problem now facing the Mao-Lin clique is not the formulation of any new economic program, but how to restore production to the pre-Cultural Revolution level . . . We doubt if they can fulfill this task."[78]

But all was not well among the top leaders themselves. In September 1971 Lin Piao, a proven supporter of Mao, suddenly turned against him. Some ROC experts offered the following explanation.[79] First, considerable acrimony had developed between the Lin Piao and Chiang Ch'ing factions, which, in complex ways, had similarly damaged personal relations between Mao and Lin. Second, although Lin fully realized he was in line to succeed Mao, he nevertheless knew he had to take certain steps of his own to arrange this transfer of power. To consolidate his position, Lin therefore tried to expand his influence in the Central Committee. These actions undoubtedly frightened Mao and convinced him that he had to get rid of Lin. Finally, Lin's position of power was at stake, because many of his military colleagues were strongly pressuring him to take action. Lin decided he had to move first, but, as we now know, Mao cleverly outsmarted Lin and dealt him and his close supporters a crippling blow. The Chinese Communists have referred to the Lin Piao affair as "the most serious and fiercest struggle" in the history of the Chinese Communist Party.[80] In fact, this event constituted something more than a simple power struggle among the very top leaders. According to one ROC expert, it had long-term consequences for the party itself.

[The Affair] further deepened the split between Party factions and within the PLA itself. It further soured Party and military relations. It had revealed Mao's real intentions of forcing the Party to serve him and members of his own family. It accelerated the factional rivalries between the local military elite and the Party Central Committee now dominated by Mao and Chiang Ch'ing. It also sabotaged any likelihood of a peaceful transfer of political power to another successor, and it condemned the Chinese Communists to an endless, harsh struggle for political power.[81]

After the Lin Piao Affair, Mao decided to allow the Cultural Revolutionary faction to take power. Mao authorized the campaign to criticize Lin Piao in 1973; later, this movement began to criticize Confucius as well as Lin Piao. At first ROC researchers were puzzled by this development. Many saw this new movement as an indirect attack on Chou En-lai.[82] But some observers disagreed with this analysis, which held that after the Tenth CCP National Congress the Maoist faction (or the group led by Chiang Ch'ing) had plotted to attack Chou.[83] New evidence strongly indicates that the campaign was nothing but a naked power struggle in which Mao attempted to unseat Chou.[84] This revelation also helps to explain the remarkable event in Tienanmen Square on March 29, 1976, which produced a series of public demonstrations leading to the bloody April 5th conflict between local militia and the people.

The Significance of the Cultural Revolution

How have U.S. and ROC experts interpreted the significance of the Cultural Revolution? From the extensive literature on this topic, we have selected studies that show that U.S. China-watchers made many different assessments of the Cultural Revolution, depending on which facet of the event interested them.[85]

Robert S. Wang attempted to determine the significance of the Cultural Revolution for China's educational system. He concluded that the CCP never set up any methods to evaluate the performance of their new educational institutions.[86] China experts who visited the PRC in the early 1970s were not at all certain about the magnitude of change produced by the Cultural Revolution. As Frederick C. Teiwes remarked, "The situation in 1973 appears different from 1965 only in degree."[87]

Some American observers in the 1970s, however, noted a fragility in the political order; the Maoist leadership continually had to marshal its forces to prevent any rolling back of the policies they had initiated during the Cultural Revolution. "The lesson for the present day is clear: great care must be taken to prevent contemporary reactionaries from reimposing their old system, the manifestations of which will appear first in the ideological superstructure. The Maoists must hit at, even violently purge, those who show themselves desirous of restoring the old and/or hindering the growth of the 'new-born things' of the Cultural Revolution."[88] Sweeping organizational changes had been possible in the 1950s partly because the regime had built on the existing community strength rooted in the pre-1949 villages and village neighborhoods. But in the late 1960s the new left-wing leadership under Mao pressed for a higher stage of rural collectivization—amalgamating production teams into brigades and making the brigades the new accounting unit. Some American observers, like William L. Parish, thought it unlikely that the regime could actually create these new mass organizations.[89]

Certain U.S. experts viewed the Cultural Revolution primarily as a mighty effort by one leader—Mao—to oppose creeping bureaucratization. But some were quick to point out that Mao only did this by taking advantage of the tensions among societal groups. Hong Yung Lee described Mao as a master manipulator, who used the following precepts to launch his attack on the state: "Obtain majority, oppose minority, destroy each group, develop the progressive forces, win over the middle roaders, isolate stubborn elements, be reasonable, and be calculative."[90] These tactics were very similar to the classic "united-front" strategy developed and applied with so much success in previous decades.

Others, like Lowell Dittmer, interpreted the Cultural Revolution as Mao's way of mobilizing the masses for struggle, self-criticism, and more struggle.[91] Still others characterized the new Maoist system created during the Cultural Revolution as one in which "power was vested more in people than in institutions."[92] Personal ties based on mutual obligation had become all-important. Leaders in Beijing exerted their power only through people bound to them by personal loyalty and patronage. At the head of this system, Mao ruled—applying coercion at will. This new, personalized system of rule eschewed bureaucratic authority, hierarchy, and institutional routine. Within this system, of course, powerful leaders used their model brigades or counties to push their special brand of politics. The result was a competition among several different socioeconomic models of community development.[93]

Finally, some political scientists, like Byung-joon Ahn, referred to the new political order of the 1970s as a mix of three political regimes whose goals included (1) institutionalizing the organizations created both before and during the Cultural Revolution, (2) transforming the behavior of the citizenry by means of political campaigns, and (3) ensuring political stability and enforcing policies originating in the party's Central Committee.[94]

Only a few U.S. experts detected social meaning in the Cultural Revolution. Edward Friedman contended that by the mid-1960s China had become so riddled with tension that some kind of social explosion was inevitable.[95] Rural people expected a better standard of living (like that in the cities), but their resources were inadequate in comparison to urban ones. In rural society, the dispossessed and deposed families of the early 1950s remained embittered, and new groups were deeply resentful of the powerful new cadre elite. These tensions were exacerbated by the continual public debate over who the new class enemies in society really were. In this muddled climate, Mao elected to base his Cultural Revolution in the cities, but, without a rural base, his revolution could not succeed.

In contrast to their U.S. counterparts, ROC communist affairs experts were appalled by the ferocity of the Cultural Revolution's impact on the intellectual community, both inside and outside the Communist Party. Reports from the mainland confirmed their worst fears that savage turmoil and brutality were widespread. Knowing that no regime since the Chin Dynasty had treated its educated elite with such barbarity, they sensed that irreparable harm was being done to Chinese society and culture.

They pointed out that sending university professors to work in the fields or to serve as janitors in their universities was not only degrading but constituted a significant loss for Chinese society. Literary people, journalists, workers in the public media, and even scientists and technicians endured suffering and death. Hsuan Mo concluded that China would pay an enormous price for the calamities that had befallen the intellectuals and "produced such a series of intractable problems for the regime."[96]

Another assessment of the Cultural Revolution stressed the spreading cynicism of party members who had lost faith in the party leadership and ideology. Warren Kuo discussed the demoralization that must have spread throughout the party's middle and lower ranks as a result of the new realization that prestigious party leaders like Liu Shao-ch'i and Lin Piao—whose writings had at one time or another served as the basic texts for study and assimilation—could fall from grace. The realization that, even after many years of devotion and sacrifice for the party, a leader could be severely criticized, humiliated, and cast out like a leper must have been particularly bewildering to these cadres. Warren Kuo attached the following significance to the Lin Piao Affair.

> The purge of Lin Piao, Mao's loyalist follower and successor, was a severe blow to the CCP, and shocked many revolutionary cadres into reassessing the true value and real significance of the Cultural Revolution and the lines laid down by the 9th Party Congress. They doubt the necessity of the Cultural Revolution and the correctness of the lines laid down by the 9th Party Congress, especially the thorough demolition of all the Party's political, financial, and cultural and educational organs at various levels, as well as the attacks and humiliation of so many cadres which can be viewed as nothing but ultra-leftist errors based upon "punitive" behavior.[97]

Many veteran cadres were rehabilitated and exonerated of their crimes after 1976, but the psychological scars of this traumatic experience must have remained.

ROC experts also viewed the Cultural Revolution as an outgrowth of the disruptive activities of the Communist Party. But more important, they considered the human costs for Chinese society of the Cultural Revolution's policies as far too high.[98] Efforts to completely undermine traditional cultural values were silently resisted throughout the country. The nation's economic engine stalled. The formerly zealous youth, who either joined the Red Guard Movement or moved to the villages as part of the rustification campaign, became disillusioned with the communist system. Some officers of the PLA became increasingly frustrated in their efforts to shoulder new political responsibilities. Other PLA officers enjoyed their new power and abused it by bullying the local party cadres. Most ROC experts believed that these consequences of the Cultural Revolution would penalize the communist regime for years to come.

CONCLUSIONS

Our selection of scholarly research that has attempted to explain the meaning of events in Communist China has included studies combining the narrative and the hypothesis-testing approaches. In American research findings, we are again struck by the great diversity of views and insights that have sprung from different perspectives and methods. Even ROC scholarship exhibits much diversity and sharp differences of opinion.

One of the important findings to emerge from American studies of the first years of the communist regime is that the land-reform policy proved to be highly successful in removing the traditional rural power elite and paving the way for the rapid, successful restructuring of private property rights and the creation of the collective farming system. At the same time, the party was able to establish a new ruling elite in the villages that was closely linked to the party. This gave the party an awesome amount of control over village life—more than even previous imperial governments had been able to exercise. This control of the rural countryside partly explains how the regime was later able to mobilize the populace for its numerous political campaigns. Nevertheless, the party never seems to have successfully institutionalized the rural elite's control over society or to have ensured this elite's compliance to party dictates.

Another important finding is that many researchers—especially among ROC experts—correctly identified the negative impact on society of the Maoist policies introduced between 1958 and 1961 to speed up the communization of China. Some American and ROC scholars also correctly ascertained that the dreadful effects of these policies produced intense intraparty factionalism and sowed the seeds of mistrust and personal dislike among the top leaders. ROC scholars, in particular, discerned that Mao's power was slipping, and that this powerful leader was not likely to go docilely into retirement.

It is interesting to compare the approaches used by both groups of scholars to study the Great Cultural Revolution. Because of their greater use of Central Committee reports and their ability to read between the lines of the party-controlled press, ROC researchers were able to follow the dynamics of intraparty struggle in great detail. They were able to accurately show how different cliques formed and which personal networks were used. Some American scholars, by virtue of their methodology, also correctly interpreted the "two lines" struggle. Most Americans, however, undervalued the importance of the power struggle of the period and the destructive effects of the Great Cultural Revolution on Chinese society.

ROC scholars were able to write more forcefully and accurately about the enormous harm resulting from Maoist policies because they were more sensitive to the damages done to the educational system, to the anguish caused by the uprooting of intellectuals and youth to live and labor in the villages, and to the suffering borne even by the purged party elite. Some American scholars argued that ideals—or even utopian impulses—motivated the Maoist policies of the period; they were, however, unable to make balanced assessments of the destructive effects these policies had on the fabric of Chinese society.

7

Understanding the Chinese Communist System

Every society develops specific features of governance, social action, economic behavior, and artistic creativity. By identifying those features that are common to a given society, or which have developed in new forms, we can achieve a greater understanding of a foreign society. It is important, then, that we try to select from our two research samples those interpretive findings that advanced new insights and offered explanations of changes and their consequences for both the new leaders of Communist China and the ordinary people.

THE COMMUNIST REGIME AND COMMUNIST SOCIETY

A view shared by many U.S. and ROC experts is that after 1949 the Chinese Communists fundamentally altered state and societal relations, breaking sharply with China's past. Edward E. Rice remarked that "the revolution that has reached its zenith under the Communists is the only one in China since the revolution of Shih Huang Ti (221–210 B.C.) that has changed the system of government and altered the configuration of society."[1] In the ROC, Warren Kuo stressed that the unification of China by the CCP was more than a new dynasty; the CCP's imposition of an alien ideology entailed a sharp break with historical trends. In commenting on the beginnings of the Cultural Revolution, Kuo offered the following interpretation of the significance of Maoist policies for China.

The severity of the current political struggle has broken all records in Chinese history. The Red Guards smashed everything connected with traditional Chinese culture under the rubric of 'destroying entirely the four legacies of the past (traditional culture, ideology, customs, and social habits).' The Maoists have tried to destroy completely China's traditional culture

. . . and they have tried to introduce a completely different, new social
system . . . This new dictatorial regime is absolutely different from any
dynasty of the past.[2]

Based on a belief that a discontinuity had occurred, some U.S. and ROC
China-watchers identified and tried to explain patterns of change. We will
now examine their scholarship in the context of three interrelated questions.
First, what were the basic features of this new system? Second, what new
elements in this system enabled it to remain viable and intact despite the great
upheavals that had occurred? Finally, what were the new difficulties that
emerged under this system?

THE PATTERN OF DOMINANCE

Edward Rice, like many others, noted that the CCP had "set up complex
organizational structures which permeated all society."[3] This accomplishment facilitated the political conquest of society by the CCP. In his case study
of Canton city and Kwangtung province between 1949 and 1968, Ezra Vogel
noted that the new political structure created by the CCP "required invasion
into what was formerly the private sector."[4] According to Vogel, the party
first recruited, trained, and educated new cadres to extend party control to
all levels of provincial governance. The party then expelled all foreigners,
tried to eliminate all opponents, and moved to re-educate the intellectuals.
The party used land reform to remove the rural elite from power and replace
them with their own cadres and organizations. By spring 1951 the PLA had
to help enforce land reform and rectify party cadres by concentrating "at first
on leaders who were most vulnerable."[5] Complete success in establishing
party dominance over society resulted in a huge party bureaucracy that rapidly became unwieldy and inefficient. The private sector was miniscule; the
dominant public sector was bloated. Political reorganizational change, rather
than economic change, turned Chinese society upside down.[6]

If political change was so pervasive, did it produce greater political participation? James R. Townsend believed it did not. According to Townsend,
although the CCP had developed the mass-line technique to mobilize people
for its war effort in the 1940s,[7] this same method, carried over into the 1950s
and early 1960s, did not succeed in developing a "high popular political
consciousness."[8] A survey study of refugees in Hong Kong conducted by
Victor C. Falkenheim in the late 1970s found that most citizens were partic-
ipating in politics (voluntarily or not) but that very few of them had any real
interest in politics.[9]

For the party and state to dominate Chinese society so effectively and pervasively, all forms of opposition had to be controlled and suppressed. Control and suppression, however, might promote an underground resistance to the central government and its policies. Nevertheless, by the mid-1950s most experts outside Communist China realized that the CCP and the state had dissuaded even those most strongly opposed to communist rule to refrain from opposition and to support the new regime. How did the CCP change the minds of their most outspoken critics and opponents? According to Robert Jay Lifton, the CCP used unique procedures to do so: brainwashing, or thought control.

In a study of a small sample of Westerners and Chinese who had undergone thought reform in the early 1950s, Robert J. Lifton found that people could indeed be made to change their beliefs and convictions in ways they never anticipated after they had been subjected to a special form of incarceration and a new routine of rewards and punishments. After interviewing a small group of refugees in Hong Kong who had formerly been strong opponents of the regime, Lifton traced how they had gradually reversed their beliefs and come around to supporting, if not endorsing, the communist regime. Lifton noted that the Chinese Communists had controlled all forms of communication with their victims, which forced them into a state of confusion and gradually broke down their self-discipline and self-control. In this newly weakened state, these victims could be gradually manipulated by an assortment of rewards and punishments that subtly altered their former beliefs, even to the point of convincing them to support the new communist system. Here is how Lifton described the method.

> The Chinese, although they utilize whatever mechanical means they have at their disposal, achieve control of greater psychological depth through a human recording and transmitting apparatus. It is probably fair to say that the Chinese Communist prison and revolutionary university produce about as thoroughly controlled a group environment as has ever existed. The milieu control exerted over the broader social environment of Communist China, while considerably less intense, is in its own way unrivaled in its combination of extensiveness and depth; it is, in fact, one of the distinguishing features of Chinese Communist practice.[10]

Following milieu control, extensive personal manipulation of the victim was employed to provoke specific patterns of behavior and emotion that appeared to have arisen spontaneously from within the victim's environment.[11] The prison wardens and guards were never satisfied with simply breaking their victims. They were motivated by the mystique of serving the party and of convincing the victim that the party's ways and purposes were correct and must be endorsed and supported for the betterment of mankind as well as for the self. Lifton's account is certainly one of the best discussions of how the CCP was able to convince the opposition to support the CCP's policies.

It is surprising that Lifton's findings about jailed victims have never been proposed to apply to Chinese society as a whole. If the party managed to successfully control the environment of its citizens—particularly, all avenues of communication—it is very understandable that opposition to party rule could never materialize and that citizens would adopt instead a pattern of compliance reinforced by a new inner belief that this behavior was proper and correct.

PATTERNS OF SOCIAL CHANGE

In the domain of social change, William L. Parish and Martin King Whyte tried to construct "a picture of the nature of the change process that could have produced the patterns" suggested by interviews of refugees in Hong Kong from sixty-three villages in Kwangtung province.[12] They observed complex changes (to which our summary remarks can scarcely do justice). First, they pointed out that whereas the income gap between towns and villages widened in the early 1950s, it "has been kept in check, and perhaps slightly reduced in recent years."[13] Income differences between villages, however, remained considerable. Second, although the state did not really increase expenditures for health, education, and welfare, it encouraged collective units to do so. Third, great changes in village leadership followed the installation of a new party-affiliated elite in the early 1950s.

Nevertheless, the authors found that much traditional behavior remained unchanged. Traditional ceremonies commemorating funerals and weddings were still common, but households spent far less on these than in the past. Exceptions included the adoption of sons, the taking of concubines, and the arrangement of marriages. Children under the age of seven still received strong, traditional family values, but children above that age who were attending school were greatly influenced by the party and state educational philosophy and teaching methods.

What of social change in the cities? Lynn T. White III tried to identify the key forces guiding Shanghai's young people in career selection and uncovered very complex social reactions to party policies and changing urban economic conditions. He noted that party policies often produced unintended social results and that the urban economy could sometimes respond by creating "hundreds of thousands of temporary jobs, most of which were not even governed by written contracts."[14] On other occasions, however, Shanghai citizens responded to party dictates. White discovered no definite pattern of social change.

PATTERNS OF DEMOGRAPHIC
AND ECONOMIC CHANGE

The absence of published data on population growth and its impact greatly hindered experts in analyzing demographic change. Some, like Leo A. Orleans, attempted to chart general growth trends and migrational patterns to show how China had struggled to provide more jobs and build a more extensive infrastructure to accommodate ever greater numbers of people.[15] To employ more people in agriculture, the regime developed many new labor-intensive farming methods. Thomas G. Rawski estimated that perhaps as many as 100 million new workers were added to the rural work force between 1957 and 1975.[16] Of course, the economy paid a high price in declining labor productivity. "Output per man-day declined sharply between 1957 and 1975, with the fall ranging from 15 to 36 percent depending upon which assumptions are chosen with regard to the labor intensity of cultivation and fertilizer."[17]

American economists spent years calculating, revising, and refining their estimates of Communist China's national income and product, industrial output, and agricultural output trends. After some debate, most experts ultimately agreed that Beijing had not falsified its statistics. Many experts tried to measure macro economic changes. Recently, Dwight Perkins compared many of these estimates to those produced by the Chinese themselves. "It is clear that the analysts who attempted to reconstruct the official series making use of as few gap-filling assumptions as possible came reasonably close to the mark. Those who made the heaviest use of assumptions that substituted for the official series were further off the mark."[18] Official statistical series showed that the Chinese gross domestic product accelerated in the 1950s but slowed during the next two decades. Nevertheless, experts like Perkins argued that the growth rate of China's economy between 1957 and 1980 was a respectable 5 percent annual rate of growth and a 3 percent per capita rate, which reflected a considerable transformation of the economy. American economists also generally agreed that China's industrial growth rate had rapidly increased but that agricultural output growth had barely kept pace with population growth.

Some years earlier, however, T. C. Liu and K. C. Yeh argued that during the first fifteen years of the regime, economic growth had been much slower than officially claimed. Many economists used their own economic time series, but they readjusted some indicators upward so that their final estimates of growth rates invariably matched the official claims. Nevertheless, in 1968 Liu and Yeh argued that the 1952 level of gross national product was definitely slightly higher than that of 1933 but that the 1952 per capita consumption was lower than that of 1933. They also concurred that the regime had invested more in 1952 than in 1933; they argued, however, that investment was increased in 1952 because consumption expenditures had been curtailed.[19] By 1957, they said, a substantial shift had occurred in the economic structure, because industrial growth had widened the gap in relative products per worker between agriculture and industry. They concluded, however, that the annual growth of GNP had increased by only 6 percent between 1952 and 1957, compared to the near 9 percent claimed by the regime—and later endorsed by most economists.

Liu and Yeh described the period 1958–65 as one of "further industrialization without growth."[20] They did not believe that future industrial growth could continue at the previous high rate without any improvement in agricultural productivity, and they postulated that future economic development was not likely to be orderly and rapid.

Although most American economists did not probe further into the significance of these fluctuating patterns of rapid growth, some pondered the following essential questions: Had high growth rates been achieved by an efficient use of scarce resources? Had the economy expanded employment and increased output by achieving greater productivity (a process that had characterized modern economic growth in the West but not in communist countries)? Thomas G. Rawski pointed out that agricultural factor productivity had declined during the years 1957–75,[21] and Anthony Tang showed that between 1952 and 1965 declining factor productivity had also been a general problem.[22] Rawski also suggested that after 1957 the rate of factor productivity growth had slowed in the producer-goods industries.[23] In other words, although the statistical record showed fairly impressive economic growth, the output from all sectors had been accompanied by enormous waste and considerable misuse of scarce resources. Although not all American experts agreed with these findings, after 1979 Chinese economists readily admitted that after 1957 the economy had become increasingly unproductive.[24]

Actually, very few American experts accurately measured production fluctuations over these three decades. After comparing the China-watchers' economic estimates with the recently released official figures, Kang Chao concluded that they "manifested a noticeable upward bias in their estimation, particularly for the years of depression. They not only understated the rates of decline by wide margins, but also misplaced the turning points."[25]

FUNCTIONAL CHARACTERISTICS OF COMMUNIST CHINA

Every society reproduces itself and experiences some kind of change over time. Every society also possesses organizations, markets, and institutions that exhibit certain functional characteristics. By functional characteristics, we mean the activities connected with organizations, markets, and institutions that allow them to perform well enough that society and economy remain integrated and can reproduce and expand without crisis. Some research, especially that produced by American scholars, tried to examine exactly how organizations and institutions worked in Communist China.

For example, the new bureaucracy became larger than any in history, and it perfected different channels of communication to control society, manage the planned economy, and provide essential services. Michel Oksenberg described seven types of communication networks in this bureaucracy and detailed the kinds of documents they used to transmit information. By means of these networks, the "existing patterns facilitated the integration of the nation (one of the major functions of the traditional system) and the total involvement and commitment of bureaucrats."[26]

By the early 1960s the production team had become the most important organization to farm the land and mobilize the rural people. In these teams, groups of households worked the land, earned much of their income, and participated in grass roots-type elections. John P. Burns described how production-team cadres were elected and argued that these production teams had some democratic content; team members could select leaders to resolve conflicts and deal with higher collective units like the brigade and commune. Although economic awards at the higher levels typically penalized the hard-working and enterprising and rewarded the lazy and inefficient, Burns contended that "the election of team cadres has democratic content, and is not the formalistic insignificant exercise previous accounts of post-Liberation rural Chinese politics have assumed."[27]

To establish its control in the cities, the CCP used traditional coolie associations to create new organizations and destroyed other organizations, like secret societies, that might block CCP efforts. Kenneth Lieberthal described how the CCP co-opted the leaders and wooed the members of coolie groups in Tientsin to develop new transport organizations. Because many of these same leaders also operated in secret societies, this tactic greatly weakened the influence of these societies. Lieberthal referred to the takeover of cities like Tientsin as a process whereby the "community building which accompanied revolutionary change in urban China itself weakened the independent social groupings with which the CCP had to deal when it first entered the cities."[28]

Despite the many zigs and zags in party-state policies, the new regime managed to dispense an adequate supply of services to satisfy popular demand—partly because the new organizations created in earlier years functioned reasonably well. David M. Lampton constructed several socioeconomic indicators for education and health services over a two-decade period, and he found that China's complex political system of 29 provinces, 2200 countries, and some 75,000 marketing systems had expanded these services to reach many more people; it had also reduced infant mortality and expanded elementary education.[29] Lampton observed that the regime pursued very different health policies depending on the particular political climate and period. He found, for example, that the many failures to provide sufficient health services to the citizenry in the 1950s did not result so much from excessive radical swings in policies, but, rather, "from the inconsistencies in leadership and programme characteristic of diverse policy-making arenas."[30] In other words, contradictory trends were set in motion in the late 1950s because the state's offering of new services was accompanied by a more fragmented political system. For instance, central organs cut their expenditures just as communes began dispensing more free medical care. Further, institutions that distributed health services in very different ways gave the appearance of policy shortcomings when this was not, in fact, the case.

Some U.S. experts explained functional aspects in the political system; others turned to the economy. In 1966 Ralph W. Huenemann described urban commodity rationing in 1954–55, particularly for grain and certain consumer necessities. Huenemann pointed out that "prices are set in both *yuan* and points, so that both currency and coupons are needed to make a purchase."[31] Circulating ration coupons could serve either as a unit of exchange and account or as money. Huenemann believed that, despite shortages and long lines, "the Chinese rationing system has functioned successfully on the whole."[32]

According to Dwight H. Perkins, in the early 1950s the CCP used a combination of price policies to fix prices for industrial crops like cotton; at other times they raised prices to encourage more supply to the market.[33] Even though the CCP steadily drew more of the peasantry into collective farming, it still relied on a mix of agricultural price policies to benefit the rapidly growing urban-industrial sector. Vivienne Shue tried to explain why rapid collectivization occurred between 1949 and 1956, using Hupei and Hunan provinces as examples. She perceived that this process had many functional aspects that enabled the regime to build a new rural order while increasing farm production. According to Shue, the CCP plotted its tactics carefully, recruited enough skilled cadres to carry out its policies quickly, and provided sufficient economic incentives during the initial stage of land redistribution to elicit peasant support for the party's rural policies.[34]

In the 1960s the CCP encouraged communes to build small-scale industries, and the number of the industries rapidly proliferated in the 1970s. In the summer of 1975 a delegation of American scholars noted that many enterprises were still operating very inefficiently, but they also contended that businesses could become more efficient over time if aided by marketing, modern input supply, and commodity specialization.[35] Most significantly, these enterprises had a functional service; they provided greatly expanded employment opportunities and more rural income. So, despite their high costs, many communes derived extra benefits from their activities.

According to Dwight Perkins, economic development had put the poor in command.[36] First by land reform and then by collectivization, the redistributive policies of the 1950s had provided enough rewards for the poor to make these new changes both possible and functional. Perkins noted that the regime had achieved a mixed economic performance, in which industry grew more rapidly than agriculture; he attributed the slow growth of agriculture to China's small amount of fertile land being formed by a large number of laborers. He argued that if Communist China had more fertile land, the regime's leaders might not have invested in industry at the expense of agriculture.[37] Despite this lopsided economic performance, most American economists contended that the Communist regime had successfully mobilized resources for rapid capital formation, an achievement that could have a high payoff in the future.

For many years the CCP appeared to concentrate on the ideological remolding of its citizens to the neglect of the education of professionals and skilled workers. Many American experts believed that the party's emphasizing of ideology at the expense of expertise damaged the regime. But one study argued that this action might never have existed. John A. Kringen analyzed the content of various magazines between 1958 and 1972 to test whether or not writers had any clear dichotomy in mind when they discussed management and ideological behavior.[38] His findings showed that various magazines expressed very contradictory views, depending on the interest group they were addressing. In fact, Kringen concluded, the concept of "red" or "expert" widely used in these sources varied greatly and was too complex to be categorized so neatly and simply. If Kringen was correct, the CCP's ideological remolding programs need not have been at odds with participant behavior in various organizations.

DYSFUNCTIONAL CHARACTERISTICS OF COMMUNIST CHINA

Organizations, markets, and institutions have functional characteristics that enable a society to remain in equilibrium, but dysfunctional characteristics can also develop and coexist in complex ways with the functional elements. By the term "dysfunction" we mean that organizations, markets, or institutions perform less efficiently than in the past; that is, new policies or rules have been imposed that make it impossible to maintain the same standards of behavior and performance as in the past.

American experts have not ignored the new dysfunctions that began to emerge within Chinese communist society. For example, Thomas P. Bernstein has shown that after land reform the CCP was never able to recruit enough dependable cadres to run the village organizations to satisfy the party.[39] Many of these cadres became disillusioned with incessant party demands and either quit their jobs or reverted to corruption. The CCP had to constantly educate and coerce rural cadres to get them to implement party policies. From the point of view of the party leadership, this chronic tendency of cadres to break ranks constituted a major dysfunction in the regime. In other words, the new socialist organizations could not work unless the majority of local cadres were committed to the communist system and were properly carrying out their duties in the new party organizations. To overcome its problems, the CCP had to recruit, replace, and discipline its local cadres. Yet the populace always found ways to influence these cadres by means of bribery and other corrupt practices. Official disenchantment with the fluctuations of party policies and with these corrupt practices therefore undermined the collective farming system.

Ying-mao Kau studied the career patterns of local officials in Wuhan city during the 1950s and early 1960s.[40] He found that the turnover rate for officials was extremely high. Moreover, to survive in office for any length of time, most officials were forced to become party generalists rather than specialists. Since it never institutionalized its early reforms, the party was compelled to introduce one campaign after another, which caused a high turnover of local officials. Although the bureaucracy continued to carry out party policies, official morale was obviously adversely affected by this high turnover.

Richard Baum cited a number of socioeconomic processes that had intensified rural-urban discontent by 1966 and that contributed greatly to the violence of the initial phase of the Cultural Revolution.[41] He found that, first, many peasants were periodically rotated to perform urban-industrial jobs at low wages and under poor living conditions, just as many industrial workers were required to work as laborers in the rural communes. Second, many of the intellectual urban youths who were sent to the villages were required to work and live in areas they found particularly distasteful.[42] Third, party stop-and-go policies, which alternately limited and expanded the farming of private plots, frustrated and angered commune workers. Fourth, many household members who had been categorized as antiparty during the 1950s were discriminated against, and they greatly resented their inferior status in society. Finally, many corrupt cadres abused their power, which angered commune and urban people alike. All of these simmering resentments were reactions to the party's various policies to rapidly build a communist society. These policies disrupted peoples' lives and careers and deprived many of new benefits and access to privileges and sources of higher income.

Perhaps the most serious dysfunction occurred in the rural economy, in the form of collectivized agriculture. John Lossing Buck, Owen L. Dawson, and Yuan-li Wu evaluated the farm output growth and the ways in which new fertilizers, irrigation, and collective organizations had contributed to that growth in the first fifteen years of the regime. Buck pointed out that the production decline after 1958 produced "extreme hunger and malnutrition, and possibly some starvation."[43]

In the mid-1960s and early 1970s the husband-and-wife team of Miriam and Ivan D. London conducted surveys in Hong Kong that provided the basis for a three-part article in 1976. They argued, for example, that there had been severe, widespread famine throughout China during the years 1960–62.[44] In part 1 they cited statements by informants—including former farmers, students, workers, and cadres—who described an incredible condition of starvation and suffering that seemed to have extended to every province of the country. In part 2 they described the harvest failures and huge loss of life that soon followed. According to this account, beggars roamed the country even in the years 1967–68. In part 3 the authors presented numerous examples of how farmers had shirked their duties in the rural collectives and expressed their extreme unhappiness with this farming system. Their research constituted the most graphic report of hunger, poverty, and misery in Communist China published by any American scholar. What made their account so powerful and paradoxical was that it appeared at a time (the mid-1970s) when there was a widespread belief in the West that the communist regime had never experienced any disaster and had eliminated poverty.

Some American experts also pointed out other problems, including the flawed incentive system in collectivized agriculture, the great loss of income from farming policies that discouraged specialization and trade, and the pricing policies that perpetually squeezed agriculture at the expense of industry.[45] Economists like Yuan-li Wu stressed the dysfunctions of a planned economy for industries like iron and steel.[46] Because managers of steel enterprises were rewarded according to the amount of steel they produced rather than according to the amount of profits generated by seeking buyers, they became insensitive to the demands of other industries. Consequently, steel inventories quickly ballooned during the 1950s and thereafter, making for a huge waste of scarce resources in this poor economy. In fact, many steel products were of such poor quality that they eventually had to be discarded. Since the planned economy could not speed up interindustry demand to reduce inventories, this dysfunction continued to plague all industries in the regime.

Certainly, the CCP leadership (and Mao himself) began to see that the

Soviet economic planning system created during the 1950s had permitted far too much power to be concentrated in the hands of the enterprise director or manager. CCP leaders increasingly viewed this new arrangement as dysfunctional because of the rigidities and waste associated with economic management. According to Franz Schurmann, the Great Leap Forward campaign was initiated partly to replace this system with collective management and, even more importantly, to shift all economic management into the hands of the party, regardless of the economic consequences.[47] For the next two decades party involvement in economic management remained substantial.

Whereas American experts described and analyzed both the functional and dysfunctional aspects of the institutions and organizations created by the CCP, ROC experts generally ignored the functional aspects and stressed the dysfunctional ones. For example, some noted how the CCP had used the tactic of the political campaign both to mobilize the masses and attack enemies of the regime and to undertake specific tasks set by the party. Vincent Chen, for example, viewed the political campaign as an instrument of coercion used to eliminate specific enemies of the new regime. "In general, apart from their professed goals, the mass campaigns have efficiently served to eliminate the enemies of the Communist regime and at the same time to improve discipline and to tighten control over the Party cadres. In turn, through the web of various mass organizations the Party as a whole is able to penetrate and consolidate its control over every segment of the population."[48] Chen also noted that the political campaign, or *yun-tung,* served to get rid of opponents of the regime; at the same time, it permitted the party to tighten its controls over society and party members. This unique instrument of coercion and mass mobilization appeared to work quite successfully in the first decade of communist rule.

Chang Ching-wen, however, pointed out that the many campaigns ultimately convinced the populace that the CCP was merely manipulating them for its particular ends; disillusionment usually followed these campaigns. "The advantages [for the CCP] lie in their use of the mass movement, but there are also disadvantages. The aims and means by which they orchestrate each campaign basically run counter to the interest of the people. Therefore, the relationship between the regime and the people always becomes sour."[49] In Chang Ching-wen's opinion, these campaigns also proved to be dysfunctional because they produced widespread popular disillusionment with and distrust for the Communist Party and its aims. In other words, the campaigns produced negative results and, especially, no tangible rewards for the hard work, energy, and time people had expended in them.

Hsuan Mo commented on the dysfunctional aspects of the CCP's rustification policy during the 1960s and 1970s. He claimed that this policy entailed enormous "cultural and educational disasters for China."[50] According to Warren Kuo, by sending perhaps seven million intellectuals and educated youth to remote and desolate areas, the regime created enormous ideological confusion among its intelligentsia, sowed widespread social discontent, and pitted the countryside against the cities.[51] Because this campaign ran counter to the personal interests of its participants, it constituted a policy of coercion. Coercion and oppression greatly demoralized the populace. Warren Kuo described this psychological process.

> The most common method for persecuting the intellectuals is by self-remolding. First, the victim is compelled to confess all his erroneous thinking and deeds and then "hand his heart to the Party" as a token of boundless loyalty to the proletariat and the dictatorship of the proletariat. Second, the victim is forced to receive education in a different environment—to go to the countryside or factories—to labor alongside peasants and workers. Excessive mental and physical suffering causes the victim to become a walking corpse that dares not think or do anything considered "erroneous" by the Peking regime.[52]

Intellectuals, in particular, bore the brunt and fury of CCP persecution and discrimination. It is quite likely that such experiences embittered and disillusioned large numbers of intellectuals during these decades even driving many to commit suicide. The dysfunctions caused by political campaigns and the transfer of urban youth and intellectuals to the villages produced a new social pathology which became widespread during the late 1960s and 1970s.

Other ROC experts argued that the policy of redistributing private property and eventually transferring virtually all private property to the collective or to the control of the unit (*tan-wei*) was a tactic that helped bring the populace under CCP control. Wang Chang-ling, for example, contended that these steps greatly circumscribed the role of the traditional family unit because control of the socialization and education of family members was transferred to the party. "Once the masses are organized, they are naturally more easily manipulated by the CCP . . . The family is no longer the main unit of social activities and education. The decline of paternal power benefited the military and bureaucratic control over society. Without private property, the Chinese people had no choice but to become dependent on the Communist regime."[53] Of course, this transformation to a new kind of psychological, social, and economic dependency coexisted with the emergence of a new privileged class in place of the traditional elite who had formerly controlled local communities.[54] This new social order required a greater reliance on personal contacts and ties than in former times, because in the past, free markets had flourished and people had been able to take advantage of commercial opportunities. Hsuan Mo supported Wang Chang-ling's argument about the emergence of a new privileged class. "With the establishment of collective ownership in China twenty years ago, landlords and propertied classes were eliminated. However, a new ruling class of Chinese Communist cadres has taken power . . . As this ruling class continues to grow, so have its privileges."[55]

ROC experts paid close attention to the role of ideology in the mass movement campaigns launched by the CCP during the 1950s and 1960s. The CCP tried to change the social and cultural norms by insisting on introducing a new brand of ideology along with the new organizations it tried to create by means of its political campaigns. The Three Red Banners campaign was a classic example of this type of policy. In 1970 Winberg Chai asserted that, by stressing ideological reform so often and so intensely, the CCP "simply hinders creativity and limits alternatives."[56] In 1975 Hsuan Mo argued that, because the CCP placed so much importance on the transformation of ideology, "it is no longer a struggle between the proletariat and the bourgeois, nor Marxism-Leninism versus Revisionism; rather, it has become a struggle between human nature and the forces representing something inhuman."[57]

In other words, the CCP tried to elicit a new kind of behavior that was abnormal to, and not in the best personal interests of, human beings. Because of the power wielded by the CCP, its policies were bound to have a powerful impact on Chinese society. ROC experts strongly believe that the social, psychological, and cultural consequences for the Chinese people have been devastating.

> From their own personal experience the broad masses of people, including many Party members and cadres, have lost their faith in Communism. This is the aftermath of more than thirty-one years of misrule by the Chinese Communists. The crisis of trust arises from lack of public faith in the CCP bureaucracy. The loss of public confidence derives from the realization that the Four Modernizations Program is unachievable by the target date, the end of this century. This three-sided crisis reflects the widespread cynicism of the people.[58]

In addition to ideological confusion, these political campaigns—with their insistence on ideological remolding—produced a new standard of survival ethics. This new ethical standard bore little relationship to anything in the past, so social and economic behavior also changed. Hsuan Mo described the new behavior.

> Between 1949 and 1976, moral education in the social and ideological sphere was on an anti-traditional morality road in Chinese Communist society . . . Moreover, three decades of experience demonstrate the destruction of the old morality, and that a fetishism for power and violence has

taken the place of morality . . . As a result of the abandonment of traditional morality in favor of Marxist practices, cadres are shameless, workers and peasants are lackadaisical, youth are depressed, intellectuals are losing their moral vigor and their sense of responsibility, and people are vying with one another for profits.[59]

Experts like Hsuan Mo believed there was little prospect that the Communist Party would take the initiative to improve its governance of China because its "absolute power enables the party to stay above the law, force the people to support its leadership, and purge dissidents and any alien ideology."[60]

The third sphere of activity in which ROC experts saw serious dysfunctions was the planned economy. For years the regime's policies produced the wrong investment decisions, stressed the construction of industries for which there was little market, slighted those industries which could have supplied more consumer products for the people, and ignored the long-term consequences of population growth for China's scarce resources. One expert described the huge economic difficulties resulting from CCP economic policies.

"Unreasonable waste and bureaucratism generated by the Stalin-style centralized economy have hamstrung the normal development of the economy. The abolishment of the system of egotism has killed incentives and thus reduced productivity."[61]

In other words, by radically curtailing private property, limiting free markets, collectivizing the economy and creating a socialist price system of regulated prices, the CCP adversely influenced economic incentives and virtually eliminated productivity as a source of economic growth for this system.

CONCLUSION

American and ROC researchers agreed in their analysis that the Chinese communist system constituted something unique, compared to former Chinese systems of governance. Their findings also converged when they identified and described the many dysfunctions of this system.

American experts made much more effective use of the research facilities offered in Hong Kong to interview refugees and subject this new information to statistical testing and social science analysis than did their ROC counterparts. This new research methodology also explains, in part, why American experts described and analyzed the new functional, as well as the dysfunctional, elements within the communist order. American social scientists were especially interested in describing how things worked in Communist China, and this motivation guided their interviews and subsequent analyses. By pay-ing attention to both the functional and dysfunctional features of the new regime, American researchers probably achieved an understanding of the regime's enormous staying power and viability even in the face of the incredible upheavals that frequently shook Chinese society. Although few, if any, American studies achieved that complex blend of functional and dysfunctional analysis that might explain why crises periodically arose and also why the leadership could resolve them, our survey sample definitely suggests how this kind of study might be carried out in the future.

ROC experts, in contrast, primarily analyzed the dysfunctions of the system—describing the social pathologies and citing the economic waste, inefficiency, and low living standards of the people. Perhaps their research findings led some of them to portray a system that was always crisis-prone and imminently in danger of collapsing into anarchy. By ignoring the functional aspects of the communist regime, ROC researchers did not really offer any important insights that would explain why this regime so successfully maintained its rule and society remained integrated for so long. Nevertheless, the ROC experts were correct in citing the many dysfunctions that, after 1978, the communist leadership eventually admitted. It now seems that these dysfunctions were chiefly responsible for forcing the leadership to reform its policies and organizations after 1978 so that it could initiate modernization.

It also seems that the Chinese experts in Taipei failed to analyze some complex socioeconomic patterns and changes that American researchers—because of their good training in social science methods—were able to undertake with considerable success. But as these patterns and changes were never understood in all their complexity, the capabilities of American experts to predict the outcomes of policy changes were not particularly noteworthy.

8

Conclusion

In an interview with Alexander Zinoviev, an academic and writer condemned to permanent exile from the Soviet Union in 1978 when a Communist Party decree revoked his Soviet citizenship for "behavior damaging to Soviet prestige," British journalist George Urban asked Zinoviev why he believed that competent Western experts could not "summon sufficient intellectual or imaginative power to get within the skin of the Soviet system."[1] Zinoviev replied as follows:

> Newtonian mechanics are a very recent discovery, and Einstein's relativity theory is even more recent. Capitalist society had existed for many centuries, but it was only in the nineteenth century that social science began to decipher the structure and describe the regularities of capitalist society. Communist society is very young indeed. Its whole history spans a mere 66 years. It is, therefore, difficult to take it in from the outside. Moreover, Western scholars approach it with their own educational background, their own values and mental models. All of this makes for distortions and incomprehensions.[2]

We have not found a similar viewpoint expressed by any dissident or émigré from the PRC. Our study strongly suggests, however, that the greater successes scored by ROC experts in understanding the general dynamics within the PRC, in predicting events and interpreting them correctly, and in explaining Communist Party leadership behavior owes much to their insiders' skills. We will recall, for example, that ROC experts frequently claimed that China's Marxist-Leninist regime (especially when Mao Tse-tung was in charge) combined the worst features of Marxist-Leninist-Stalinist ideological dogmatism and political despotism with the autocratic behavior, bureaucratism, and corruption that had exemplified China's political traditions for the past 2000 years.

This same view has recently been advanced by PRC dissidents in their periodical *Chung-kuo chih ch'un* (China Spring), now published in New

York City. Many Chinese scientists and scholars studying in North America write in this journal under a *nom de plume*. Here we can find "insider" interpretations of how the communist system evolved in China and still functions.[3] Some argue that the behavior of Mao Tse-tung and Teng Hsiao-p'ing, the party cadres, and the intellectuals produced a new system unlike any in Chinese history. Others even go so far as to blame the Chinese intellectuals for creating the special conditions under which China first became a Marxist-Leninist country. One writer complained that by embracing Marxism-Leninism for the purpose of making China wealthy and strong, "China's leading intellectuals threw out individual freedom, cast out respect for the individual, and disregarded independent thought. With both arms extended, those intellectuals embraced Stalinism. In some malevolent way, Stalinism then enhanced the reactionary elements of Chinese culture in their state of mind. The result was to greatly increase the successes of the Chinese Communist totalitarian political system."[4] These dissidents, who grew up under the Chinese communist system, now consider Marxism-Leninism largely responsible for the establishment of a totalitarian system that gradually revived the worst habits of traditional Chinese political behavior.

But our task here is not to present an interpretation of contemporary Chinese dissident writings published in the United States. We merely point out that these "insiders" produced interpretations similar to those advanced by ROC experts over the past several decades. As already argued, ROC experts were also insiders of a sort, so it should not be surprising that their intuitive grasp of Chinese political behavior and thought enabled them to reach conclusions similar to those found in *China Spring*.

American scholarship on Communist China was more diverse, ranging from praise of this regime's revolutionary policies to descriptions and explanations of how the CCP established its rule over the world's largest society. Chinese scholarship in the ROC presented a more defined perspective and a stronger critique of the failures and disasters that had occurred in Communist China. A small group of American scholars, however, interpreted Communist China in the same way as the ROC experts.

Different training and different cultural-linguistic backgrounds explain the variation in research approaches and findings between (most) American and ROC experts. Yet these differences did not prevent a small group of Americans from making interpretations of the general dynamics of Communist China similar to those of their ROC counterparts. Further, although these Chinese and American experts pointed out very different functional and dysfunctional aspects of the regime, in retrospect the analyses of both groups appear to have been equally valid.

Our survey also showed that there have been some serious misunderstandings of this regime. ROC experts certainly failed to ascertain why this system could remain intact and survive many crises without fragmenting into oblivion. Many American experts undervalued the huge costs to Chinese society when the regime imposed its new policies to transform the values, norms, and behavior of the populace. What are the main conclusions to emerge from our review of how different groups of experts tried to understand a complex, closed society like that of Communist China over a thirty-year period?

THE PROBLEM
OF MISUNDERSTANDING
A FOREIGN SOCIETY

We have stressed how difficult it is for researchers to try to understand the events and developments in a foreign society—especially one that is closed to outsiders and that publishes little information about itself. Outsiders are bound to distort and misunderstand such a society. We point out four main kinds of misunderstanding that have characterized research on Communist China and that probably equally apply to research on similar regimes of the twentieth century.

First, American and ROC scholars accurately described the methods and institutions of control the CCP had imposed on society, but they had difficulty in understanding exactly how these new controls influenced the behavior and thought of the Chinese people. The CCP had unified China far more quickly than anyone had believed possible. The communist leadership had also confounded their domestic opposition by imposing a single-party government set of controls on the society and economy within the incredibly short period of seven years. From all appearances, this accomplishment had the support of the populace and even its approval.

The available information was interpreted largely in terms of how the CCP established new control. But very few American or ROC experts fully understood why these controls had been established so quickly and what they actually meant for the people. When a society is rapidly turned upside down, and many new organizations are created to replace older ones, social action and thought are bound to be powerfully affected in subtle and far-reaching ways. It was therefore extremely difficult for American and ROC experts to understand what this extraordinary experience meant for both the common people and their leaders. Only a few refugee interviews were conducted in the 1950s—by American journalists and a few social scientists. This information—while extremely valuable—could not be further corroborated. When more systematic interview research was conducted in Hong Kong during the 1960s and after, it became dangerous to generalize about the entirety of China from interviews with refugees who came primarily from nearby Kwangtung province.

It now appears, however, that when China was subjected to such rapid change in the 1950s, its people must have experienced considerable trauma, and certain social groups must have suffered extreme hardship. Although it has appeared that the first seven years of the regime were relatively stable, perhaps they were not. Perhaps the new conditions that were soon to produce the cataclysmic changes in China had already materialized in these early years.

The CCP's miraculous social engineering, rarely matched in modern times, produced major, unintended consequences for both the leadership and the people. As some scholars in the U.S.—and most scholars in the ROC— correctly noted, the main figures in the CCP leadership perceived the successes and failures of CCP policies in the pre-1957 period very differently. Because expectations of what party policies were supposed to produce also varied greatly, political factions were already forming within the CCP at a time when all outward appearances suggested that party unity and harmony still prevailed. Political factionalism worsened after 1957, and it remains the driving force of Chinese politics and socioeconomic change to the present day.

The new system of controls that had been put in place by the CCP before 1957 was never institutionalized or sufficiently modified to accommodate the diverse conditions within the country. The social groups that had been displaced from power and prestige were replaced by a very different sociopolitical coalition of local leadership that was very closely linked to the CCP. Additionally, a huge new state bureaucracy had been built and was rapidly growing. The impact of these changes on society is still little known, but it must have been immense.

Not only did few scholars really understand the profound changes in Chinese society that flowed from the new system of control created by the CCP, but few ever developed any new conceptual categories and terms to evaluate the influence of these new social engineering policies for both the state and society. This same defect continued to characterize scholarly studies in later decades, when the CCP leadership introduced even more dramatic policy changes.

We are only now becoming aware of the enormity of the tragedy that occurred between 1958 and 1962, when perhaps as many as twenty to thirty million people needlessly died; untold millions suffered humiliation and misery from the punitive actions of socialist organizations; and confusion, despair, and cynicism spread rapidly throughout Chinese society. All of these calamities were directly caused by the CCP's policies and its new methods of control. Although most ROC experts understood these developments, only a few American experts understood them. It is ironic that nearly three decades passed before American experts on the USSR accurately understood the indescribable horrors experienced by the Soviet Communist Party and the Russian people in the Stalinist 1930s, it took roughly the same amount of time for most American experts to realize the full extent of the tragedy that unfolded in China between 1958 and 1962.

But misunderstanding how CCP rule influenced Chinese society did not end here. During the late 1960s and 1970s most American scholars still failed to accurately describe and interpret the impact of CCP policies and controls on the Chinese people. Again, most ROC experts seem to have accurately understood the devastating impact of the Great Cultural Revolution on Chinese society. Only after 1978 did CCP leaders admit and foreigners report an equally grim picture of the tragedy and suffering in Chinese society.

What still seems only dimly realized is that whereas in the 1960s and 1970s, many youth, party members, the intelligentsia, and their families and friends suffered during the 1950s, a much smaller segment of society—namely, the traditional elite and their families and supporters—also had suffered. Put differently, policies that proclaimed to build the good society in the 1950s became intolerable in the 1960s and 1970s, when virtually everyone in Chinese society was adversely affected. But the events of the 1960s and 1970s were by-products of the same monumental social engineering policies that had victimized the landlords and their families in the early 1950s.

It now seems valid to say that far too many American scholars failed to understand the high costs borne by Chinese society as a result of the social engineering policies of the CCP and its leaders after 1949. The new policies imposed by the CCP had far greater damaging effects on Chinese society than the country's leaders ever expected.

A second misunderstanding of scholars (particularly, of many American experts) had to do with the behavior of the political elite. Whereas many of these experts correctly understood that policy differences divided the CCP leadership, only a few really understood how personal relationships influenced the struggle for political power within the CCP. We now know that factionalism has been the driving force in Chinese communist political behavior ever since the party unified the country (and probably even before). It still constitutes the most significant systemic feature of this regime. Although it is difficult to understand where policy differences among the top elite end and the intraparty struggle for political power begins, personal ties and networks competing for political power and influence must always be taken into account when analyzing Chinese communist political behavior.

Because trust and loyalty can be built only by means of personal ties in Chinese communist politics, and because personal ties are the only means by which a party power-holder can translate power into political action, there have been persistent attempts by party leaders to, first, build a faction, and subsequently, manipulate opposing factions in order to gain control over them. Further, although power has inevitably concentrated in the hands of a few top leaders, rarely have these leaders agreed on all issues. Therefore, the contest for power appears to rage continuously in this type of political system.

A third misunderstanding concerns the enormous role played by ideas in the shaping of policies and, particularly, in disputes over policy differences in Communist China. American and ROC experts have often undervalued the importance ideas had for those exercising power. The new communist leaders who unified China possessed a very definite philosophy of history and human behavior, which set them apart from previous Chinese leaders. They shared the general philosophy of Marxism-Leninism with other communist regimes but were influenced in complex ways by Mao Tse-tung's writings. Their political conduct and policies were always closely governed and shaped by this mix of ideas. Therefore, any insightful analysis of leadership behavior must be linked to these ideas and must take into account when and how these ideas changed.

American scholars have long debated to what extent the CCP leaders were genuine Marxist-Leninists and to what extent they were influenced either by Mao's thought or by Chinese political tradition. The issue has still not been resolved to everyone's satisfaction. But a small group of American specialists, along with most ROC scholars, generally tried to interpret Chinese communist leadership behavior according to a well-defined core of Marxist-Leninist ideas that the leadership used to justify and organize the communist governance of state and society. Although there was always considerable flexibility of political action (especially when Mao's influence predominated), CCP leaders were guided by those Marxist-Leninist principles that granted supreme power to the party and its dogma. Future research should never ignore the central role that Marxist-Leninist ideas continue to play in Chinese communist policy-making and leadership behavior.

A fourth misunderstanding arose from the misconception (especially on the part of many ROC experts) that the regime did not possess the basic functional elements to enable it to resolve serious political and economic crises and still maintain party dominance over society. Many American social scientists acknowledged these functional elements and elaborated on them in considerable detail. Future experts must be able to understand both the functional and the dysfunctional elements of the communist regime if they are to accurately assess the developments in Chinese society.

ACHIEVING A BETTER
UNDERSTANDING OF
COMMUNIST CHINA

Why did some scholars successfully avoid certain misunderstandings, whereas others did not? What can be done to improve our research skills so that we can better understand Communist China in the future?

The answer to these questions, we believe, will require identifying the minimal skills necessary to better understand any foreign society. These include a skillful, imaginative use of social science methods; access to relevant historical documents and a profound understanding of language and culture; and a thorough knowledge of the ideas and philosophy shared by those who rule.

Possession of those three skills varied greatly among both American and Chinese scholars, and rarely did any scholar possess all three. ROC scholars were particularly adept at examining and comprehending large quantities of complex CCP documents and other forms of information put out by the regime. They also knew how individuals and groups behaved in this society, and, especially, within the CCP itself, because many had been members of the party and knew how it conducted its affairs and how its members treated one another. Most of the ROC scholars, however,—especially the first generation—were poorly trained in social science methodology. The generation that emerged in the late 1970s and 1980s was better equipped to apply social-science research techniques and formulate questions like American social scientists.

Most American scholars, on the other hand, had been trained in the tradition of the positivist social sciences. They tried to explain patterns of behavior in terms of observable behavioral relationships that could be measured. The first generation, educated in the 1950s and 1960s, were poorly trained in the Chinese language and relied, for the most part, on translated documents and information from the public media. The next generation, trained in the late 1960s and 1970s, possessed far better language skills and were capable of both conducting extensive fieldwork in Hong Kong and making careful analyses of the Chinese communist press reports and official documents. We suspect, however, that few possessed the empathy and understanding of Chinese behavior that only comes from a profound understanding of both Chinese language and culture—or that could be acquired by personal experience within the CCP. Finally, some American experts lacked the necessary skill to understand communist theory and practice. The reason for this deficiency deserves more consideration than we can provide here.

Even though some of these skills were effectively mastered and used by both scholarly groups, we contend that it was the rare scholar who commanded all three. We should mention, however, that American scholars of Chinese descent who were educated in China, Hong Kong, or Taiwan and transplanted to American academic institutions produced remarkably high-quality scholarship, particularly in economic and political studies of Communist China.

Although expending an enormous amount of time and energy to master the basic skills necessary to study and understand a foreign society like Communist China, some American, and most ROC experts, managed to transcend their biases and produce valid research findings about this regime. Although scholars in both communities labored under enormous handicaps, much of their research accurately described the developments inside Communist China. Some puzzles remain, however, which we will briefly cite in the hope that others will find answers.

In the late 1960s and 1970s many popular books and articles described the policies and experiments of the communist regime in China in a favorable light. The hostility and fear with which the American public had long regarded China turned to curiosity, and there was even a twinge of sympathy for the goals this regime appeared to be trying to achieve. President Nixon's trip to Peking in 1972 added impetus to this new momentum and led to even more statements about the successes of the Chinese regime.

It is extremely difficult to gauge how much the favorable reporting about Communist China was influenced by the writings of American experts. We now realize that much diversity of interpretation and viewpoint has characterized American research on Communist China. But it is not clear that this diversity was fully recognized during the period when so many experts were reporting favorably on developments inside Communist China. After 1978 the diversity within the profession declined, and a scholarly interpretation emerged that was much closer to the descriptive typology adhered to by ROC scholars and those American experts whose writings we subsumed under the Chinese communist regime typology. Why is it, then, that some scholarly interpretations of the regime were at variance with those circulating in the popular media during the late 1960s and 1970s, particularly during the Cultural Revolution?

This brings us to our final puzzle. Despite the paucity of information on Communist China, many American experts deliberately ignored the research and publication of documents by ROC scholars. Although a handful of American scholars used these materials to great advantage, it was not until the mid-1970s that more American scholars began to take advantage of the research findings and communist documents published by ROC scholars. Why? We think the answer is that many American scholars were very prejudiced in their assessment of ROC scholarship and believed that the communist documents published by ROC scholars were forged. Whatever the reason for this past divergence, a convergence of interpretations has been gradually taking place in these two scholarly communities in recent years. This new development leads us to our final comment about future research approaches for understanding Communist China.

TOWARD A BETTER RESEARCH METHODOLOGY FOR UNDERSTANDING FOREIGN COMMUNIST SOCIETIES

Experts in both the United States and the ROC have steadily improved their research skills, but we believe that few experts will be able to effectively combine all three of the research skills cited above. Therefore, other means must be found to enhance our capabilities to understand foreign societies like Communist China.

The adoption of a new research strategy, which we call the internationalization of research on foreign, communist societies, could accomplish this feat. By "foreign, communist societies" we mean all foreign societies dominated by a party whose leaders are committed to the philosophical ideals and thoughts embodied in Marxism-Leninism. Since 1917 most countries that have undergone political revolution have invariably become ruled by Marxist-Leninist regimes. To be sure, there is neither agreement nor friendship among many of these countries, but the fact remains that the twentieth century has witnessed the spread of Marxist-Leninist regimes in the regions of Asia, Africa, Latin America, and Eastern Europe. Marxism-Leninism is perhaps the greatest political force of our time.

To help American scholars achieve a better understanding of communist regimes—especially like that in China—we urge that the human and physical resources of countries friendly to the United States be pooled with those of our own country to mount major cooperative studies of Marxist-Leninist regimes.

In addition to international conferences, there should be more exchanges of personnel to collaborate on research projects and improve individual skills. Documents should be jointly published and distributed. Finally, collaborative research efforts by experts from different countries should be encouraged. Such sharing of resources could enhance the mastery of the three basic skills we have outlined, nurture new research that might have higher scholarly merit, and greatly elevate our understanding of Marxist-Leninist societies.

NOTES

PREFACE

1. John King Fairbank, "The New China and the American Connection," *Foreign Affairs*, October 1972, p. 36.

2. Galeazzo Santini, "A Great Wall of Philosophy," *Successo* 13, no. 11 (November 1971): 95–96.

3. Miriam London and Ivan D. London, "The Other China: Hunger, Part 1: The Three Red Flags of Death," *Worldview* 19, no. 5 (May 1976): 4.

4. *Jen-min jih-pao*, 1 October 1979, p. 1.

1 ■ THE PROBLEM AND OUR APPROACH

1. Max Weber, *Economy and Society: An Outline of Interpretive Sociology*, vols. 1 and 2 (Berkeley, Los Angeles, and London: University of California Press, 1978).

2. Francois Furet, "Beyond the *Annales*," *The Journal of Modern History* 55, no. 3 (September 1983): 389–410.

3. Hara Kakuten, "Mantetsu chōsabu no rekishi to Ajiya kenkyū" (The history of the South Manchuria Railway Research Bureau and Asian research), *Ajiya keizai* 4 (1979): 48–65. This essay was the first of many installments on the history of this remarkable research organization.

4. See Social Sciences Research Council, *Annual Report, 1958–1959* (New York: Social Sciences Research Council, 1959). See p. 24 for a list of the ten committee members.

5. John M. H. Lindbeck, *Understanding China: An Assessment of American Scholarly Resources* (New York: Praeger, 1971), p. 79. (This amount does not include the funds spent by public and private institutions of higher education to support contemporary China studies.)

6. These figures are based on information contained in the annual SSRC reports

for the years 1969–70 to 1978–79. We are grateful to Sophia Sa of the SSRC for making these materials available to us.

7. The samples in this study are selections from major China studies journals, monographs, and conference volumes. From the United States, we referred to, among others, *The China Quarterly, Asian Survey, The Journal of Asian Studies,* and *Problems of Communism.* We also made use of important monographs produced by major university presses and a number of conference volumes sponsored by the Social Science Research Council's Contemporary China Committee. From the Republic of China, we selected the journals *Issues & Studies, Fei-ch'ing yueh-pao (FCYP), Chung-kung yen-chiu (CKYC),* and *Tung-ya chi-k'an (TYCK).* Only on rare occasions did we refer to other periodicals. We also used the essays included in the published proceedings of each of the Sino-American Conferences on Mainland China (an annual event that began in 1970) and a variety of monographs written by Chinese experts in Taiwan. We have not included a bibliography, but the Index and Notes list all works and authorship.

We deeply regret that we were unable to include the excellent research on Communist China produced in Hong Kong, Japan, Europe, the socialist-bloc countries of Eastern Europe, and the Soviet Union. But an analysis of this large, complex body of literature would require a separate study in itself.

8. The reason we decided to only review scholarship in the years 1949 through 1978 is because the third plenum of the Eleventh CCP Central Committee of late 1978 marked a watershed in PRC history. At that plenum Teng Hsiao-p'ing won the final showdown against Hua Kuo-feng and began to initiate a new policy course for the country. The new leadership also began to speak more candidly about China's governance and development in the years between 1949 and 1978.

9. To protect the individuals concerned, we have not mentioned those who had affiliations with the Chinese Communist Party.

10. The evidence for this assertion is based on private interviews between the authors and leading ROC Communist China experts.

11. Henry G. Schwarz, "The Ts'an-'ao Hsiao-hsi: How Well Informed Are Chinese Officials About the Outside World?", *The China Quarterly,* no. 27 (July–September 1966): 56.

12. Warren Kuo, *Tui-fei tou-cheng shih-shih* (Facts about the political struggle against the Chinese Communists) (Taipei: Bureau of Investigation, 1963), p. 153.

13. These documents were later published by the Bureau of Intelligence, Republic of China (Taipei, 1970). An English version has been published by the Hoover Institution (Charles Price Ridley, trans., and C. S. Chen, ed., *Rural People's Communes in Lien-Chiang* [Stanford: Hoover Institution Press]).

14. The Landing Craft Documents have been collected at the Institute for the Study of Chinese Communist Problems, Taipei.

15. On November 5, 1970 major newspapers in Taipei, Taiwan, ROC published the entire text of the revised draft of the constitution of the People's Republic of China that was to be approved by the Fourth People's Congress.

16. *CKYC,* 6, no. 4 (April 1972): 4–5.

17. Ibid., 6, no. 7 (July 1972): 1–12 and 98–102.

18. "The Political Report Given by Chou En-lai at the CCP 10th National Congress," *CKYC* 7, no. 9 (September 1973): 38–40.

19. The Chinese journal *Fei-ch'ing yueh-pao* (*FCYP*) has also published a number of these documents.

20. Wang Hsiao-t'ang, "Four-Clean Movement and the Cultural Revolution," *CKYC* 1, no. 1 (January 1967): 31.

21. "The CCP's New Policy Towards Minorities on the Mainland," *FCYP* 1, no. 6 (July 1959): 5. We should point out that the name of the journal *Fei-ch'ing yueh-pao* is translated *Bandit Monthly*. ROC scholars, following the policy of their government, regarded the CCP as an illegitimate party that did not represent the will of the Chinese people. They therefore referred to the CCP as "bandits," using this pejorative term to denote that illegitimacy. Many American scholars regarded giving such a title to a scholarly journal as an indication of blatant bias, and they refused to take the journal and its contents seriously. We will merely remark here that this attitude also represents a failure to understand how cultural values are reflected by language. We would urge that rhetoric be ignored and that only the substance of scholarship be judged for its veracity. In July 1985 the journal's name became *Chung-kuo ta-lu yen-chin* [Mainland China Studies].

22. Karel Kovanda, "Chasing China's Shadows," *Problems of Communism* (January-February 1984), pp. 73–77. "Administratively, China is divided into some 2,300 counties. Probably not more than 200 of them ever welcomed a foreign visitor. The cumulative observations of *all* foreigners then reveal nothing about perhaps 2,100 entire counties in China, counties where altogether, figuring conservatively, some 500 million people live" (ibid., p. 74).

23. See W. G. Runciman's observation that "ideal types of descriptive theory are generated by extracting, or even forcing, a similarity between observations which, as reported, could not be seen of themselves to fall under the common rubric" *A Treatise on Social Theory: The Methodology of Social Theory*, vol. 1 [Cambridge: Cambridge University Press, 1983], p. 293.

For an excellent example of the development of an "ideal" descriptive type and an analysis of the behavior of the Soviet regime, see R. V. Burk, "The Arcane Art of Kremlinology," *Encounter* 60, no. 3 (March 1983): 20–30. Burk's essay inspired us to organize Chapters 2 and 3 on the basis of descriptive typology, and we acknowledge our intellectual debt to his essay.

2 ■ UNDERSTANDING BY MEANS OF TYPOLOGIES: RESEARCH IN THE UNITED STATES

1. Carl J. Friedrich and Zbigniew Brzezinski, *Totalitarian Dictatorship and Autocracy* (Cambridge: Harvard University Press, 1956), pp. 9–10.

2. Walter W. Rostow, *The Prospects for Communist China* (New York: John Wiley and Sons and The Technology Press of MIT, 1954), p. 299.

3. Ibid.

4. T. T., "The Intellectual in the New China," *Problems of Communism* 2, no. 2 (1953): 4.

5. For a discussion of the end of the united-front strategy to attack the bourgeois class, see W. M., "The Chinese Communists and the 'Bourgeoisie,'" *Problems of Communism* 1 (1952): 1–4. The party also made frequent, intense efforts to remold the thought of party cadres. For comments about this development, see S. B. Thomas, *Government and Administration in Communist China* (New York: Institute of Pacific Relations, 1953), Appendix on An Tzu-wan's report on rectifying the party, January 7, 1953.

6. Richard L. Walker, *China Under Communism: The First Five Years* (New Haven: Yale University Press, 1955), p. 24.

7. Ibid., chap. 2 describes how the party established its dominance over Chinese society. Some historians strongly objected to Walker's description of the way in which the Communist Party established its hegemony in China, eliminated its opposition, and began creating a new socialist society. See Mary C. Wright's review of Walker's book in *The Far Eastern Quarterly* 15, no. 2 (February 1956): 274–76. Wright's very negative review is puzzling, for she did not criticize the totalitarian typology Walker used to analyze Communist China's first five years. Instead, she castigated Walker for writing a chaotic and confusing book (ibid., p. 276).

8. H. Arthur Steiner, "Trade Unions in Mao's China," *Problems of Communism* 2, no. 5 (March-April 1956): 33.

9. Norris P. Smith, "Mao's Forced March to Collectivization," *Problems of Communism* 5, no. 5 (September-October 1956): 23–28.

10. Benjamin Schwartz, "New Trends in Maoism?", *Problems of Communism* 4, no. 6 (July-August 1957): 7.

11. Ibid., p. 7.

12. Arthur F. Wright, "The Chinese Monolith, Past and Present," *Problems of Communism* 4, no. 4 (July-August 1955): 8.

13. Roderick MacFarquhar, "Totalitarianism Via Industrialization? The Case of Communist China," *Problems of Communism* 5, no. 7 (September-October 1958): 7. Also see note 4.

14. Robert C. North, "Peiping on the March: The Eighth Congress of the CCP," *Problems of Communism* 6, no. 1 (January-February 1957): 24.

15. Stanley Rich, "The Communes—Mao's 'Big Family,'" *Problems of Communism* 8, no. 1 (January-February 1959): 5.

16. A. Doak Barnett, *Communist China in Perspective* (New York: Frederick A. Praeger, 1962), p. 28.

17. John K. Fairbank, *The United States and China* (Cambridge: Harvard University Press, 1958), p. 314.

18. Richard L. Walker, "Collectivization in China: A Story of Betrayal," *Problems of Communism* 4, no. 1 (January-February 1955): 11–12.

19. Shau Wing Chan and Yuan-li Wu, "Popular Discontent in Communist China," *Problems of Communism* 4, no. 4 (July-August 1955): 16–17.

20. Karl A. Wittfogel, "Forced Labor in Communist China," *Problems of Communism* 5, no. 4 (July-August 1956): 40.

21. Yuan-li Wu, *An Economic Survey of Communist China* (New York: Bookman Associates, 1956), pp. 322–37. Wu estimated that roughly twenty-three million persons had been involved in transport, labor export, government farms, telecommunications, water conservancy, and other projects. His figure was based on estimates produced by Nationalist Chinese sources in 1955.

22. A. Doak Barnett, *Communist China: The Early Years, 1949–55* (New York: Frederick A. Praeger, 1964), p. 203.

23. Ibid., pp. 208–9.

24. Barnett, *Communist China in Perspective,* p. 40.

25. See Gilbert Rozman, ed., *The Modernization of China* (New York: The Free Press, 1981), p. 3.

26. The terms "transformative" and "accommodative" are described in detail in Thomas A. Metzger, *Escape From Predicament* (New York: Columbia University Press, 1977). See his last two chapters.

27. "The First Decade," *The China Quarterly,* no. 1 (January-March 1960): 19–20.

28. Richard D. Baum, "Red and Expert: The Politico-Ideological Foundation of China's Great Leap Forward," *Asian Survey* 4, no. 9 (September 1964): 1048–57.

29. John Wilson Lewis, "Revolutionary Struggle and the Second Generation in Communist China," *The China Quarterly,* no. 21 (January-March 1965): 127.

30. Benjamin Schwartz, "Modernization and the Maoist Vision—Some Reflections on Chinese Communist Goals," *The China Quarterly,* no. 21 (January-March 1965): 3. In 1971 Donald J. Munro would note that even in the 1950s Mao believed that people were easily educated and that means could be found for changing their values and behavior. Mao's position had already pitted him against the government's Ministry of Education. See "The Malleability of Man in Chinese Marxism," *The China Quarterly,* no. 48 (October-December 1971): 609–40. See also Joseph R. Levenson, "Communist China in Time and Space: Roots and Rootlessness," *The China Quarterly,* no. 39 (July-September 1969): 10. "Mao would transform the peasants (and everybody else) through voluntarism . . . politics takes command, superstructure takes priority, over the substructural means of production—and of destruction" (ibid.).

31. Tang Tsou, "The Cultural Revolution and the Chinese Political System," *The China Quarterly,* no. 38 (April-June 1969): 64. See also his article, "Revolution, Reintegration, and Crisis in Communist China: A Framework for Analysis," in Ping-ti Ho and Tang Tsou, eds., *China in Crisis—China's Heritage and the Communist Political System,* vol. 1, book 1 (Chicago: University of Chicago Press, 1968), pp. 277–347.

32. Richard D. Baum, "Ideology Redivivus," *Problems of Communism* 16, no. 3 (May-June 1967): 7.

33. Tang Tsou, "The Cultural Revolution," p. 85. For comments on Mao's struggle against entrenched bureaucracy, see Maurice Meisner, "The Maoist Legacy and Chinese Socialism," *Asian Survey* 17, no. 11 (November 1977): 1016–27 and idem, *Mao's China: A History of the People's Republic* (New York: The Free Press, 1977), chap. 20.

34. Lloyd E. Eastman, "Mao, Marx, and the Future Society," *Problems of Communism* 18, no. 3 (May-June 1969): 21–26.

35. Richard M. Pfeffer, "The Pursuit of Purity: Mao's Cultural Revolution," *Problems of Communism* 18, no. 6 (November-December 1969): 21.

36. Gordon A. Bennett, "China's Continuing Revolution: Will It Be Permanent?", *Asian Survey* 10, no. 1 (January 1970): 17.

37. John Bryan Starr, "Conceptual Foundations of Mao Tse-tung's Theory of Continuous Revolution," *Asian Survey* 11, no. 6 (June 1971): 610–28.

38. Harry Harding Jr., "China: Toward Revolutionary Pragmatism," *Asian Survey* 11, no. 1 (January 1971): 51.

39. James R. Townsend, "Chinese Populism and the Legacy of Mao Tse-tung," *Asian Survey* 17, no. 11 (November 1977): 1015. Mao's utopian goals were supposed to be achieved by means of unusual hard work, unending diligence, great sacrifice, and the cultivation of the virtue of unselfishness. See Maurice Meisner, "Utopian Goals and Ascetic Values in Chinese Communist Ideology," *The Journal of Asian Studies* 28, no. 1 (November 1968): 101–10.

40. Tang Tsou, "Mao Tse-tung Thought, the Last Struggle for Succession, and the Post-Mao Era," *The China Quarterly,* no. 71 (September 1977): 498–527.

41. Roderick Macfarquhar is an Englishman, but he was at Columbia University when he was doing his research for this study. See "Problems of Liberalization and the Succession at the Eighth Party Congress," *The China Quarterly,* no. 56 (October-December 1973): 645–46. For other developments during the 1950s, see R. P. Suttmeier's essay ("Party Views of Science: The Record from the First Decade," *The China Quarterly,* no. 44 [October-December 1970]: 146–68), which points out that cadres were supposed to make science serve the masses and use the traditional, indigenous legacy to produce new scientists who were both red and expert.

42. For a study that exhibits some fundamental philosophical differences between Mao and Liu by 1958, see Stuart R. Schram, "Mao Tse-tung and Liu Shaoch'i, 1939–1969," *Asian Survey* 12, no. 4 (April 1972): 275–93.

43. Andrew J. Nathan, "Policy Oscillations in the People's Republic of China: A Critique," *The China Quarterly,* no. 68 (December 1976): 729. Nathan (ibid., p. 70) criticizes scholars who interpret "the pattern of policy change in China in terms of a combination of cyclical and secular patterns, to refer to policy oscillations in passing while presenting a chronology which actually indicates secular change, to offer the oscillations model explicitly as just a convenient simplification; or to ignore oscillations entirely in discussing the development of policy."

44. Ramon H. Myers, "Scarcity and Ideology in Chinese Economic Development," *Problems of Communism* 27 (March-April 1978): 87. This review essay examines seven economic studies. See also Alexander Eckstein, *China's Economic Development: The Interplay of Scarcity and Ideology* (Ann Arbor: University of Michigan Press, 1975).

45. Yuan-li Wu, "Planning, Management, and Economic Development in Communist China," in *An Economic Profile of Mainland China* (New York: Praeger, 1968, pp. 97–119 and "Communist Economic Planning vs. Capitalism as a Model for Development," in Milorad M. Drachkovitch, ed., *Marxist Ideology in the Contemporary World* (New York: Praeger for Hoover Institution on War, Revolution, and Peace, 1966), pp. 126–39.

46. Kuan-I Chen, "Economic Fluctuations in a Planned Underdeveloped Economy—A Case Study of Mainland China, 1952–65," *Asian Survey* 12, no. 4 (April 1972): 349–62.

47. Alexander Eckstein, "Economic Growth and Change in China: A Twenty-Year Perspective," *The China Quarterly*, no. 54 (April-June 1973): 221.

48. Robert Michael Field, "Civilian Industrial Production in the People's Republic of China, 1949–74," in Joint Economic Committee, Congress of the United States, *China: A Reassessment of the Economy* (Washington, D.C.: U.S. Government Printing Office, 1975), p. 149.

49. Ibid., p. 156.

50. Leo A. Orleans, "China's Environomics: Backing Into Ecological Leadership," in U.S. Congress, *China: A Reassessment of the Economy*, pp. 116–44.

51. Robert F. Dernberger, "Radical Ideology and Economic Development in China: The Cultural Revolution and Its Impact on the Economy," *Asian Survey* 12, no. 12 (December 1972): 1058–66.

52. Ibid., p. 1064.

53. Victor H. Li, "The Role of Law in Communist China," *The China Quarterly*, no. 44 (October-December 1970): 66–111.

54. Carl Riskin, "Small Industry and the Chinese Model of Development," *The China Quarterly*, no. 46 (April-June 1971): 272.

55. Martin King Whyte, *Small Groups and Political Rituals in China* (Berkeley: University of California Press, 1974), p. 17.

56. Other organizations that might be included here are the labor camps, where citizens are made to work and reform their thoughts; the new agricultural living unit called the brigade, which is organized like the model village of Tachai in Shansi province; and the new industrial living unit, such as the industrial community of Taching in Heilungkiang province. Numerous articles describe these and other organizations created by the party after 1949.

57. Ezra F. Vogel, "From Friendship to Comradeship: The Change in Personal Relations in Communist China," *The China Quarterly*, no. 21 (January-March 1965): 46.

58. Ibid., p. 59.

59. Rensselaer W. Lee III, "The *Hsia Fang* System: Marxism and Modernization," *The China Quarterly*, no. 28 (October–December 1966): 61.

60. Paul E. Ivory and William R. Lavely, "Rustication, Demographic Change, Development in Shanghai," *Asian Survey* 17, no. 5 (May 1977): 442.

61. Lucian W. Pye, *The Spirit of Chinese Politics* (Boston: MIT Press, 1968), p. 4.

62. Lucian W. Pye, *China: An Introduction* (Boston: Little, Brown and Company, 1972), p. 339.

63. Ibid., pp. 349–50.

64. Ibid., p. 352. Richard H. Solomon, a student of Pye, has extended this line of analysis in a detailed study of Maoist political behavior. See Richard H. Solomon, *Mao's Revolution and the Chinese Political Culture* (Berkeley: University of California Press, 1971). Solomon tries to show that the socialization of young Chinese continued to reinforce traditional values toward authority even after 1949. The personal desire for authority still conflicts with the personal reluctance to conform to modern organizational authority. Solomon, like Pye, uses political cultural analysis to explain why Maoist transformational thinking and policies prevailed after 1949 and why the regime has still been only partially successful in creating modern organizations in which authority is dispersed. See also Richard H. Solomon, "Mao's Effort to Reintegrate the Chinese Polity: Problems of Authority and Conflict in Chinese Social Processes," in A. Doak Barnett, ed., *Chinese Communist Politics in Action* (Seattle and London: University of Washington Press, 1969), pp. 271–361.

65. For criticism of the Joint Committee on Contemporary China, see the report by Moss Roberts ("Some Problems Concerning the Funding of Contemporary China Studies—A Reply to Professor Fairbank," *Bulletin of Concerned Asian Scholars* 3, nos. 3 and 4 [Summer-Fall 1971]: 113–38). See also the same journal, 5, no. 1 (July 1973): 72–76. The following quotation conveys some of the rhetorical fervor of concerned Asian students and professors in expressing their concern about the importance of studying Communist China.

> During the past sixty years, one of the world's great cultures has been transformed by a profound revolution which touches virtually every aspect of life in that society. As China continues to struggle to fully control her own destiny and to put her revolutionary ideals into practice, the rest of the world looks on with no little fascination tinged with a certain amount of envy, residual misunderstanding, skepticism, and admiration.

(John Berninghausen and Ted Huters, "Introductory Essay," *Bulletin of Concerned Asian Scholars* 8, no. 2 [January–March 1976]: 2.) See also James Peck, "The Roots of Rhetoric: The Professional Ideology of America's China Watchers," *Bulletin of Concerned Asian Scholars* 2, no. 1 (October 1969): 59–69. Peck perceived many of his generation as revolutionary Marxists who contended that China in the nineteenth and twentieth centuries had been exploited and made subordinate to American capitalism. "Instead of an evolving world order of independent self-determining states under the benevolent protection of America, the revolutionary Marxist sees capitalism as necessarily generating conditions that develop one part of the world system at the expense of another" (ibid., p. 65).

66. John G. Gurley, *China's Economy and the Maoist Strategy* (New York: Monthly Review Press, 1976), p. 5.

67. Victor Lippit, "Economic Development and Welfare in China," *Bulletin of Concerned Asian Scholars* 4, no. 2 (Summer 1972): 84, and idem, *Land Reform and Economic Development in China* (White Plains, N.Y.: International Arts and Sciences Press, 1974), chap. 3.

68. Carl Riskin, "Maoism and Motivation: Work Incentives in China," *Bulletin of Concerned Asian Scholars* 5, no. 1 (July 1973): 11.

69. Stephen Andors, "The Dynamics of Mass Campaigns in Chinese Industry: Initiators, Leaders, and Participants in the Great Leap Forward, the Cultural Revolution, and the Campaign to Criticize Lin Biao and Confucius," *Bulletin of Concerned Asian Scholars* 8, no. 4 (October-December 1976): 38.

70. Phyllis Andors, "Social Revolution and Woman's Emancipation in China During the Great Leap Forward," *Bulletin of Concerned Asian Scholars* 7, no. 1 (January-March 1975): 33–42. For another essay that credits revolutionary policies for contributing to a great improvement in the status of women, see Norma Diamond, "Collectivization, Kinship, and the Status of Women in Rural China," *Bulletin of Concerned Asian Scholars* 7, no. 1 (January-March 1975): 25–32.

71. Carl Riskin, "The Chinese Economy in 1967," in Michael Oksenberg, Carl Riskin, Robert A. Scalapino, and Ezra F. Vogel, eds., *The Cultural Revolution, 1967 in Review*, Michigan Papers in Chinese Studies, no. 2 (Ann Arbor: University of Michigan, 1968), pp. 53–54.

72. Stephen Andors, *China's Industrial Revolution: Politics, Planning, and Management, 1949 to the Present* (New York: Pantheon Books, 1977), p. 221.

73. Stephen Andors, ed., *Workers and Workplaces in Revolutionary China* (White Plains, N.Y.: M. E. Sharpe, 1977), p. ix.

74. Andors, "Dynamics of Mass Campaigns in Chinese Industry," p. 43.

75. Benedict Stavis, "How China is Solving Its Food Problem," *Bulletin of Concerned Asian Scholars* 7, no. 3 (July-September 1975): 22–38.

76. Roland Berger, "Financial Aspects of Chinese Planning," *Bulletin of Concerned Asian Scholars* 6, no. 2 (April-August 1974): 16 [Translated from the French]. (We have cited this article because it fits so well into our "ideal" type.)

77. Gurley, *China's Economy and the Maoist Strategy*, p. 13.

78. Paul Harper, "The Party and the Unions in Communist China," *The China Quarterly*, no. 37 (January-March 1969): 118. The party also controlled young people by means of the party-led Youth League, which became an instrument of the party and had close "affinity with the Party" (Victor Funnell, "The Chinese Com-

munist Youth Movement, 1949–1966," *The China Quarterly,* no. 42 [April-June 1970]: 126). Funnell is an Australian, but we have cited his essay because it falls under this "ideal" type.

79. Harper, "The Party and the Unions in Communist China," p. 119.

80. Allan Spitz, "Maoism and the People's Courts," *Asian Survey* 9, no. 4 (April 1969): 258.

81. Ibid., p. 262. Therefore, "within the framework of Chinese Communist legality, justice is mostly administered without formal court trials, and the role of the judiciary proper is secondary to that of administrative authority" (Gene T. Hsiao, "Communist China: Legal Institutions," *Problems of Communism* 14, no. 2 [March-April 1965]: 112).

82. George Ginsburg and Arthur Stahnke, "The People's Procuratorate in Communist China: The Period of Maturation," *The China Quarterly,* no. 24 (October-December 1965): 53–91.

83. Paul Hollander, "Privacy: A Bastion Stormed," *Problems of Communism* 12, no. 6 (November-December 1963): 1–2.

84. Adam Oliver, "Rectification of Mainland China Intellectuals, 1964–65," *Asian Survey* 5, no. 10 (October 1965): 489.

85. James P. Harrison, "The Ideological Training of Intellectuals in Communist China," *Asian Survey* 5, no. 10 (October 1965): 491.

86. Lucy Jen Huang, "The Role of Religion in Communist Chinese Society," *Asian Survey* 11, no. 7 (July 1971): 695.

87. Victor C. Falkenheim, "County Administration in Fukien," *The China Quarterly,* no. 59 (July-September 1974): 540.

88. Ralph L. Powell and Chong-kun Yoon, "Public Security and the PLA," *Asian Survey* 12, no. 12 (December 1972): 1083.

89. Ibid., p. 1093.

90. Chu-yuan Cheng, "The Power Struggle in Red China," *Asian Survey* 6, no. 9 (September 1966): 469.

91. Peter R. Moody, "Policy and Power: The Career of T'ao Chu, 1956–66," *The China Quarterly,* no. 54 (April-June 1973): 267–93.

92. Franz Michael, "The Struggle for Power," *Problems of Communism* 16, no. 3 (May-June 1967): 21. See also Franz Michael, *Mao and the Perpetual Revolution* (New York: Barron's Educational Series, 1977), chap. 7.

93. Philip Bridgham, "The Fall of Lin Piao," *The China Quarterly,* no. 55 (July-September, 1973): 427–49.

94. Ibid., p. 448.

95. Parris H. Chang, "Mao's Last Stand?", *Problems of Communism* 25, no. 4 (July-August 1976): 15.

96. For an account of the arrest of Chiang Ch'ing and her colleagues—the resolution of a power struggle—see Andres D. Onate, "Hua Kuo-feng and the Arrest

of the 'Gang of Four,'" *The China Quarterly,* no. 75 (September 1978): 540–65.

97. William Whitson, "The Field Army in Chinese Communist Military Politics," *The China Quarterly,* no. 37 (January-March 1969): 1–30. For a critique of Whitson's analysis and a different explanation of PLA factionalism, see William L. Parish, Jr., "Factions in Chinese Military Politics," *The China Quarterly,* no. 56 (October-December 1973): 667–69. For yet another view of PLA factionalism, see William Pang-yu Ting, "A Longitudinal Study of Chinese Military Factionalism, 1949–1973," *Asian Survey* 15, no. 10 (October 1975): 896–910.

98. Michael Oksenberg and Steven Goldstein, "The Chinese Political Spectrum," *Problems of Communism* 23, no. 2 (March-April 1974): 9.

99. Ibid., p. 13.

100. Alan P. L. Liu, "The 'Gang of Four' and the Chinese People's Liberation Army," *Asian Survey* 19, no. 9 (September 1979): 819.

101. Harry Harding, Jr., "China After Mao," *Problems of Communism* 26, no. 2 (March-April 1977): 1–18.

102. Choh-ming Li, "Economic Development," *The China Quarterly,* no. 1 (January-March 1960): 46–47.

103. Yuan-li Wu, "On China's Descending Spiral," *The China Quarterly,* no. 12 (October-December 1962): 51.

104. Edwin F. Jones, "The Impact of the Food Crisis on Peiping's Policies," *Asian Survey* 2, no. 10 (December 1962): 10. Another study very critical of agricultural performance is John Lossing Buck, Owen L. Dawson, and Yuan-li Wu, *Food and Agriculture in Communist China* (New York: Frederick A. Praeger, 1966).

105. John Wilson Lewis, "China's Secret Military Papers: 'Continuities' and 'Revelations,'" *The China Quarterly,* no. 18 (April-June 1964): 68–78 and J. Chester Cheng, "Problems of Chinese Communist Leadership as Seen in the Secret Military Papers," *Asian Survey* 4, no. 6 (June 1964): 861–72. These documents were translated by J. Chester Cheng, *The Politics of the Chinese Red Army* (Stanford: Hoover Institution Press, 1966).

106. Wen-shun Chi, "Water Conservancy in Communist China," *The China Quarterly,* no. 23 (July-September 1965): 53.

107. Edwin P. Reubens, "Under-Employment Theory and Chinese Communist Experiences," *Asian Survey* 4, no. 12 (December 1964): 1203.

108. Anthony M. Tang and Bruce Stone, *Food Production in the People's Republic of China* (Washington, D.C.: International Food Policy Research Institution, 1980), p. 13.

109. Ralph L. Powell, "Soldiers in the Chinese Economy," *Asian Survey* 11, no. 8 (August 1971): 758.

110. Martin King Whyte, "Corrective Labor Camps in China," *Asian Survey* 13, no. 3 (March 1973): 253–69.

111. Frederick C. Teiwes, "The Purge of Provincial Leaders, 1957–1958," *The China Quarterly,* no. 27 (July-September 1966): 32. Teiwes remarks that these

purges were "accomplished smoothly and apparently with remarkable organisational continuity despite their coincidence with a radical new policy departure" (ibid.).

112. See Frederick C. Teiwes, *Politics and Purges in China: Rectification and the Decline of Party Norms, 1950–1965* (White Plains, N.Y.: M. E. Sharpe, 1979), chap. 9 and idem, "'Rules of the Game' in Chinese Politics," *Problems of Communism* 28, nos. 5–6 (September-December 1979): 67–76.

113. Merle Goldman, "Hu Feng's Conflict With the Communist Literary Authorities," *The China Quarterly,* no. 12 (October-December 1962): 136.

3 ■ UNDERSTANDING BY MEANS OF TYPOLOGIES: RESEARCH IN THE REPUBLIC OF CHINA

1. Warren Kuo, "Mainland China Studies in the R.O.C.," *Proceedings of the First Sino-American Conference on Mainland China* (Taipei: The Institute of International Relations, 1971), pp. 13–16.

2. "Seminar on Methodology of Communist China Studies," *China Times Magazine,* July 4–10, 1982, pp. 57–62.

3. Ibid., p. 62.

4. Cheng Hsüeh-chia, *A Review of the Chinese Communist Party in the Past Thirty Years* (Taipei: China Times Press, 1980), pp. 1–56 and Li T'ien-min, "The Study of the Chinese Communist Personality," in *Proceedings of the Second Sino-American Conference on Mainland China* (Taipei: The Institute of International Relations, 1972).

5. Chen Yü-ch'ang, "The Political Theories of the Chinese Communists," *Monograph on the CCP Politics* (Taipei: The Institute of International Relations, 1973), p. 11.

6. Wu An-chia, "The Nature of the Chinese Communists," *Chin-tai Chung-kuo* (Modern China), February 1983, pp. 171–73.

7. Ibid., p. 163.

8. Warren Kuo, "Personal Dictatorship or Collective Leadership?", *Issues & Studies* 10, no. 12 (September 1974): 48.

9. Warren Kuo, "Reforming the Chinese Communist Leadership System," *Proceedings of the Tenth Sino-American Conference on Mainland China* (Berkeley: University of California, 1981), p. 41.

10. Wu An-chia, "Nature of the Chinese Communists," p. 168.

11. Tsui Chui-yien, "Does Mao Tse-tung's Thought Originate in the Chinese Tradition?", *Issues & Studies* 4, no. 7 (April 1968): 1–8 and Teng Kung-hsuan, "Maoism vs. Chinese Cultural Tradition," *Issues & Studies* 4, no. 9 (June 1968): 1–8.

12. Hsing Kuo-ch'iang, "A Brief Analysis of Mao Tse-tung Thought After Mao's Death," *Issues & Studies* 12, no. 11 (November 1976): 55.

13. Teng Kung-hsuan, "Maoism vs. Chinese Cultural Tradition," p. 1.

14. Ibid., p. 7.

15. Warren Kuo, "Mainland China Studies in the R.O.C.," pp. 13–16; Tsui Chui-yien, "Mao Tse-tung's Thought"; and Teng Kung-hsuan, "Maoism vs. Chinese Cultural Tradition."

16. Warren Kuo, "Communist China in the Post-Mao Period: Possible Development of the Power Struggle," *Fei-ch'ing yueh-pao (FCYP)* 19, no. 5 (November 1976): 8.

17. Chu Hsin-min, "Mao Tse-tung's Personality Model and Behavior Rule," *Tung-ya chi-kan* (East Asian Quarterly) 10, no. 3 (January 1979): 134–44.

18. Warren Kuo, "Personal Dictatorship or Collective Leadership?", p. 51.

19. Hsing Kuo-ch'iang, "Analysis of Mao Tse-tung Thought," p. 61.

20. Yung Wei, "Culture, Ideology, and Elite Conflict: Toward a 'Middle Range' Interpretation of Chinese Communist Behavior," in *Proceedings of the Eighth Sino-American Conference on Mainland China,* Institute of International Studies, University of South Carolina, May 17–20, 1979. (Columbia, S.C.: The Institute of International Studies, 1979), p. 226.

21. Warren Kuo, "Personal Dictatorship or Collective Leadership?", p. 53.

22. Ibid., p. 53.

23. Ibid., pp. 52–53.

24. Cheng Hsüeh-chia, *From the Cultural Revolution to the CCP Eleventh National Congress* (Taipei: Li-min Publishing Co., 1978), p. 14.

25. K'ung Teh-liang, "A Brief Review of CCP Activities During the Past Fifty Years," *Issues & Studies* 7, no. 10 (July 1971): 39.

26. Warren Kuo, "Communist China in the Post-Mao Period," p. 8.

27. Li T'ien-min, "The Big Struggle on the Chinese Mainland," *Issues & Studies* 2, no. 11 (August 1966): 7.

28. Yeh Hsiang-chih, "A Review of the CCP's Intra-party Struggles," *Chung-kung yen-chiu (CKYC)* 6, no. 11 (November 1972): 4.

29. Warren Kuo, "Possible Outcome of the Recent CCP Intra-Party Struggle," *FCYP* 19, no. 12 (June 1977): 8.

30. Chang Cheng-pang, "The Evolution of Mao-Lin Clique's Strategy to Seize Power," *FCYP* 10, no. 3 (April 1967): 13–19 and idem, "The CCP's Intra-party Struggle After the CCP Tenth National Congress," *Monograph on the CCP's Intra-party Struggle* (Taipei: The Institute of International Relations, 1973), pp. 658–76.

31. Yao Meng-hsuan, "Issues of the CCP Intra-Party Struggle," *FCYP* 16, no. 2 (April 1973): 13.

32. K'ung Teh-liang, "Review of CCP Activities," p. 42.

33. Warren Kuo, "Peace Offensives and the United Front Tactics," *Issues & Studies* 15, no. 3 (March 1979): 14–15.

34. Warren Kuo, "Personal Dictatorship or Collective Leadership?", p. 43.

35. Yin Ch'ing-yao, *PRC's Foreign Policy and Foreign Relations* (Taipei: The Institute of International Relations, 1973), p. 21.

36. Hsiang Nai-kwang, "Historical Lessons of the Chinese Communist Negotiation Policy," *CKYC* 6, no. 8 (August 1972): 55.

37. Chang Ching-wen, "An Analysis of the Members of the Ninth CCPCC," *FCYP* 12, no. 3 (May 1969): 14–17; Kung Teh-liang, "A General Analysis of the CCP Ninth National Congress," *FCYP* 12, no. 13 (May 1969): 7–13; and Yao Meng-hsuan, "Some Questions Concerning the Ninth National Congress of the CCP," *Issues & Studies* 5, no. 10 (July 1969): 16–30.

38. Hsiao Yeh-hui, "Power Infrastructure of the CCP Top Level Hierarchy and Its Future Direction of Struggle," *CKYC* 6, no. 9 (September 1973): 5–9; Kung Teh-liang, "A Comprehensive Analysis of the CCP Tenth National Congress," *FCYP* 16, no. 8 (October 1973): 7–13; and Ying Ch'ing-yao, "The CCP Tenth National Congress and Peiping's Foreign Policy," *FCYP* 16, no. 9 (November 1973): 13–19.

4 ■ VERIFICATION OF TYPOLOGIES

1. "Resolution of Certain Questions About the History of Our Party Since the Founding of the People's Republic," *Jen-min jih-pao* (People's Daily), July 1, 1981, pp. 1–5. For this quote, see p. 2. (Henceforth referred to as "Resolution.")

2. For a copy of this report in Chinese, see Liao Kai-lung, "Historical Experiences and Our Road of Development, part 1, printed by an unknown CCP school in 1980; reprinted by *Fei-ch'ing yueh-pao* (*FCYP*) 24, no. 2 (August 1981): 96. (Henceforth referred to as *Report.*)

3. *Ta-kung-pao,* Hong Kong, 4 July 1980, p. 1.

4. *Report,* pt. 1, p. 96.

5. Ibid., p. 97.

6. Ibid. For these two quotes in sequence, see pp. 90 and 100.

7. "Resolution," p. 3.

8. *Report,* pt. 1, p. 95.

9. "Resolution," p. 2.

10. *Report,* pt. 1, p. 100.

11. "Resolution," p. 2.

12. *Report,* pt. 1, p. 100.

13. *Jen-min jih-pao,* 15 September 1980, p. 1.

14. "Teng Hsiao-p'ing's Speech at the Enlarged Meeting of the CCP Political Bureau," *Issues & Studies* 17, no. 3 (March 1981): 81.

15. Richard Bernstein, *From the Center of the Earth* (Boston and Toronto: Little, Brown and Company, 1982), p. 100.

16. Steven W. Mosher, *Broken Earth: The Rural Chinese* (New York: The Free Press, 1983), pp. 63–64.

17. Fox Butterfield, *China: Alive in the Bitter Sea* (Toronto, New York, and Sydney: Bantam Books, 1982), p. 95.

18. Ibid., p. 95.

19. Editorial, "Communist Cadres Ought to Speak the Truth," *Jen-min jih-pao*, 30 June 1980.

20. Mosher, *Broken Earth: The Rural Chinese*, p. 40.

21. Butterfield, *China: Alive in the Bitter Sea*, p. 273.

22. Bernstein, *From the Center of the Earth*, pp. 45–46.

23. *The Japan Times*, 28 April 1984, p. 7. On September 11, 1984 Beijing's State Statistical Bureau responded to queries submitted by the Associated Press and confirmed that between 1959 and 1962 "over 10 million people died of unnatural death due to both man-made factors and serious natural disasters." See *Times Tribune*, 12 September 1984, p. A-9.

24. George E. Taylor, "Communist China—The Problem Before Us," *Asian Survey* 1, no. 2 (April 1961): 33.

25. John Kenneth Galbraith, *A China Passage* (Boston: Houghton Mifflin, 1973), pp. 136–37.

26. John K. Fairbank, "To China and Back," *New York Review of Books*, 19 October 1972, pp. 10–12.

27. John K. Fairbank, "On the Death of Mao," *New York Review of Books*, 14 October 1976, p. 3.

28. Quoted in Paul Hollander, *Political Pilgrims* (New York: Harper Colophon Books, 1983; Oxford: Oxford University Press, 1981), p. 344.

29. Edward Friedman, "The Innovator," in Dick Wilson, ed., *Mao Tse-tung in the Scales of History* (Cambridge, England and New York: Cambridge University Press, 1977), p. 320.

30. Michel Oksenberg, "Mao's Policy Commitments, 1921–1976," *Problems of Communism* 25, no. 6 (November-December 1976): 19 and 22.

31. *The New York Review of Books*, 14 October 1976, p. 3.

32. Ross Terrill, *800,000,000: The Real China* (Boston and Toronto: Little, Brown and Company, 1971), p. 40.

33. Ibid., p. 228.

34. Ibid., p. 232.

35. Ross Terrill, "Peking: Trying to Make China Work," *The Atlantic*, July 1983, p. 28.

5 ■ *UNDERSTANDING COMMUNIST CHINA BY MEANS OF PREDICTION*

1. Quoted in John Gross, *The Oxford Book of Aphorisms* (New York and Oxford: Oxford University Press, 1983), p. 325.

2. Richard L. Walker, "Collectivization in China: A Story of Betrayal," *Problems of Communism* 4, no. 1 (January-February 1955): 11–12.

3. Peter S. H. Tang, "Power Struggle in the Chinese CP: The Kao-Jao Purge," *Problems of Communism* 4, no. 6 (November-December 1955): 24.

4. This view can be found in some of the works cited in Richard L. Walker's perceptive review of eight studies on Communist China ("China Under Mao," *Problems of Communism* 18, no. 1 [January-February 1969]: 28–30).

5. Walter W. Rostow, *A Comparison of Russian and Chinese Societies Under Communism* (Cambridge: Center for International Studies, MIT, 1955), p. 16.

6. Ibid., p. 24.

7. In the late 1940s and 1950s some of America's most brilliant public-affairs experts, such as Walter Lippmann, predicted that the Soviet Union would move away from communist ideology and adopt a platform based on nationalistic interests, which would make diplomatic accord between East and West more feasible. See Ronald Steel, *Walter Lippmann and the American Century* (New York: Vintage Books, 1981), pp. 428–29.

8. A. Doak Barnett, *Communist China in Perspective* (New York: Frederick A. Praeger, 1962), p. 68.

9. Ibid., pp. 69–70.

10. Ibid., p. 67.

11. Donald S. Zagoria, "Strains in the Sino-Soviet Alliance," *Problems of Communism* 9, no. 3 (May-June 1960), p. 11.

12. Zbigniew Brzezinski, "Pattern and Limits of the Sino-Soviet Dispute," *Problems of Communism* 9, no. 5 (September-October 1960): 6. But in early 1962 Arthur A. Cohen correctly stated that "Mao and his associates have abandoned hope of a viable working relationship with the present leaders of Soviet Communism and that the rift between the two Communist leaderships, instead of mending is, on the contrary, becoming still deeper and more difficult to resolve" (*Problems of Communism* 11, no. 4 [July-August, 1962]: 63).

13. Barnett, *Communist China in Perspective*, p. 85.

14. Ibid., p. 86.

15. Ibid., p. 87.

16. *Wen-t'i yu yen-chiu (WTYYC)* [*Issues & Studies*] 1, no. 6 (September 1956): 202–5.

17. *WTYYC* 3, no. 10 (January 1959): 67.

18. The Three Red Banners included (1) the Socialist General Line, (2) the Great Leap Forward, and (3) the People's Communes.

19. Editorial, "An Analysis of Peoples' Communes, *Fei-ch'ing yueh-pao (FCYP)* 1, no. 8 (September 1958): 82.

20. "Organization and Distribution in the PRC's People's Communes," *FCYP* 11, no. 10 (October 1958): 27–40.

21. "Where Do People's Communes Go From Here?", *FCYP* 1, no. 12 (January 1959): 119 and 123.

22. "A Review of International Affairs, 1958," *WTYYC* 3, no. 10 (January 1959): 60–61. See also "The 6th Plenum of the CCP 8th National Congress and Mao's Resignation," *WTYYC* 3, no. 10 (January 1959): 65–67 and "On the CCP's Agricultural 'Great Leap Forward' and the Basic Farming System," *WTYYC* 4, no. 1 (April 1959): 21–25.

23. Same sources as in note 22.

24. "Industrial and Agricultural Production Exposes Severe Crises on the Chinese Mainland," *FCYP* 2, no. 7 (August 1959): 31–37.

25. For one example, see Thomas P. Bernstein, "Starving to Death in China," *The New York Review of Books,* 16 June 1983, pp. 36–38. See also Liang Heng and Judith Shapiro, *Son of the Revolution* (New York: Knopf, 1983).

26. Robert F. Emery, "Recent Economic Developments in Communist China," *Asian Survey* 6, no. 6 (June 1966): 304.

27. Michel Oksenberg, "Communist China: A Quiet Crisis in Revolution," *Asian Survey* 6, no. 1 (January 1966): 1.

28. Ibid., p. 1.

29. Michel Oksenberg, "China: Forcing the Revolution to a New Stage," *Asian Survey* 7, no. 1 (January 1967): 14.

30. A. Doak Barnett, *China After Mao* (Princeton, N.J.: Princeton University Press, 1967), p. 68.

31. Ibid., p. 69.

32. Ibid., p. 116.

33. Parris H. Chang, "The Second Decade of Maoist Rule," *Problems of Communism* 18, no. 6 (November-December 1969): 11.

34. Tang Tsou and Morton H. Halperin, "Maoism at Home and Abroad," *Problems of Communism* 14, no. 4 (July-August 1965): 13.

35. For relevant discussion of Beijing's assistance to Southeast Asian guerrilla insurgency, see the section entitled "The Pacific and Asia" in each year's *International Communist Yearbook* for the years 1965 through 1983 (Stanford: Hoover Institution Press).

36. Tsai Hsuan, "The Campaign of 'Study Mao Thoughts,'" *(FCYC)* 9, no. 2 (February 1966): 22–26; K'ung Teh-liang, "Learning of Thought of Mao Tse-tung on the Chinese Mainland," *FCYP* 9, no. 1 (February 1966): 21–24; Wang Changling, "A Brief Comment on the Wu-han Affair," *FCYP* 9, no. 3 (April 1966): 50–54; and Chou Chia-tung, "The Launching of the 'Study Chiao Yu-yu Movement' and the Campaign to Purge Intellectuals on the Chinese Mainland," *FCYP* 9, no. 3 (April 1966): 55–59.

37. Li Ping-hsüeh, "The Current Situation Concerning the Thought-Rectification Campaign on the Chinese Mainland," *FCYC* 9, no. 5 (May 1966): 1.

38. Chen Yu-ch'ang, "Power Struggle and 'Three Family Village Affair,'" *FCYC* 9, no. 6 (June 1966): 12.

39. Ibid.

40. "A Monthly Review of the Major Events on the Chinese Mainland," *FCYP* 9, no. 4 (May 1966): 2. This same article also predicted the purge of Lo Jui-ch'ing, the PLA's top general, which occurred in late 1966. Chen Kuang also forecasted that "the purge campaign will further spread to the Party organs at the provincial and municipal levels and when the CCP holds the 9th Party National Congress, it will confirm Lin Piao as Mao's successor" ("The Cultural Revolution and the CCP's Intra-Party Struggle," *FCYC* 9, no. 10 [October 1966], p. 29).

41. Wang Chang-ling, "Purges and the Factional Rivalry on the Chinese Mainland," *FCYP* 9, no. 5 (June 1966): 7–13; Cheng Yu-cheng, "'The Purge of the Three Family Village' and the Power Struggle on the Chinese Mainland," *FCYC* 9, no. 6 (June 1966): 1–12; and Chen Yu-chang, "Certain Key Points about the Cultural Revolution," *FCYC* 9, no. 7 (June 1966): 1–10.

42. Tseng Yung-hsien, "The Political Rectification Campaign on the Chinese Mainland," *FCYP* 9, no. 6 (July 1966): 7.

43. Li T'ien-min, "The Big Struggle on the Chinese Mainland," *Issues & Studies* 11, no. 11 (August 1966): 1–14. Li offered this interesting observation: "A careful assessment of the great turmoil will lead one to realize that it is the commune system in the rural areas which gave rise to the ideological turmoil now undermining the foundation of the Peiping regime" (12).

44. Another ROC China-watcher, Shu Hui, predicted in September 1966 that the Red Guard movement would soon fan out from the schools from which it had originated and involve all other organizations, becoming, in effect, a national political movement. He also believed the Red Guards would take military action and arm themselves. All of these developments occurred in 1967. (See Shu Hui, "An Analysis of the Red Guard Movement on the Chinese Mainland," *FCYC* 9, no. 9 [September 1966]: 1–8.)

45. Gordon A. Bennett, "China's Continuing Revolution: Will It Be Permanent," *Asian Survey* 10, no. 1 (January 1970): 17.

46. Harry Harding, Jr., "China: Toward Revolutionary Pragmatism," *Asian Survey* 11, no. 1 (January 1971): 51–67.

47. Daniel Tretiak, "Is China Preparing to Turn Out? Changes in Chinese Levels of Attention to the International Environment," *Asian Survey* 11, no. 3 (March 1971): 219–37.

48. Harry Harding, Jr., "China: The Fragmentation of Power," *Asian Survey* 12, no. 1 (January 1972): 14.

49. Parris H. Chang, "Regional Military Power: The Aftermath of the 'Cultural Revolution,'" *Asian Survey* 12, no. 12 (December 1972): 1013.

50. Parris H. Chang, "Decentralization of Power," *Problems of Communism* 21, no. 4 (July-August 1972): 74.

51. See Martin K. Whyte, "'Red vs. Expert': Peking's Changing Policy," *Problems of Communism* 21, no. 6 (November-December 1972): 18–27.

52. Richard Wich, "The Tenth Party Congress: The Power Struggle and the Succession Question," *The China Quarterly*, no. 58 (April-June 1974): 248.

53. Alan P. L. Liu, "Control of Public Information and Its Effects on China's Foreign Affairs," *Asian Survey* 14, no. 10 (October 1974): 950.

54. Parris H. Chang, "The Passing of the Maoist Era," *Asian Survey* 16, no. 11 (November 1976): 1010. Writing in the summer of 1976, Chang saw the Beijing regime lurching toward "praetorian politics," because the rules of the game had dissolved within party politics. See his "Mao's Last Stand?", *Problems of Communism* 25, no. 4 (July-August 1976): 16–17.

55. Allen S. Whiting, "China After Mao," *Asian Survey* 17, no. 11 (November 1977): 1028.

56. Harry Harding, Jr., "China After Mao," *Problems of Communism* 26, no. 2 (March-April 1977): 1–18.

57. Maurice Meisner, "The Maoist Legacy and Chinese Socialism," *Asian Survey* 17, no. 11 (November 1977): 1027. Meisner predicted the "permanence of bureaucracy and its dominance over society" (ibid.).

58. Joyce K. Kallgren, "China 1979: The New Long March," *Asian Survey* 19, no. 1 (January 1979): 18. In their predictions of developments in the post-Mao period, American China-watchers preferred to be cautious and to define more carefully the ongoing processes within China. See Harding, "China After Mao," pp. 15–18.

59. Robert Michael Field, "Chinese Agriculture in the 1970s: Production, Consumption, and Trade," *Asian Survey* 13, no. 10 (October 1973): 908–13.

60. Kuan-I Chen and Robert T. Tsuchigane, "An Assessment of China's Foodgrain Supplies in 1980," *Asian Survey* 16, no. 10 (October 1976): 931–47.

61. Alexander Eckstein, "Economic Growth and Change in China: A Twenty-Year Perspective," *The China Quarterly*, no. 54 (April-June 1973): 241. A. Doak Barnett (*China and the Major Powers in East Asia* [Washington, D.C.: The Brookings Institution, 1977], p. 269) also saw continuing economic growth in China.

62. Chang Ching-wen, "An Analysis of the Newly Elected 9th CCP Central Committee," *FCYP* 12, no. 3 (April 1969): 17.

63. These findings are discussed in greater detail in "An Analysis of the Situation in Mainland China After the CCP 9th National Congress," *WTYYC* 8, no. 9 (June 1969): 1–17.

64. Li T'ien-min, "Mao-Lin Relationship and the Future of Lin Piao," *Proceedings of the First Sino-American Conference on Mainland China* (Taipei: The Institute of International Relations, 1970).

65. "New Developments in the Chinese Communist Internal Struggle," *Chungkung yen-chiu (CKYC)*, 7, no. 1 (January 1973): 4.

66. Chung Tao, "The Return of Teng Hsiao-p'ing and the CCP's Internal Crisis," *CKYC* 7, no. 5 (May 1973): 16.

67. Chang Cheng-pang, "On the Cultural Revolutionaries," *CKYC* 8, no. 10 (October 1974): 40.

68. For ROC commentators' predictions about Teng's future, see Editorial Board, "Major Events on the Chinese Mainland," *FCYP* 18, no. 8 (February 1976): 1–7 and Editorial Board, "Major Events on the Chinese Mainland," *FCYP* 18, no. 9 (March 1976): 1–7. It should be mentioned, however, that some ROC experts erroneously predicted Chou En-lai's successor. Li T'ien-min, for example, believed that Chang Ch'un-ch'iao would follow Chou, but Mao instead engineered the selection of Hua Kuo-feng.

69. Chang Cheng-pang, "On the Cultural Revolutionaries," *CKYC* 8, no. 10 (October 1974): 39–46.

70. Ch'iu K'ung-yuan, "An Observation on the Power Transition Within the CCP," *FCYP* 18, no. 6 (December 1975): 10.

71. Li T'ien-min, "Communist China After Chou En-lai," *FCYP* 18, no. 7 (January 1976): 10.

72. Warren Kuo, "Communist China in the Post-Mao Period: Possible Development of the Power Struggle" (Address delivered on September 30, 1976 at the Armed Forces University); later published in *Issues & Studies* (12, no. 11 [November 1976]: 15).

73. Ibid., p. 20.

74. Cheng Hsüeh-chia, "On the Death of Mao Tse-tung," *Chuang-hua tsa-chih*, October 1976, p. 13.

75. Ibid., p. 14.

76. Li T'ien-min, "The Cultural Revolution: Its Past and Future," *The 5th Sino-American Conference on Mainland China* (Taipei: The Institute of International Relations, July 1976), pp. 212–24. The Tienanmen Incident occurred in Beijing on April 5, 1976.

77. Ibid., pp. 212–24.

78. Li Chiu-i, "A Brief Analysis of Hua Kuo-feng's Past and His Future Moves," *FCYP* 13, no. 6 (December 1976): 27.

79. Editorial Board, "The Significance of the October 6th Coup D'état and the Trends Originating from That Incident," *CKYC* 10, no. 11 (November 1976): 4–5.

80. Ch'iu K'ung-yuan, "The October Coup in Peking and Its Aftermath," *Issues & Studies* 13, no. 1 (January 1977): 1–11.

6 ■ *UNDERSTANDING BY MEANS OF*
INTERPRETATION OF THE EVENT

1. Thomas P. Bernstein, "Leadership and Mass Mobilization in the Soviet and Chinese Collectivization Campaigns of 1929–30 and 1955–56: A Comparison," *The China Quarterly*, no. 31 (July-September 1967): 1–47.

2. Ibid., p. 45.

3. Philip Bridgham, Arthur Cohen, and Leonard Jaffe, "Mao's Road and Sino-Soviet Relations: A View From Washington, 1953," *The China Quarterly*, no. 52 (October-December 1972): 670–98.

4. Ibid., p. 671.

5. Ibid., p. 676.

6. Ibid., p. 695.

7. Chao Yu-shen, "The Three Transformations in the PRC," *Monograph on Politics in the People's Republic* (Taipei: The Institute of International Relations, 1975), pp. 92–122. (In Chinese)

8. Other ROC experts also observed the CCP's successes in carrying out its five major campaigns between 1949 and 1953, but they contended that, because of the speed and harshness of these campaigns, the CCP paid a high price; it simultaneously used up its good will with the populace and demoralized many party cadres. They further argued that these campaigns damaged the economy and society, which made the country especially weak and vulnerable during future campaigns.

9. Instead of citing Teiwes' many essays, we will mention only his *Politics and Purges in China: Rectification and the Decline of Party Norms* (White Plains, N.Y.: M. E. Sharpe, 1979).

10. Frederick C. Teiwes, "'Rules of the Game' in Chinese Politics," *Problems of Communism* 38, nos. 5–6 (September-December 1979): 69.

11. Because vital information about the purging of Kao Kang and Jao Hsu-shih in 1954 is still lacking—particularly on the impact of this incident on the behavior and morale of the Central Committee membership—Teiwes does not allude to it. We also ignore it, but readers should ponder whether or not this purge set into motion the subsequent erosion of party political norms.

12. Michel Oksenberg, "The Exit Pattern From Chinese Politics and Its Implications," *The China Quarterly*, no. 67 (September 1976): 507.

13. Ibid., pp. 517–18.

14. K'ung Teh-liang, "A Brief Review of CCP Activities During the Past Fifty Years," *Issues & Studies* 7, no. 11 (August 1971): 53–63.

15. Ibid., p. 61.

16. Wang Hsüeh-wen, "The Nature and Development of the Great Proletarian Cultural Revolution," *Fei-ch'ing yueh-pao* (*FCYP*) 11, no. 4 (May 1968): 24–30.

17. Tsen Yung-hsien, "An Analysis of the P'eng-Huang Incident," *Monograph on the Intra-party Struggle of the Chinese Communist Party* (Taipei: The Institute of International Relations, 1975), pp. 249–62.

18. Ibid., p. 261.

19. Many studies analyze the political developments of 1966–67, especially the social dynamics underlying the Cultural Revolution, but they ignore the complex origins of the movement before 1966. Some of these studies will be considered when we examine the process of the Cultural Revolution itself.

20. See Franz Michael, "The Struggle for Power," *Problems of Communism* 16, no. 3 (May-June 1967): 18–20 for one account of how Mao tried to reconquer the party.

21. Gene T. Hsiao, "The Background and Development of 'The Proletarian Cultural Revolution,'" *Asian Survey* 7, no. 6 (June 1967): 389–404.

22. Charles Neuhauser, "The Chinese Communist Party in the 1960s: Prelude to the Cultural Revolution," *The China Quarterly,* no. 32 (October-December 1967): 7.

23. Harry Gelman, "Mao and the Permanent Purge," *Problems of Communism* 15, no. 6 (November-December 1966): 2–14. See also Byung-Joon Ahn, "The Politics of Peking Opera, 1962–1965," *Asian Survey* 12, no. 12 (December 1972): 1066–81. Ahn sees the Cultural Revolution as originating from the satires written about Mao's late 1950s policies under the "guise of artistic and academic themes" (ibid., p. 1066). Because Mao lacked the power to ban plays and articles criticizing him, he organized his followers (like Chiang Ch'ing) to criticize his literary detractors.

24. Richard D. Baum, "Ideology Redivivus," *Problems of Communism* 16, no. 3 (May-June 1967): 1.

25. Philip Bridgham, "Mao's 'Cultural Revolution': Origin and Development," *The China Quarterly,* no. 29 (January-March 1967): 1–35.

26. Richard M. Pfeffer, "The Pursuit of Purity: Mao's Cultural Revolution," *Problems of Communism* 18, no. 6 (November-December 1969): 22.

27. Ibid.

28. An argument similar to Pfeffer's can be found in Maurice Meisner, *Mao's China* (New York: The Free Press, 1977), chap. 17.

29. Chalmers Johnson, "The Two Chinese Revolutions," *The China Quarterly,* no. 39 (July-September 1969): 12–29.

30. Tang Tsou, "The Cultural Revolution and the Chinese Political System," *The China Quarterly,* no. 38 (April-June 1969): 63–91.

31. Paul J. Hiniker, "The Cultural Revolution Revisited: Dissonance Reduction or Power Maximization," *The China Quarterly,* no. 94 (June 1983): 282–303. Hiniker refers to this explanation as a theory of cognitive dissonance.

32. Li Min-hua, "The Cultural Revolution in Mainland China," *Monograph on the Politics of the People's Republic* (Taipei: The Institute of International Relations, 1975), p. 167.

33. Ting Kuang-hua, "The Power Struggle Between Mao Tse-tung and Liu Shao-ch'i," *FCYP* 6, no. 4 (January 1967): 31–36.

34. K'ung Teh-liang, "A Brief Review of CCP's Activities During the Past Fifty Years," pt. 3, *Issues & Studies* 7, no. 12 (September 1971): 78–89. See also pt. 2 of the same article in *Issues & Studies* 7, no. 11 (August 1971): 78–89.

35. Tsen Yung-hsien, "An Analysis of the P'eng-Huang Incident," *Monograph on the Politics of the People's Republic* (Taipei: The Institute of International Relations, 1975).

36. For this line of argument, see the following writings: Ting Kuang-hua, "The Power Struggle Between Mao Tse-tung and Liu Shao-ch'i," *FCYP* 6, no. 4 (January

1967): 31–36; K'ung Teh-liang "Brief Review of the CCP's Activities," pt. 3, pp. 78–89; and Li T'ien-min, "The Big Struggle on the China Mainland," *Issues & Studies* 2, no. 11 (August 1966): 1–14.

37. Wu Nan-hsing, *Notes of the Three-Family Village* (Beijing: People's Literary Press, 1979), p. 61. (First published in 1961.)

38. Ibid., p. 8.

39. Wang Chang-ling, "A Comparative Study of the Ideological Lines of Mao Tse-tung and Liu Shao-ch'i," *FCYP* 10, no. 10 (November 1967): 14–18, and *FCYP* 10, no. 11 (December 1967): 33–38.

40. See also Wang Hsüeh-wen, "The Nature and Development of the Great Proletarian Cultural Revolution," *FCYP* 11, no. 4 (May 1968): 24–30.

41. Chen Li-sheng, *The Cultural Revolution and Political Struggle on the China Mainland* (Taipei: Li-min Publication Co., 1974), p. 7.

42. Chalmers Johnson, "China: The Cultural Revolution in Structural Perspective," *Asian Survey* 8, no. 1 (January 1968): 1–15.

43. Ibid., p. 1.

44. The precise analytical model explicating this interpretation can be found in Lowell Dittmer, *Liu Shao-ch'i and the Chinese Cultural Revolution: The Politics of Mass Criticism* (Berkeley, Los Angeles, and London: University of California Press, 1974), pp. 298–99. The empirical evidence for this interpretation is presented in chapters 9 and 10.

45. Lowell Dittmer, "'Line Struggle' in Theory and Practice: The Origins of the Cultural Revolution Reconsidered," *The China Quarterly*, no. 72 (December 1977): 707.

46. Hong Yung Lee, *The Politics of the Chinese Cultural Revolution: A Case Study* (Berkeley, Los Angeles, and London: University of California Press, 1978), p. 5.

47. Ibid., p. 9.

48. Barry Burton, "The Cultural Revolution's Ultra Left Conspiracy: The 'May 16 Group,'" *Asian Survey* 11, no. 11 (November 1971): 1029–53.

49. Juliana Pennington Heaslet, "The Red Guards: Instruments of Destruction in the Cultural Revolution," *Asian Survey* 12, no. 12 (December 1972): 1032–47. See also John Israel, "The Red Guards in Historical Perspective: Continuity and Change in the Chinese Youth Movement," *The China Quarterly*, no. 30 (April-June 1967): 1–32. Hong Yung Lee, using Kwangtung as a case study, also postulated that the radical students in the Cultural Revolution tried to redress grievances rather than promote group interests. See Hong Yung Lee, "The Radical Students in Kwangtung during the Cultural Revolution," *The China Quarterly*, no. 64 (December 1975): 645–83. For a more recent work, see Stanley Rosen, *Red Guard Factionalism and the Cultural Revolution in Guangzhou (Canton)* (Boulder, Colo.: Westview Press, 1982). See also the review of this work by Lynn T. White III (*Journal of Asian Studies* 62, no. 4 [August 1982]: 936–38).

50. Gardel Feurtado, "The Formation of Provincial Revolutionary Committees,

1966–68: Heilungkiang and Hopei," *Asian Survey* 12, no. 12 (December 1972): 1031.

51. Parris H. Chang, "Mao's Great Purge: A Political Balance Sheet," *Problems of Communism* 18, no. 2 (March-April 1969): 1–10.

52. Parris H. Chang, "Decentralization of Power," *Problems of Communism* 21, no. 4 (July-August 1972): 67–74. For a more complex view of this same thesis, see Lewis M. Stern, "Politics Without Consensus: Center-Province Relations and Political Communications in China, January 1976-January 1977," *Asian Survey* 19, no. 3 (March 1979): 260–80. For another argument, which emphasizes the new, important role of the army in provincial and national politics, see Gene T. Hsiao, "The Background and Development of 'The Proletarian Cultural Revolution,'" *Asian Survey* 7, no. 6 (June 1967): 389–404.

53. Parris H. Chang, "Regional Military Power: The Aftermath of the Cultural Revolution," *Asian Survey* 12, no. 12 (December 1972): 1010. For support of this viewpoint, see George C. S. Sung, "China's Regional Politics: A Biographical Approach," *Asian Survey* 15, no. 4 (April 1975): 346–65.

54. Robert A. Scalapino, "The CCP's Provincial Secretaries," *Problems of Communism* 25, no. 4 (July-August 1976): 18–35. See also Gordon Bennett's analysis of 158 provincial secretaries and deputy secretaries in the newly created provincial committees between December 4, 1970 and August 24, 1971, which showed that a large share of these secretaries came from outside their current province ("Military Regions and Provincial Party Secretaries: One Outcome of China's Cultural Revolution," *The China Quarterly*, no. 54 [April-June 1973]: 294). This observation suggests that less decentralization had taken place at the provincial level than had been assumed.

55. Harvey Nelsen, "Military Forces in the Cultural Revolution," *The China Quarterly*, no. 51 (July-September 1972): 444–74.

56. Victor C. Falkenheim, "Continuing Central Predominance," *Problems of Communism* 21, no. 4 (July-August 1972): 83.

57. Harry Harding, Jr., "China: The Fragmentation of Power," *Asian Survey* 12, no. 1 (January 1972): 1–15.

58. Richard M. Pfeffer, "Serving the People and Continuing the Revolution," *The China Quarterly*, no. 52 (October-December 1972): 620. Many works could be mentioned here. See Rensselaer W. Lee III, "Ideology and Technical Innovation in Chinese Industry, 1949–1971," *Asian Survey* 12, no. 8 (August 1972): 647–61, which describes how the Cultural Revolution encouraged workers to compare their work experiences and introduce many innovations. See also the cluster of works mentioned in chapter 2 that relate to the revolutionary socialist regime typology.

59. See Gordon A. Bennett, "China's Continuing Revolution: Will It Be Permanent?", *Asian Survey* 10, no. 1 (January 1970): 2–17.

60. Philip Bridgham, "Mao's Cultural Revolution: The Struggle to Consolidate Power," *The China Quarterly*, no. 41 (January-March 1970): 1–25.

61. Philip Bridgham, "The Fall of Lin Piao," *The China Quarterly,* no. 55 (July-September 1973): 427–49.

62. Ying-mao Kau and Pierre M. Perrolle, "The Politics of Lin Piao's Abortive Military Coup," *Asian Survey* 14, no. 6 (June 1974): 573–74.

63. John Bryan Starr, "China in 1974: Weeding Through the Old to Bring Forth the New," *Asian Survey* 15, no. 1 (January 1975): 1.

64. Merle Goldman, "China's Anti-Confucius Campaign, 1973–74," *The China Quarterly,* no. 63 (September 1975): 461.

65. Parris H. Chang, "The Anti-Lin Piao and Confucius Campaign: Its Meaning and Purposes," *Asian Survey* 14, no. 10 (October 1974): 871–86.

66. A. James Gregor and Maria Hsia Chang, "Anti-Confucianism: Mao's Last Campaign," *Asian Survey* 19, no. 11 (November 1979): 1077.

67. Edward E. Rice, "The Second Rise and Fall of Teng Hsiao-p'ing," *The China Quarterly,* no. 67 (September 1967): 494–500.

68. Chen Li-sheng, *The Cultural Revolution and Political Struggle in the Chinese Mainland* (Taipei: Li-min Publication Co., 1974), pp. 17–18. See also Cheng Hsüeh-chia, *The Cultural Revolution and the Intra-party Struggle of the CCP* (Taipei: Chang Wang Publication Co., 1969), pp. 1–16.

69. Cheng Hsüeh-chia, *Cultural Revolution and Intra-party Struggle,* p. 4.

70. Chen Li-sheng, *Cultural Revolution and Political Struggle,* pp. 99–100.

71. For a discussion of Liu's clique, of local party leaders' resistance to the Cultural Revolution, and of the violent clashes that occurred throughout mainland China, see K'ung Teh-liang, "An Analysis of the Current Conditions Surrounding the Cultural Revolution," *FCYP* 9, no. 10 (November 1966): 13–16; Su Hui, "The New Development of the Power Struggle in China," *FCYC* 1, no. 2 (February 1967): 10–15; and Wang Chang-ling, "The Power Struggle in Mainland Provinces and Cities," *FCYP* 10, no. 1 (February 1967): 36–42.

72. Wang Chang-ling, "The Great Cultural Revolution and the Red Guards," *Issues & Studies* 3, no. 2 (November 1966): 4–13; Wang Hsüeh-wen, "The Background of the Red Guards Movement," *FCYP* 9, no. 8 (September 1966): 14–20; and Shu Hui, "An Examination of the Red Guards Movement," *Fei-ch'ing yen-chiu (FCYC)* 9, no. 9 (September 1966): 1–9.

73. Cheng Hsüeh-chia, *Cultural Revolution and Intra-party Struggle,* p. 10.

74. Wang Chang-ling, "The Essence of the Cultural Revolution," *FCYP* 10, no. 3 (May 1967): 25.

75. K'ung Te-liang, "A Brief Review of the CCP Activities During the Past Fifty Years," pt. 1 *Issues & Studies* 7, no. 10 (July 1971): 35.

76. Chang Ching-wen, "Problems Facing the Mao-Lin Clique After the 9th National Congress," *Issues & Studies* 5, no. 12 (September 1962): 12.

77. Hsuan Mo, "Revolutionary Criticism and Ideological Confusion in Communist China," *Monograph on Politics of the People's Republic* (Taipei: The Institute of International Relations, 1975), p. 176.

78. Chang Ching-wen, "Problems Facing the Mao-Lin Clique," p. 18.

79. Li T'ien-min, "On the Lin Piao Incident," *Monograph on Chinese Communism* (Taipei: The Institute of International Relations, 1973), pp. 274–95 and Li Min-hua, "The Cultural Revolution on the Chinese Mainland," *Monograph on Politics of the People's Republic* (Taipei: The Institute of International Relations, 1975), pp. 145–67.

80. Radio Lanchow, September 17, 1972; in *Foreign Broadcasting Information Service (FBIS)*, September 19, 1972, p. H-1.

81. Chuan Tsun, "A Reappraisal of the Mao-Lin Relations and the Lin Piao Incident," *FCYP* 17, no. 4 (June 1974): 30.

82. Hsiang Nai-kuang, "An Analysis of Peking's Second Cultural Revolution," *Chung-kung yen-chiu (CKYC)* 8, no. 3 (March 1974): 4–7.

83. Li T'ien-min, "Chou En-lai: After the CCP 10th National Congress," *Issues & Studies* 10, no. 3 (December 1973): 10–20 and Li T'ien-min, "Why Did Mao Tse-tung Launch the Movement to Criticize Lin Piao and Confucius?", *Proceedings of the Fourth Sino-American Conference on Mainland China* (Taipei: The Institute of International Relations, 1975). Li Chung-ta also disagreed that the target of the movement was Chou En-lai. See Li Chung-ta, "The Movement to Criticize Lin Piao and Confucius as Viewed From Another Angle," *FCYP* 17, no. 2 (April 1974): 22–27.

84. Wang Jo-shui, deputy editor-in-chief of *Jen-min jih-pao*, made these revelations. (See "The Lesson We Got from the Cultural Revolution," *Min-Pao Monthly* 15, no. 2 [February 1980]: 2–15.)

85. Many conferences and books have been devoted to this topic. See Stuart R. Schram, ed. *Authority, Participation, and Cultural Change in China* (Cambridge: Cambridge University Press, 1973). Although the volume was written primarily by European scholars, Stuart R. Schram, an American, edited it and wrote the longest essay on the events leading up to the Cultural Revolution. The book focuses entirely on the impact of the Cultural Revolution on China.

86. Robert S. Wang, "Educational Reforms and the Cultural Revolution: The Chinese Evaluation Process," *Asian Survey* 15, no. 9 (September 1975): 758–74.

87. Frederick C. Teiwes, "Before and After the Cultural Revolution," *The China Quarterly*, no. 58 (April-May 1974): 348.

88. Thomas W. Robinson, "China in 1973: Renewed Leftism Threatens the 'New Course,'" *Asian Survey* 14, no. 1 (January 1974): 11. For a similar view, developed in a different way, see Byung-Joon Ahn, "The Cultural Revolution and China's Search for Political Order," *The China Quarterly*, no. 58 (April-May 1974): 249–85.

89. William L. Parish, "China—Team, Brigade, or Commune?", *Problems of Communism* 25, no. 2 (March-April 1976): 51–65.

90. Hong Yung Lee, "Mao's Strategy for Revolutionary Change: A Case Study of the Cultural Revolution," *The China Quarterly*, no. 77 (March 1978): 62.

91. Lowell Dittmer, "Mass Line and Mass Criticism in China: An Analysis of

the Fall of Liu Shao-ch'i," *Asian Survey* 13, no. 8 (August 1973): 772–92 and idem, "The Structural Evaluation of 'Criticism and Self-Criticism,'" *The China Quarterly,* no. 56 (October-December 1973): 708–29.

92. Michel Oksenberg and Richard Bush, "China's Political Evolution, 1972–81," *Problems of Communism* (September-October 1982): 3. The views expressed in this article about the significance of the Cultural Revolution for the leaders and people are very different from those expressed by Michel Oksenberg (*China: The Convulsive Society* [New York: Foreign Policy Association: 1970]). Oksenberg's study tried to explain the meaning of the Cultural Revolution in terms of China's intellectual debates and modernization instead of in terms of the kind of political order that was evolving in the late 1960s.

93. Edward Friedman, "The Politics of Local Models, Social Transformation and State Power Struggles in the People's Republic of China: Tachai and Teng Hsiao-p'ing," *The China Quarterly,* no. 76 (December 1978): 873–90.

94. Byung-joon Ahn, "The Cultural Revolution and China's Search for Political Order," *The China Quarterly,* no. 58 (April-June 1974): 284.

95. Edward Friedman, "Cultural Limits of the Cultural Revolution," *Asian Survey* 9, no. 3 (March 1969): 138–201.

96. Hsuan Mo, "Revolutionary Criticism and Ideological Confusion in the People's Republic," *Monograph on Politics of the People's Republic* (Taipei: The Institute of International Relations, 1975), p. 175.

97. Warren Kuo, "A Study of Mao Tse-tung's Successor," *Issues & Studies* 10, no. 4 (January 1974): 31.

98. Warren Kuo, "The Evolution of the Chinese Communist Party," *Proceedings of the 4th Sino-American Conference on Mainland China* (Taipei: The Institute of International Relations, 1974).

7 ■ UNDERSTANDING THE CHINESE COMMUNIST SYSTEM

1. Edward E. Rice, "A Radical Break With the Past," *Problems of Communism* 23, no. 5 (September-October 1974): 16.

2. Warren Kuo, "China Studies in the ROC," *Fei-ch'ing yueh-pao* (*FCYP*) 14, no. 11 (December 1971): 14.

3. Rice, "Radical Break With the Past," p. 17.

4. Ezra F. Vogel, *Canton Under Communism: Programs and Politics in a Provincial Capital, 1949–1968* (Cambridge: Harvard University Press, 1969), p. 351.

5. Ibid., p. 117. Few studies have pointed out this strategy used by the CCP to crush its opponents.

6. Ibid., p. 351.

7. James R. Townsend, *Political Participation in Communist China* (Berkeley and Los Angeles: University of California Press, 1967), pp. 51–69.

8. Ibid., chap. 7. Townsend has re-emphasized this point in a later study. See his *Politics in China* (Boston: Little, Brown and Company, 1974), chap. 8. Townsend concludes his study by pointing out that, although many citizens were actively involved with the new political system, and, if given access, more would have responded, the regime had not yet highly institutionalized its new political arrangements.

9. Victor C. Falkenheim, "Political Participation in China," *Problems of Communism* 27, no. 3 (May-June 1978): 18–32. The author interviewed a sample of thirty-seven informants to elicit his findings.

10. Robert Jay Lifton, M.D., *Thought Reform and the Psychology of Totalism: A Study of "Brainwashing" in China* (New York: W. W. Norton and Company, 1961), p. 420.

11. Ibid., p. 422.

12. William L. Parish and Martin King Whyte, *Village and Family in Contemporary China* (Chicago: The University of Chicago, 1978), p. 9.

13. Ibid., p. 71. See also Martin King Whyte ("Inequality and Stratification in China," *The China Quarterly*, no. 64 [December 1975], pp. 684–711), who concludes that after the early 1950s income distribution remained relatively unchanged and that urban-rural stratification differences remained sharp.

14. Lynn T. White III, *Careers in Shanghai* (Berkeley, Los Angeles, and London: University of California Press, 1978), p. 227.

15. Leo A. Orleans, *Every Fifth Child: The Population of China* (Stanford: Stanford University Press, 1972).

16. Thomas G. Rawski, *Economic Growth and Employment in China* (New York and Oxford: Oxford University Press, 1979), p. 117.

17. Ibid., p. 119.

18. Dwight H. Perkins, "Research on the Economy of the People's Republic of China: A Survey of the Field," *The Journal of Asian Studies* 42, no. 2 (February 1983): 350. The economic literature is so large and varied that we will not attempt to refer to all studies.

19. Ta-chung Liu, "Quantitative Trends in the Economy," in Alexander Eckstein, Walter Galenson, and Ta-chung Liu, eds., *Economic Trends in Communist China* (Chicago: Aldine, 1968), p. 143.

20. Ibid., p. 168.

21. Rawski, *Economic Growth and Employment in China*, p. 121.

22. Anthony M. Tang, "Input-Output Relations in the Agriculture of Communist China, 1952–65," in W. A. Douglas Jackson, ed., *Agrarian Policies and Problems in Communist and Non-Communist Countries* (Seattle: University of Washington Press, 1971), pp. 289–95.

23. Thomas G. Rawski, "The Growth of Producers Industries, 1900–1971," in Dwight H. Perkins, ed., *China's Modern Economy in Historical Perspective* (Stanford: Stanford University Press, 1975), pp. 224–25.

24. See, for example, Xu Dixin et al., *China's Search For Economic Growth: The Chinese Economy Since 1949* (Beijing: New World Press, 1982), p. 16. Many other Chinese sources could also be cited.

25. Kang Chao, "The China-Watchers Tested," *The China Quarterly*, no. 81 (March 1980): 104.

26. Michel Oksenberg, "Methods of Communication Within the Chinese Bureaucracy," *The China Quarterly*, no. 57 (January-March 1974): 39.

27. John P. Burns, "The Election of Production Team Cadres in Rural China: 1958–74," *The China Quarterly*, no. 74 (June 1978): 296.

28. Kenneth Lieberthal, "The Suppression of Secret Societies in Post-Liberation Tientsin," *The China Quarterly*, no. 54 (April-June 1973): 266.

29. David M. Lampton, "Performance and the Chinese Political System: A Preliminary Assessment of Education and Health Policies," *The China Quarterly*, no. 75 (September 1978): 509–39.

30. David M. Lampton, "Health Policy During the Great Leap Forward," *The China Quarterly*, no. 60 (October-December 1974): 668.

31. Ralph W. Huenemann, "Urban Rationing in Communist China," *The China Quarterly*, no. 26. (April-June 1966): 51.

32. Ibid., p. 57.

33. Dwight H. Perkins, *Market Control and Planning in Communist China* (Cambridge: Harvard University Press, 1966), chap. 1.

34. Vivienne Shue, *Peasant China in Transition: The Dynamics of Development Toward Socialism, 1949–1956* (Berkeley, Los Angeles, and London: University of California Press, 1980), chap. 8.

35. Dwight H. Perkins and the American Rural Small-Scale Industry Delegation, eds., *Rural Small-Scale Industry in the People's Republic of China* (Berkeley, Los Angeles, and London: University of California Press, 1977), chap. 4.

36. Dwight H. Perkins, "The Central Features of China's Economic Development," in Robert F. Dernberger, ed., *China's Development Experience in Comparative Perspective* (Cambridge: Harvard University Press, 1980).

37. Ibid., p. 148.

38. John A. Kringen, "An Exploration of the 'Red-Expert' Issue in China Through Content Analysis," *Asian Survey* 15, no. 8 (August 1975): 693–707.

39. Thomas P. Bernstein, "Problems of Village Leadership After Land Reform," *The China Quarterly*, no. 36 (October-December 1968): 1–22.

40. Ying-mao Kau, "The Urban Bureaucratic Elite in Communist China: A Case Study of Wuhan, 1949–65," in A. Doak Barnett, ed., *Chinese Communist Politics in Action* (Seattle and London: University of Washington Press, 1969), pp. 216–67.

41. Richard Baum, "Elite Behavior Under Conditions of Stress: The Lesson of the 'Tang-Ch'uan P'ai' in the Cultural Revolution," in Robert A. Scalapino, ed., *Elites in the People's Republic of China* (Seattle and London: University of Washington Press, 1972), pp. 552–55.

42. Many other essays reporting the dysfunctional aspects of this relocation policy could be cited, but one very good one is Thomas P. Bernstein, "Urban Youth in the Countryside: Problems of Adaptation and Remedies," *The China Quarterly,* no. 69 (March 1977): 75–108. See also Thomas P. Bernstein, *Up to the Mountains and Down to the Villages: The Transfer of Youth from Urban to Rural China* (New Haven, Conn.: Yale University Press, 1977).

43. John Lossing Buck, Owen L. Dawson, and Yuan-li Wu, *Food and Agriculture in Communist China* (New York and Washington: Frederick A. Praeger, 1966), pp. 50–51.

44. Miriam London and Ivan D. London, "The Other China," pt. 1, *World View* 19, no. 5 (May 1976): 4–11; ibid., pt. 2, 19, no. 6. (June 1976): 43–48; ibid., pt. 3, 19, nos. 7–8 (July-August 1976): 25–26 and 35–37.

45. See Dennis L. Chinn, "Income Distribution in a Chinese Commune," *Journal of Comparative Economics,* no. 2 (September 1978): 246–65; Dennis L. Chinn, "Cooperative Farming in North China," *Quarterly Journal of Economics* 94, no. 2 (March 1980): 279–98; and Dennis L. Chinn, "Team Cohesion and Collective-Labor Supply in Chinese Agriculture," *Journal of Comparative Economics* 3, no. 4 (December 1979): 375–94. For policies affecting farm income, see Ramon H. Myers, "Wheat in China—Past, Present, and Future," *The China Quarterly,* no. 74 (June 1978): 297–333. For policies affecting farm prices, see Kang Chao, *Agricultural Production in Communist China, 1949–1965* (Madison, Milwaukee, and London: University of Wisconsin Press, 1970), pp. 62–63.

46. Yuan-li Wu, *The Steel Industry in Communist China* (New York, Washington, and London: Frederick A. Praeger, 1965), pp. 154–55.

47. Franz Schurmann, *Ideology and Organization in Communist China* (Berkeley and Los Angeles: University of California Press, 1966), pp. 220–308, esp. p. 279.

48. Vincent Chen, "The Significance of the Mass Campaign in Mainland China," *Issues & Studies* 7, no. 10 (July 1971): 57.

49. Chang Ching-wen, "The Mass Movement of the Chinese Communists," *Monograph on the Politics of the People's Republic* (Taipei: The Institute of International Relations, 1975), p. 80.

50. Hsuan Mo, "The Revolutionary Criticism and Ideological Confusion in Mainland China," *Monograph on the Politics of the People's Republic* (Taipei: The Institute of International Relations, 1975), p. 179.

51. Warren Kuo, "Oppression and Persecution in Communist China," *Issues & Studies* 13, no. 4 (April 1977): 19.

52. Ibid., p. 19.

53. Wang Chang-ling, "The Evolution of the Family System in Mainland China," *Fei-ch'ing yen-chiu (FCYC)* 12, no. 10 (December 1969): 54 and Wang Chang-ling, "The Social Classes in the Chinese Mainland," *FCYP* 13, no. 2 (April 1970): 24–29.

54. Wang Chang-ling, "The Changes in the Social Structure in the Chinese Mainland," *FCYP* 11, no. 11 (January 1969): 38–43.

55. Hsuan Mo, "Built-in Traumas in Communist China," *Issues & Studies* 17, no. 5 (May 1981): 49.

56. Winberg Chai, "The Impact of Ideology Upon Public Policy in Mainland China," *Issues & Studies* 6, no. 9 (June 1970): 35.

57. Hsuan Mo, "Revolutionary Criticism and Ideological Confusion," p. 189.

58. King-yuh Chang, "Current Situation in Mainland China," *Issues & Studies* 17, no. 7 (July 1981): 12–13.

59. Hsuan Mo, "Built-in Traumas in Communist China," p. 56.

60. Ibid., p. 51.

61. S. J. Chang, "An Analysis of the Current Situation on the China Mainland," *Issues & Studies* 17, no. 5 (May 1981): 29.

8 ▪ *CONCLUSION*

1. George Urban, "Portrait of a Dissenter As a Soviet Man," *Encounter* 62, no. 4 (April 1984): 10. This interview continued in *Encounter* 62, no. 5 (May 1984): 30–38.

2. Urban, "Portrait of a Dissenter," (April 1984): 10.

3. See *Chung-kuo chih-ch'un (CKCC)*, no. 14 (August 1984), which contains many essays that describe the characteristics of the Chinese communist system.

4. Chai Chih-ch'eng, "Lun Chung-kung chi-chuan cheng-t'i chih ken-yuan" (The origins of the totalitarian political system in communist China) (*CKCC*), no. 14 (August 1984), p. 38.

INDEX

Ahn, Byung-joon, 105, 156
American Council of Learned Socie-
  ties, 2
American studies of Communist China:
  early beginnings, 2; difficulties of re-
  search, 10–12
Andors, Phyllis, 31
Andors, Stephen, 30–31
Antirightist struggle, 53

Banister, Judith, 59
Barnett, A. Doak, 20–21, 65–67, 70–
  71
Baum, Richard D., 91, 118
Bennett, Gordon A., 24, 73, 158
Berninghausen, Richard H., 142
Bernstein, Richard, 56, 59
Bernstein, Thomas P., 84–85, 118
Bloch, Marc, 1
Bridgman, Philip, 35, 91, 98
Brzezinski, Zbigniew, 17, 66
Buck, John Lossing, 119
Bulletin of Concerned Asian Scholars,
  29
Burns, John P., 115
Burton, Barry, 96
Bush, Richard, 161
Butterfield, Fox, 57–58

Catastrophes, 10, 37, 54, 59, 106, 119,
  128, 149

Central Intelligence Agency (CIA), 4,
  35
Chai, Winberg, 122
Chang, Cheng-pang, 7, 78–79
Chang, Ching-wen, 76–77, 103, 120
Chang, Ch'un-ch'iao, 62, 80
Chang, Maria Hsia, 99
Chang, Parris H., 36, 71, 74–75, 97,
  99, 153
Chang, Wen-t'ien, 89
Chao, Hsien-yün, 42
Chao, Hung-tse, 8
Chao, Yu-shen, 85–86
Ch'en, I, 94
Chen, Kuang, 152
Chen, Kuan-i, 25, 76
Chen, Li-sheng, 94, 99–100
Ch'en, Po-ta, 36, 98–99
Chen, Vincent, 120
Chen, Yü-ch'ang, 42, 72
Ch'en, Yun, 79, 87
Cheng, Chu-yuan, 35
Cheng, Hsüeh-chia, 42, 46, 80, 100–
  101
Cheng, J. Chester, 37
Cheng feng movement, 34
Chiang, Chen-ch'ang, 8
Chiang, Ch'ing, 73, 77–80, 94, 103–4
Chiang, Hsin-li, 8
China Quarterly, 8
Chinese communist regime, 32; typol-

Chinese communist regime (*cont.*)
ogy, 33; verification of typology, 60–61
Chinese communist totalitarian system, 40; typology, 41; verification of typology, 60–61
Ch'iu, K'ung-yuan, 81
Chou, Chia-tung, 72
Chou, En-lai, 9, 71–72, 74, 77–79, 87, 97–99, 104
Chou, Hsiao-chou, 89
Chou, Yang, 73, 99
Chou, Yu-shan, 8
Chu, Hsin-min, 45
Chu, Wen-lin, 7
Chung, Tao, 78
Chung-kuo chih ch'un [China Spring], 125, 165
Class struggle, 42
Cohen, Arthur A., 150
Communes, 53, 68, 87, 116–17, 152
Communist Party reports, 52–53
Communist-totalitarian China, 17; typology, 17; Stalinist-totalitarian, 19; costs imposed by totalitarian rule, 20–21; verification of typology, 59–60; description of China, 126
Corruption, 57–58
Counter-attacking the Right-deviationist Wind, 78
Cult of personality, 46, 55
Cultural Revolution, *see* Great Proletarian Cultural Revolution

Dawson, Owen L., 119
Defense, Department of (U.S.), 4
Democracy Wall movement, 81
Demographic change, 113
Dernberger, Robert, 26
Descriptive typology, 13–15, 137
Dittmer, Lowell, 95, 105

Eastman, Lloyd, 24
Economy: performance, 26, 32, 37, 58–59, 61–62, 69, 113–14, 119, 123; economic organization, 26; fluctuations, 26; income redistribution, 30; land reform, 30; industrial organization, 31; labor unions, 33; productivity, 38, 113; predictions, 66; policies, 116
Eckstein, Alexander, 25–26, 76
Eighth Party Congress, 19, 25, 67
Emery, Robert F., 70

Fairbank, John King, 2, 20, 62
Falkenheim, Victor C., 97, 110
Febvre, Lucien, 1
Field, Robert Michael, 26, 76
Fifth National People's Congress, 55
Ford Foundation, 3
Foreign area studies, early beginnings, 1–2
Foreign policy: united front tactics, 50; predictions, 60–61, 74; expansionism, 67
Four Clean movement, 10, 91, 137
Four Modernizations program, 122
Friedman, Edward, 105
Friedrich, Carl, 17
Fuertade, Gardel, 96
Fukien province, 8, 34, 97
Funnell, Victor, 143

Galbraith, John Kenneth, 61
Gelman, Harry, 91
Ginsburg, George, 34
Goldman, Merle, 39, 99
Goldstein, Steven, 36
Gotō, Shimpei, 1
Great Leap Forward campaign, 6, 23, 54, 120
Great Proletarian Cultural Revolution, 15, 23, 32–33, 35–36, 38, 44, 51, 54–55, 69–81, 155; origins, 89–94; interpretation, 89–107; as a process, 94–104; significance, 104–7
Gregor, A. James, 99
Gurley, John, 32

Halperin, Morton H., 71, 74
Harding, Harry, Jr., 24, 37, 74–75, 97

Harper, Paul, 33
Heaslet, Juliana Pennington, 96
Hiniker, Paul J., 92
Hollander, Paul, 34
Hsia fang campaign, 27, 91
Hsiao, Gene T., 90, 144
Hsiao, Yeh-hui, 7
Hsiao-tsu, 27
Hsieh, Fu-chih, 94
Hsing, Kuo-ch'ang, 45
Hsiung, Tse-chien, 8
Hsuan, Mo, 7, 103, 106, 120–23
Hu, Feng, 39
Hu, Yao-pang, 36, 53
Hua, Kuo-feng, 36, 52, 55, 75, 80–81
Huai-Jen Hall incident, 73
Huang, K'e-ch'eng, 89, 93
Huenemann, Ralph W., 116
Huters, Ted, 142

Income redistribution, 30, 117, 121
Industrial organization, 31; Soviet-style
   factory management, 31; wages, 31
Institute for the Study of Chinese Com-
   munist Problems (ISCCP), 6–8
Institute of International Relations
   (IIR), 6–9
Intellectuals, 34; control of, 34; thought
   reform of, 34, 111–12, 117; cam-
   paigns against, 38–39; persecution
   of, 121, 129
Issues & Studies, 9
Ivory, Paul, 28

Jao, Hsu-shih, 65
Johnson, Chalmers, 92, 95
Joint Committee for Contemporary
   China Studies, 2–3, 27, 142
Jones, Edwin F., 37

Kang, Chao, 114
Kao, Kang, 65
Kau, Ying-mao, 98, 118
Khrushchev, Nikita, 91
Kovanda, Karel, 137
Kringen, John A., 117

Kuan, Meng-hüeh, 85
K'ung, Teh-liang, 46, 48, 72, 87–88
Kung-tso t'ung-hsun [Bulletin of Activi-
   ties], 37
Kuo, Warren, 7, 42–45, 48–49, 79–80,
   106, 109, 121
Kwangtung province, 112, 128

Labor camps, 20, 38, 139, 141
Labor unions, 33
Lampton, David M., 115–16
Landing Craft Documents, 8, 136
Land reform, 84–85, 118
Lavely, William, 28
Lee, Hong Yung, 96, 105, 157
Lee, Rensselaer W., III, 158
Legal system, 26, 144; People's Courts,
   34; People's Procuratorate, 34
Lewis, John Wilson, 23, 37
Li, Chiu-i, 81
Li, Choh-ming, 37
Li, Chung-ta, 160
Li, Hsien-nien, 79
Li, Min-hua, 92
Li, T'ien-min, 7, 42, 47, 73, 77, 79–
   80, 152, 154
Li, Victor, 26
Liang-ke, ssu-ling-pu [two headquar-
   ters], 88
Liao, Kai-lung, 53
Lieberthal, Kenneth, 115
Lifton, Robert Jay, 111–12
Lin, Chen, 7
Lin, Li-kuo, 9
Lin, Piao, 8–9, 36, 48, 72–73, 77, 90–
   95 *passim,* 98–99, 101–3, 106; con-
   flict with Mao, 103; conflict with
   party members, 103
Ling, Ting, 34
Lippitt, Victor, 30
Lippmann, Walter, 150
Liu, Alan P. L., 37, 75
Liu, Shao-ch'i, 25, 35, 65–73 *passim,*
   78, 87–90, 92–94, 96, 98–102, 106
Liu, Sheng-chi, 8
Liu, T. C., 113–14

Lo, Jui-ch'ing, 78, 93, 99
London, Ivan D., 119
London, Miriam, 119
Lu, Ting-i, 73, 78, 99–100
Lushan plenum, 98

MacFarquhar, Roderick, 19, 25
Mao, Tse-tung, 9–10, 17–19 *passim,*
   23–29 *passim,* 36–49 *passim,* 54–55,
   62, 67–106, 119, 125–26, 130; authority challenged, 87; conflict with
   Liu Shao-ch'i, 88; conflict with P'eng
   Teh-huai, 89; return to power, 90;
   conflict with party leaders, 90, 92,
   98, 102; tactics and strategies, 95,
   100, 105; purging of opponents, 97,
   99; struggle with Lin Piao, 103; policies, significance of, 108–9
Marxist-Leninist theory, 42–43, 130
May 7th cadre schools, 62, 97
Meisner, Maurice, 75, 153
Metzger, Thomas A., 22
Michael, Franz, 35, 90
Modernization, 22, 124; standards of
   evaluation, 16–17; accommodative,
   22–23, 139; transformative, 22–24,
   139
Modernizing communist regime, 21; typology, 22; verification of typology,
   60
Moody, Peter, 35
Mosher, Steven W., 56, 58
Munro, Donald J., 139

Nathan, Andrew, 25, 140
Nelsen, Harvey, 97
Neuhauser, Charles, 91
Ninth National Congress (also Ninth
   Party Congress), 51, 106
North, Robert C., 19
Notes of the Three-Family Village, 90,
   93, 100

Oksenberg, Michel, 36, 62, 70, 87,
   115, 161

Oliver, Adam, 34
Orleans, Leo A., 26, 113
"Outline of 'Project 571'", 9

Parish, William L., 105, 112
Peck, James, 142
P'eng, Chen, 72–73, 78, 87, 90, 99–
   100
P'eng, Teh-huai, 38, 78, 87, 89, 91, 93
People's Liberation Army (PLA), 35–
   36, 38, 48, 73, 92, 94–95, 97, 99,
   107
Perkins, Dwight H., 113, 116–17
Perrolle, Pierre M., 98
Pfeffer, Richard M., 24, 91, 97
P'i-Lin p'i-K'ung [Anti–Lin Piao and
   Anti-Confucius Campaign], 98
Political control, 33, 35, 43, 56, 110–
   12, 115, 120–21; county administra-
   tion, 34; instruments of, 34, 45;
   power struggle and factionalism, 35–
   37, 47–48, 50, 87, 130; party leader
   groupings, 36
Political norms, 28–29, 38, 86–87
Political pathologies, 50
Polity: instability, 28; leadership, 28,
   87; bureaucratic communication, 115;
   elite behavior, 129
Population fertility (Shanghai), 28
Powell, Ralph L., 38
Prediction: political, 65–83; economic,
   70; foreign policy, 70–71
Production team, 115
Public Security Bureau, 35, 41
Pye, Lucian, 28–29

Rawski, Thomas G., 113–14
Red Guards, 48, 70, 73, 90, 94–96,
   100–102, 152, 157
Redistribution of property, 30, 117, 121
Research approaches, 12–14; narrative,
   13; social-science theory, 13; descriptive typology, 13–16; verification of
   typologies, 59–61

Research in Republic of China (ROC), 4–5; origins of Communist China research, 5; evolution of Communist China research, 6; research staff and institutions, 7–8; difficulties of research, 10–11

Research on Communist China in the United States: bias, 9–10; difficulties, 9–12; research approach, 12–14; approach of this study, 14–15

Revolutionary Councils, 97

Revolutionary socialist regime, 29; typology, 29; verification of typology, 60

Rice, Edward E., 99, 109–10

Riskin, Carl, 26, 30–31

Rostow, Walter, 17, 65

Runciman, W. G., 137

Salisbury, Harrison, 62

Scalapino, Robert A., 97

Schurmann, Franz, 120

Schwartz, Benjamin, 17, 23

Schwarz, Henry G., 8

Shih, Huang Ti, 109

Shu, Hui, 152

Shue, Vivienne, 116

Sino-Soviet split, 6

Smith, Norris P., 17

Socialist Education campaign, 91, 93

Socialist transformation, 15; predictions, 64–67; interpretation, 84–86

Social Sciences Research Council, 2–3

Society: values, 27, 142; social relations, 27, 46, 121–22; political values, 28; control of groups and behavior, 34, 44; social deviancy, 46–47; conditions, 62–63, 122; social change and mobility, 112, 118

Solomon, Richard H., 142

Spitz, Allan, 34

Stahnke, Arthur, 34

Stanford University–Taipei Language Center, 4

Starr, John Bryan, 24, 98

State, Department of (U.S.), 4

Steiner, Arthur, 17

Suttmeier, R. P., 140

Tang, Anthony M., 38, 114

T'ang, Chen-lin, 94

Tang, Peter S. H., 65

Tang, Tsou, 71, 92

Tan-wei [unit], 121

T'ao, Chu, 35

Taylor, George, 2, 60

Teiwes, Frederick C., 38, 86–87, 104

Teng, Hsiao-p'ing, 25, 36, 52, 55, 70–81 *passim*, 87–88, 90, 93–95, 99, 126

Teng, Kung-hsuan, 44

Teng, T'o, 72–73, 91, 93

Tenth National Congress, 51

Terrill, Ross, 63

Three Red Banners campaign, 15, 53, 59, 68–69; interpretation of, 86–89, 122

Tienanmen Square event, 1976, 104

Townsend, James R., 24, 110, 140, 162

Tretiak, Daniel, 74

Tsai, Hsiao-ch'ien, 7

Tsai, Hsuan, 72

Tsan-k'ao hsiao-hsi [Reference News], 8, 136

Ts'ao, Po-i, 42

Tsen, Yung-hśien, 89

Tseng, Yung-hsien, 73

Tsou-hou-men [going through the back door], 57

Tsuchigane, Robert T., 76

Tu-li wang-kuo [independent kingdom], 100

Understanding Communist China: comparative approach, 4; nature of communist society, 109, 125; character of party dominance over society, 110; social change, 112; economic change, 113–14; functional characteristics, 114–17; dysfunctional characteristics,

Understanding Communist China (*cont.*)
    117–23; by ROC and American ex-
    perts, 123–24; by Chinese scientists
    and scholars abroad, 126; comparing
    American and ROC experts, 127–31;
    difficulties, 127–30; future prospects
    of, 133
United-front tactics, 42, 49–50, 138;
    foreign policy, 50
United Research Institute, 3
Urban, George, 125

Vogel, Ezra, 27, 110

Walker, Richard L., 17, 64
Wang, Chang-ling, 101, 121
Wang, Hsüeh-wan, 88
Wang, Hung-wen, 80
Wang, Li, 94
Wang, Robert S., 104
Wang, Tung-hsin, 80
Water conservancy projects, 20, 37–38

Weber, Max, 1
White, Lynn T., III, 112
Whitson, William, 36
Whyte, Martin King, 27, 112, 162
Wich, Richard, 74
Wright, Mary C., 138
Wu, An-chia, 8, 43
Wu, Han, 72, 89, 91, 100
Wu, Yuan-li, 20, 24, 37, 119, 139

Yang, Shang-k'un, 78
Yao, Meng-hsuan, 48
Yao, Wen-yuan, 72, 80, 89
Yeh, Chien-ying, 79, 94
Yeh, K. C., 113–14
Yeh, Po-t'ang, 8
Yin, Ch'ing-yao, 7, 42, 50
Yung, Wei, 7, 45
Yun-tung [political campaign], 120

Zagoria, Donald S., 66
Zinoviev, Alexander, 125

Understanding Communist China

ISBN 0-8179-8342-2   >>$9.95